HERBS
AND
SPICES

How hard and uncertaine it is
to describe in words the true proportion of Plants...
they best do know who have
deepliest waded in this sea of Simples.

John Gerard, *Herball*, 1597

Seventeenth-century Europe delighted in lively seasoning. The love of herbs is echoed in this engraving. "Herb Gardener at Work," by Adamus Lonicerus, from the *Kreuterbuch*, pub- lished in Frankfurt in 1679. Opposite, the flow- er of the saffron, throughout its history the most expensive spice in the world.

WAVERLEY ROOT
ROY GENDERS · NIKA S. HAZELTON
PAULA WOLFERT

HERBS
AND
SPICES

THE PURSUIT
OF FLAVOR

EDITED BY
WAVERLEY ROOT

McGRAW-HILL BOOK COMPANY

NEW YORK   ST. LOUIS   SAN FRANCISCO

A McGraw-Hill Co-Publication

Library of Congress Cataloging in Publication Data

Main entry under title:
Herbs and spices.
  1. Cookery (Herbs) 2. Herbs. 3. Spices.
4. Herb gardening. I. Root, Waverley Lewis,
1903 -
TX 819.H4H46 641.6'57 80-18563

ISBN 0-07-053591-4

Original Design:
ROBERT TOBLER

Editor:
DAVID BAKER

Managing Editor:
FANCINE PEETERS

Designers:
PHILIPPE MAAG
ERNST HODEL

Picture Procuration:
RUTH RÜEDI

Production Manager:
FRANZ GISLER

Graphic Artist:
FRANZ CORAY

Printed and bound by:
MLADINSKA KNJIGA, LJUBLJANA, YUGOSLAVIA

Composition by:
BASLER ZEITUNG, BASEL, SWITZERLAND

Photolithography by:
PHOTOLITHO HEGO, LITTAU, SWITZERLAND

Printed in Yugoslavia

CONTENTS

PREFACE   7
WAVERLEY ROOT

INTRODUCTION
THE PURSUIT OF FLAVOR   8
WAVERLEY ROOT

REFERENCE SECTION I
CHOOSING YOUR HERBS AND SPICES   27
PAULA WOLFERT

PLANT LEXICON   40
ROY GENDERS

FROM THE GARDEN TO THE KITCHEN   73
ROY GENDERS

REFERENCE SECTION II
GROWING AND PROCESSING   105
ROY GENDERS

THE ART OF SEASONING   120
NIKA S. HAZELTON

REFERENCE SECTION III
COOKING WITH HERBS   137
PAULA WOLFERT

SEASONERS OF THE WORLD   152
WAVERLEY ROOT

GLOSSARY   184
PICTURE CREDITS   185
INDEX   186

PREFACE

Wheat and beef, rice and fish are the prose of food, herbs and spice are its poetry. Poets and seasoners perform the same function: they add grace (chervil, Robert Herrick) or even force (pepper, Dryden). Seasoners appeal with silent subtlety to another sense than taste—smell: the sachet of lemon verbena in the clothes closet, the clove-studded orange called a pomander, the herb nosegay still carried on ritual occasions by English judges.

What practice woos the senses more deliciously than that of sowing herbs in the paths of the knot-garden, so that when they are trod upon their crushed leaves waft a cloud of perfume to the nostrils? This is a pleasure which can be savored even more brutally: "Luxury of luxuries," wrote Edna Walling. "You haven't lived if you have not lain flat on your middle on a thyme lawn." A. E. Housman would have agreed: "Here of a Sunday morning/My love and I would lie,.../And I would turn and answer/Among the springing thyme."

Poets have always been sensitive to herbs, beginning with the greatest of them all. "I know a bank whereon the wild thyme blows," Puck sang, and Ophelia wept: "There's rosemary, that's for remembrance; pray you love, remember. There's fennel for you, and columbines; there's rue for you, and here's some for me; we may call it herb of grace o' Sundays."

"I crave the stain of tears," cried Robert Frost, "the aftermath of almost too much love, the sweet of bitter bark and burning clove."

Sang Solomon: "Thy plants are an orchard of pomegranates, with pleasant fruits; samphire, with spikenard, spikenard and saffron, calamus and cinnamon, with all trees of frankincense; myrrh and aloes, with all the chief spices."

Seasoners are the poetry of food, and its music too. Consider the trumpet note of the chili, the shrill piccolo of chives; sage, the blatant trombone. The crisp clarity of watercress sweeps across the senses like a harp glissando, the velvety sweetness of cinnamon is the muted horn, the lush huskiness of nutmeg the deep chalumeau octave of the clarinet.

Seasoners have an affinity for woodwinds. The crystal flute recalls angelica, the reedy oboe, mustard, the English horn caraway, and the bassoon, clown of the orchestra, horseradish. The conservative strings are wedded to the conservative flavorers: parsley, bay leaf, celery, even sage; but the viola has heard of saffron, the cello of onions, the bass viol of turmeric.

Capers sound ringingly, like the pure peal of the celesta. In the percussion, spices are kings: coriander seed rattles the head of the snare drum; the note of the bass kettledrum is black pepper, of the tenor drum, white pepper; cloves are a clash of cymbals. What is garlic? The tuba. And sugar? The bass drum.

Altogether a full symphony of tastes.

WAVERLEY ROOT

Borage, wrote John Gerard in his *Herball* (1597), "makes men and women glad and merry, driving away all sadnesse, dulnesse, and melancholy... and quieteth the phrenticke or lunaticke person."

The Pursuit of Flavor

WAVERLEY ROOT

Seasoning was invented by Neolithic Man, possibly the most astute creature in human history. When, for the first time, he deliberately added salt to his food to improve its taste, he launched the second gastronomic revolution. The first, of course, was cooking; to a certain extent it had opened the way for the second. When meat was first roasted, on a spit over an open fire, the juices which escaped from it took some of the flavor with it (we do not know how soon it occurred to prehistoric cooks to encase meat in a coating of clay and throw it into the fire, thus sealing in the juices and the taste). Loss of flavor in cooking was intensified when Neolithic Man, again the inventor, devised earthenware vessels sufficiently resistant to heat so that they could be placed over a fire. Boiling became common (it had, however, existed earlier when heated stones dropped into a hollow in a rock filled with water brought it to the boiling point). Boiling leached even more flavor from foods than roasting. The most important factor in making the second gastronomic revolution inevitable, however, was another sort of revolution, a revolution in the very nature of human society. Once more it was the work of Neolithic Man: he invented agriculture.

When the first wandering tribes planted seeds from plants they had found growing wild and had perforce to stay in the same place until the seeds grew and ripened, they exchanged a nomadic for a sedentary existence. They also changed the character of their diet. Before the advent of agriculture, game had played a much more important role in their nutrition than vegetables, and game came self-seasoned. (So did the saltwater fish which prehistoric man took when he lived near a coast.) Herbivorous animals added flavor to their flesh by regular visits to salt licks; carnivorous animals acquired it by eating the herbivores; man got it by eating both. As the proportion of vegetables to game increased, food became less interesting. Vegetables were apt to be less tasty than animals. True, some roots were spicy or sweet, some plants were peppery; but many others were dull and uninspiring. Besides, the most important vegetable foods were cereals. Some of their grains, crunched whole, possessed a certain nuttiness; but by the time they had been reduced to flour, they needed some sort of a fillip to become palatable.

We may presume, of course, that during the pre-agricultural period tastiness was not a particularly pertinent factor. Man ate to survive rather than to derive pleasure from what he was eating. But if at first he did not perceive a difference between his new diet and the old in terms of taste, there was another element which forced it upon his attention. When he began to eat more vegetable foods and fewer animal foods, he found himself also eating less salt. The presence of salt, it has been remarked, is felt only in its absence.

Neolithic Man may not have felt its absence at first in the form of a diminution of flavor; but he would have felt it instinctively, as animals do, in a diminution of health. Salt, the primordial seasoner, the only important food which comes from the mineral kingdom, is essential to well-being; so salt was added to vegetables to replace the salt which had been lost with meat. Prehistoric man could hardly have failed to notice that in adding salt, he had also added flavor. An aesthetic factor had been applied to eating, nutrition had become gastronomy, and the human race was launched upon the adventure of the pursuit of flavor. Man began to build up what would become a richly variegated treasury of tastes, some subtle, some strong, some caressing, some overwhelming. He drew his seasoners from the inexhaustible resources of the vegetable kingdom in the form of herbs, spices, and condiments.

The twin sources of Egyptian fertility, the heat of the sun and the waters of the Nile, are symbolized in the upper panel of this depiction of the Garden of Ialu, the Egyptian paradise, found in one of the best preserved and most highly decorative of the tombs of western Thebes. Aton the sun god, identified by his circle-crowned cross, the holy ankh, seated in a Nile boat, is flanked by two baboons, sacred to Thoth, god of learning—including the art of agriculture, the subject of two central panels. At the bottom we see ancient Egyptian plants, which included many herbs and spices—more widely used for embalming than for food.

8

Most herbs and spices entered the Western world as medicines before they were used for seasoning. Collectors of antiques prize the handsome porcelain jars in which they were stored, lined up in long rows on the shelves of medieval pharmacies, like the one below, pictured in the *Hortus Sanitatis* (Strasbourg, ca. 1497).

In medieval belief, witches brewed their evil potions from such ingredients as snakes and cocks which had betrayed their diabolic nature by laying eggs, as in this drawing published in Augsburg in 1508, and also from herbs—yew and the deadly hemlock in *Macbeth*,—but also from the innocent garlic, onion, anise, and parsley.

WHAT IS AN HERB?

"Anything that grew out of the mould / Was an excellent herb to our fathers of old," wrote Kipling, who was not exaggerating the area of meaning once covered by the word "herb." In early English usage "herb" was more or less synonymous with "vegetable." Later the name was restricted to vegetables, or parts of vegetables,

a woody, stem, which, after the plant has bloomed and set its seed, dies down to the ground, whether it is minded to rise again the following year or not. This definition is not perfect, but nobody yet has formulated one which is; all definitions leave out some plants which we perceive, unmistakably, as herbs, and let in others which, just as unmistakably, are not. Sage, thyme, and rosemary, indisputably herbs, do not conform strictly to the botanical definition, for all three have more or less woody stems, though they do not form true bark. The botanical definition would rule out laurel, an evergreen woody-trunked tree or shrub which gives us bay leaves, one of our commonest herbs, but would let in the banana, which it would occur to no one to call an herb. And where does one classify the undisciplined castor oil plant, which has a fleshy stem in temperate zones and a woody one in the tropics?

For the pharmacist, an herb is a plant whose properties permit using it as a medicine (or an anti-medicine, for a poisonous plant may be an herb, like the hemlock which removed Socrates from this world). Most of the herbs we think of today as seasoners were employed as medicines before they were used in food. They served for centuries as the principal medicaments of man; kept in pharmacies in dried form so that they might be available all year round, they gave the English language the word "drug," from the Anglo-Saxon *drigan,* to dry. They were gathered wild by specialists in wortcraft, a skill requiring much knowledge, since so many plants

which grew aboveground: a turnip was a vegetable but its leafy top was an herb. Molière did not tell us whether he was thinking of aboveground or underground growth when he wrote in *Les Femmes Savantes* of a woman *"épluchant ses herbes,"* peeling her herbs, but it is evident that in his time French, like English, covered more ground than it does today.

What does "herb" mean now?

For the botanist, an herb is a plant with a fleshy, not

possess beneficial properties that Emerson once defined a weed as "a plant whose virtues have not yet been discovered." Today the most used herbs have been transferred to cultivation; some of them have become so thoroughly dependent on man that they could not survive if he abandoned them.

For the sorcerer—and there are many sorcerers still practicing today if you look for them in the right places—an herb is a plant capable of producing magical effects, usually operative only if the occult rules of the game have been properly observed. In Christian times and places, one such condition is often that the appropriate plant must be picked on St. John's Eve or Day, which bestow particular potency on philters. In other times and places the rules were different; in Babylon, for instance, magic-working herbs were plucked by moonlight, when they were steeped in the power of the moon god, Sin.

And for the cook, an herb is primarily a plant which adds flavor to food—a seasoner. It adds flavor to drinks too, such as herbal teas and wines, but these are beyond the scope of this work; let us note only, for the record,

Many seasoners are versatile in their uses, as for instance fennel. The seeds, often ground for Indian curries, are a spice. The flowers *(right)* serve as an herb in French pickles, and so do the leaves *(center right)*, cooked with fish or raw in salads. The bulbs *(far right)* are eaten as a vegetable in Italy. And what name can we give to dried fennel twigs, when sea bass is cooked over them to pick up their delicate aroma?

that in medieval times it was customary both to precede and follow a meal with an herbal drink; and their modern descendants have in their names, in French at least, preserved for us a reminder of the properties which accounted for this practice—the herb-flavored vermouth taken before a repast is an *apéritif,* an arouser of the appetite; the herb-flavored liqueur taken after it is a *digestif.*

For the cook an herb is also a challenge and an oppor-

Cinnamon (also cassia)

Clove (also capers)

tunity—a challenge to his creative ability, which is enabled through seasoners to manifest refinement or imagination, an opportunity to rise above the routine, the humdrum, and the commonplace by using them, in the art which appeals to the sense of taste, as a painter uses highlights in the art which appeals to the sense of sight or a musician uses grace notes in the art which appeals to the sense of hearing.

All of us have instinctive feelings about the nature of herbs which transcend the restrictions of formal definitions. One of them is that herbs are green and leafy, like parsley, cress, or chervil. When we use other parts of herbs than their leaves, we deny them the name of herb. Mustard, nasturtium, and coriander are herbs when we use their leaves; when we use their seeds, we class them with spices. Coriander, indeed, even changes its name completely when it changes its function: we call the seeds coriander, but the leaves Chinese parsley.

In the case of fennel, the leaves are herbs, the seeds are spices, and the roots are vegetables.

We feel also that herbs, more than other seasoners, are mild, modest, gentle, and caressing (though there are exceptions). The cook uses herbs when he wants to woo us or seduce us, when the effect he seeks is delicate, refined, or subtle; but when he wants to shock or startle us, when he seeks the spectacular or the sensational, he turns to spices.

WHAT IS A SPICE?

Nobody knows. Or at least, nobody yet has been able to put into words a definition which can encompass all, or even most, spices, and exclude all, or even most, non-spices. In another sense, everybody knows; it is a matter of feeling. If you are asked whether cinnamon or nutmeg or clove are herbs or spices, you will answer unhesitatingly that they are spices. But if you can put into words a description of the peculiarities of spices which will enable anyone unfamiliar with them to identify them unmistakably, you will prove yourself more skillful than any lexicographer so far.

For herbs one has at least a botanical description, even though it has exceptions, a grouping which exists in nature. But spices form no botanically describable family. Of herbs we can say that they are characterized by the fact that usually the parts eaten for all of them are the same, their leaves, but we have no such help in isolating spices. They may come from the bark (cinnamon), the buds (cloves), the flowers (saffron), the fruits (allspice), the roots (ginger), the seeds (caraway), or even from secretions (balm, a gum).

Faced with this confusion, the dictionary makers have had recourse to subterfuge. Webster's unabridged dictionary defines a spice as "any of various aromatic vegetable products... used in cookery to season food." It supplements this information by giving as examples a number of indisputable spices; but if you substitute examples chosen among herbs, the definition would serve just as well for them. *The Grand Larousse Encyclopédique* proposes similarly fuzzy distinctions: a spice is "an aromatic substance used for seasoning"; a herb "a vegetable substance used in function of the suave and aromatic odor which it gives off"; a condiment "a substance added to foods to season them." The definitions are virtually interchangeable.

In desperation, food writers have attempted to describe spices in terms of extraneous circumstances which apply to most of them—for instance, the sort of climate in which they flourish. "True spices," wrote Rosemary Hemphill in *Spices and Savour*, "are aromatic plants usually indigenous to hot countries." It is a fact that the seasoners we tend to think of as spices are as a rule stronger and more pungent than those we tend to think

A study of English recipes of the fifteenth century leaves one with the impression that to the cook the spices were a good deal more important than the food itself.... Ginger, pepper, mace, cloves, cinnamon, and galingale [were] specified for ninety percent of the meat and fish dishes.   Elizabeth David

Saffron
(also dill)

Allspice
(also chilies)

Ginger
(also licorice)

Caraway
(also mustard)

of as herbs; and it seems to be the further fact that the heat of spices may be attributed to the heat of the sun which beats down upon them in torrid climates. The fragrance of spices is often lodged in their essential oils; and, as books on medicinal herbs can tell you, all plants producing essential oils need strong sunshine to do so. The sunshine which has transferred its heat to most of our common spices is that of tropical Asia. It may well be that our present difficulty in defining them is in part a difficulty of language, itself rooted in an accident of geography. Tropical Asia was *terra incognita* to Mediterranean peoples at the time when they were developing the vocabulary which the Occidental civilization is obliged to use today in talking about seasoners.

The Venerable Bede (A.D. 672/3–735), the great English monk, scholar, and theologian, left a detailed list of the spices stocked in his monastery at the time of his death. Spices had by then become so rare in Britain that his supply was handed down as a precious legacy, and each of his seventeen seasoners was inventoried in the monastery records.

They did not even suspect the existence of these exotic flavorers; it is hardly surprising that they failed to evolve a concept which would take them all in, or a word to express such a concept.

Our word "spice" comes from the Low Latin *species,* whose origin precedes the period when the spices of the East reached the West. Language was slow to perceive that a new category of *species* had made its appearance, and required a new word to describe it. As late as the time of Gregory of Tours (538–594), *species* was still a word so imprecise that it covered such diverse products as wheat, oil, and wine, among others. If it was desired to single out seasoners, it was necessary to say "aromatic species," and this could stand for herbs as well as spices. Gradually, however, "spice" came to mean especially the hot seasoners which came from the Far East. This geographical basis—an explanation for the character of spices rather than a description of them—was resorted to by the *Encyclopédie* of 1755, which specified that "spice" did not apply to native plants (i.e., native to the Occident) but only to Oriental drugs and aromatic substances. Like Webster's today, it had to clarify its meaning by citing specific examples.

Nearly two and a half centuries later, we are still without a satisfactory definition of what is essential to spicehood. We must identify spices one by one, as we come upon them, by the extent to which each one appeals to instinct or to reason as belonging to this category. A spice, in short, is a seasoner which seems to those familiar to it to be a spice. This seems to be the best that we can do.

13

WHAT IS A CONDIMENT?

If we are on unsound ground in attempting to define spices, when we attempt to define condiments we are on quicksand. Webster's dictionary does the best it can. A condiment, it tells us, is "something usually pungent, acid, salty, or spicy, added to or served with food to enhance its flavor." Something! The vaguest of words! The difficulty about defining condiments is that condiments do not exist. They do not exist, that is, in nature. Herbs can be grouped into a single category on the basis of a botanical distinction; it exists in nature. Spices can be described, one by one, in terms of their character-

istics, whereupon we perceive that there do exist among them certain common factors (heat, pungency) which permit us to fit them also into a single category; those characteristics exist in nature. The substances used as condiments by man possess no common elements in nature. "Condiment" does not describe a thing, it describes the use to which men put many different things—or "something." Any food can become a condiment when it is used to season other foods; but no food is a condiment in itself. All natural substances used

as condiments have other independent roles to play. One might expect to find exceptions, foods used for seasoning and only for seasoning, among, for example, what the Middle Ages, mixing up culinary nomenclature a little more, called disdainfully "the strong spices of the poor" (which were nevertheless not neglected by the rich), the members of the onion-garlic family. The onion does indeed play an extremely important role as a seasoner, but it is not confined to that role: consider the sweet excellence of creamed onions. You might think that garlic has no function except that of lending flavor to other foods, though not if you are familiar with southwestern France, one of whose specialities is *tourin,* a thin garlic soup, which, believe it or not, is subtle, delicate, and restrained in flavor.

Some vegetables are used oftener as condiments than for their own sake, horseradish for instance, but even horseradish is also eaten alone, as an appetite-provoking prelude to a repast, like ordinary radishes, raw, dipped before each bite into a little heap of salt on the plate. Other vegetables are, on the contrary, usually eaten for their own merits, but are sometimes drafted to add flavor to other foods, carrots or celery for instance.

Vegetable oils, used on salads or in cooking, are condiments, and so are vinegar and mayonnaise, but these are products fabricated by man, which fall outside the scope of this work. We will not concern ourselves with the bewildering variety of artificial condiments which man has devised to enliven his food, such as New England cranberry sauce with turkey, Pennsylvania Dutch sweet and sour relishes, Louisiana tabasco, American ketchup, English Worcestershire sauce, European four spices, Chinese five powders, Indian curries and chutneys, southeastern Asia's all-purpose *nuoc mam,* Ethiopia's berberé pepper (misnamed, for it is not one spice but a combination of fourteen or more), or Morocco's *ras el hanout,* which is a mixture of thirty. Much less will we allow ourselves to be diverted into the far-flung reaches of this subject. We are at a far cry

It is quite surprising that the use of pepper
has come so much into fashion...
pepper has nothing in it that can plead as a recommendation
to either fruit or berry, its only desirable quality
being a certain pungency; and yet it is for this that we import it
all the way from India. Who was the first to make trial
of it as an article of food? And who, I wonder, was the man
that was not content to prepare himself
by hunger only for the satisfaction of a greedy appetite?

Pliny the Elder, writing in Rome in the first century A.D.

from herbs and spices when we meet kirsch poured over slices of pineapple as a condiment; or chorizo sausage adding its spiciness to Spanish *paella*; or anchovy fillets on a breaded veal chop or in a *salade niçoise*; or bits of chopped meat in sauces, salads, or omelets; or grated cheese sprinkled on pasta or in minestrone.

They may be, by virtue of their function, genuine condiments; but we will restrict ourselves here primarily to the seasoning plants provided by Nature, altered as little as possible by the mischievous manipulations of man.

THE EVOLUTION OF FLAVOR

The pursuit of flavor did not progress in orderly crescendo from the epoch when Neolithic Man first started it on its way to our own times. It knew its ups and downs. Some periods and places were characterized by excessive use of the strongest spices; others used hardly any. There has probably never been in the whole history of the world a time when its seasoners were utilized to their full potential. There are today something like 2,500 recognized species of edible herbs, of which the great majority are neglected. It is probably safe to assume that the total number of spices falls far below this figure, but any attempt to count them has apparently been discouraged by the imprecision of their definition, by disagreement about their classification as species, subspecies, varieties, and subvarieties, and by the relative inaccessibility of many of the regions where they grow most abundantly. There is perhaps no reliable confirmable indisputable precise enumeration of spices more recent than the early fourteenth century, when the spice merchants of Florence were dealing with a recorded 288 species. As for condiments, since al-

The Arkesilas bowl, named for the place at which it was found and dated between 565 and 560 B.C., depicts silphium, one of the most popular—and most expensive—seasoners of antiquity. It was nevertheless allowed to die out from sheer neglect. It seems to have been a close relative of asafetida; the Roman author Apicius called for it in several of his recipes, in the form of a gum. There is still no unanimous agreement on what it was, but the best guess may well be that it was *Laserpitium latifolium,* laserwort. If so, it did not really become extinct, for this plant still grows wild in mountainous areas of Germany, Switzerland, Italy, and France; but it is no longer used in cooking.

most any food can be pressed into service to add flavor to others, they are uncountable. The number of its seasoners, for all practical purposes, is infinite.

It seems to be the astonishing fact that one of the underprivileged periods in the history of seasoning, in the Occident at least, is our own, while one of the richest came at the very beginning of the recorded history of our civilization, in Babylon. One account of the death of Sardanapalus (648 B.C.?) attributes his death not to the usual version—that he set fire to his own palace and his

household with it in a rather excessive attempt to escape from a feared invasion—but to the circumstance that he burned so many herbs to enjoy the aromatic fragrance of their fumes that he suffocated in the smoke. Hippocrates (ca. 460 B.C.) is said to have employed four hundred herbs (but as medicines rather than as seasoners), twice as many as the Western world uses today. The spice trade was well organized in the Middle East of antiquity: when Joseph was sold into slavery by his brothers, the purchasers were spice merchants.

Rome, for the first five centuries of its existence, was a model of austerity. It used few seasoners and disapproved of those who did. Oriental gourmandise and luxury weakened the moral fiber, the early Romans held, and they felt that the Easterners, softened by self-indulgence, swathed in rich fabrics, breathing clouds of incense, and exhausted by the pleasures of the bed and the table, must eventually succumb to the force of Roman arms. In fact they did. The legions conquered the spice eaters of the East and the spices of the East conquered the legions. A turning point in the history of gastronomy occurred in 185 B.C. when the Roman Asiatic Army returned from their conquests bringing with them the aromatic herbs and spices of the East and an acquired taste for them, along with cooks from the Greek colonies in Asia Minor skillful at using seasoners in cooking.

Rome was not lost in a day. Comparative sobriety was maintained through the golden age of Augustus, that is to say until A.D. 14, but restraint went by the board through the reigns of Tiberius, Gaius, and Claudius; Rome had foundered in the excesses of the table by the advent in A.D. 54 of Nero (who had the streets beneath his feet spread with saffron when he entered Rome, and burned more cinnamon than Rome imported from Araby in a year on the funeral pyre for the empress Poppaea, in remorse at having killed her by a kick in the stomach). Camel caravans plying the Silk Road from the Far East and Arab ships sailing eastward with the monsoon and returning when the winds shifted provided Rome with all the important Old World herbs known to us today except tarragon and angelica, and all the Old World spices except nutmeg. The cookbook of Apicius named the seasoners which were expected to be at hand in any well-stocked kitchen: the length of his list would frighten a restaurant pantryman today. The food of the Empire ended in an orgy of overseasoning in which the stronger spices dominated, but herbs also played an important role, though they were gentler and more subtle handmaidens of taste.

The Romans in their turn degenerated, their strength also sapped by excess, including excess in seasoning. The Barbarians got along very easily without them when the Western world was deprived of seasoners because the collapse of the Roman Empire was accompanied by the collapse of its network of communications. Virtually all the seasoners of classical times had been imported from the East. When the galleys abandoned the oceans and the docks of Ostia became overgrown with grass (and wild mint, one of the few herbs which had taken root in southern Europe), Europe was almost totally deprived of herbs and spices. The pursuit of flavor had become becalmed in the doldrums. The art of seasoning was among the casualties of the aesthetic holocaust which supplanted the grandeur that was Rome by the drabness that was the Dark Ages.

In England the use of herbs declined with the departure of the Roman legions; by 735 they had become so rare and precious that the most important part of the legacy the Venerable Bede left to be shared among the brethren of his monastery was the contents of his spice cupboard, described by Maxime McKendry in *Seven Centuries of English Cooking* as "lavender, aniseed, buckwheat, cinnamon, cloves, cubebs, cumin, coriander, cardamom (called grains of paradise), cypress roots (called garmgale, galmgale, or galyngale) [this was not genuine galingale but chufa, which grows in England], ginger (both raw and preserved), gromic [?], licorice, dried prunes, raisins, pepper, and sugar, which was thought of as a spice and used medicinally. Sugar was expensive, having been brought with the rest of these food treasures from the Far East by caravan and by Genoese and Venetian vessels from Alexandria."

In France, Charlemagne may be credited with having tried to resuscitate the use of herbs, for in the list of plants he ordered grown in his domains were chervil, chives, costmary, cress, dill, fennel, fenugreek, lovage, mint, parsley, rosemary, and other aromatic plants.

The return of aromatics to cooking lagged until the Crusaders invaded the Holy Land; once more it was an army which brought the spices of the East to the West. They might have begun to seep back into Europe earlier, when the Saracens became the rulers of Sicily in the ninth century, or in the eighth, when the Moors took over much of Spain, and even penetrated France as far as Poitiers before Charles Martel stopped them in 732.

As good as money in the ancient world, spices twice saved Rome. In 408, when the city was threatened by Alaric the Goth, he was bought off by a tribute including pepper. In 452, when Attila the Hun *(left)* menaced Rome in his turn, he was bribed to desist by a tribute including pepper and cinnamon.

But there was little contact between the Islamic world in southernmost Europe and the Christian world to the north except with sword or scimitar in hand, and it was indeed with sword in hand that the Crusaders recovered the fragrances of the East for twelfth-century Europe.

Spices now began to play an important, almost a dominant, role in the economy, and thus in the history, of Europe. The astute Venetians ferried the Crusaders to the Holy Land, charging fares so profitable that they were able to build up a fleet of three thousand galleys and sailing ships. On their return voyages, the Venetian craft brought back the precious spices which made Venice a rich and powerful state; a little later they would also contribute mightily to the prosperity of Genoa. (When Western navigators reached the Spice Islands, Portugal and Holland too would wax rich on spices.) So far as vegetable foods were concerned, much of Europe had, onions and garlic apart, been living largely on a tasteless diet of mosses and mallows. Its people fell almost with folly on the new flavors. Oddly enough,

Charlemagne, in his *Capitulare de Villis*, gave instructions about the plants he wanted grown on his domains. His list included many herbs, but he probably thought of them less as seasoners than as medicines. He is said to have had a method of diagnosis for his ailments peculiarly his own: he tossed his sword into the herb garden, trusting to God to make it fall among the plants his health required.

those who made least use of them were their first importers. The abstinence of the Genoese is perhaps easy to understand, for the exigencies of geography imposed upon the sailors of a nation of sailors (where the tastes of sailors shaped the tastes of the whole population) long deep-water voyages from Asia Minor to the west coast of Italy, during which their nostrils were assailed day after day by the pungent odors rising from their battened hatches which soon ceased to be seductive and became, for them, suffocating stenches. As they neared the Ligurian coast, the offshore breezes carried out to

them, even before they could see land, the fresh cleansing fragrance of the hillside herbs, first of all basil, then as now the favorite seasoner of Genoa. Once ashore, they sought refuge from the heady spices in their homely herbs. But the Venetian ships, plying the narrow Adriatic, and when they were out of it, hugging the coasts and navigating by church steeples, were never out of touch with the odors of the green plants of the earth nor overwhelmed by a surfeit of spiciness. Yet they too were moderate in the pursuit of flavor; Venetian cooking today still uses spices sparingly. It must have been that the Venetians thought of spices less in terms of taste than in terms of value.

Inland, spices were greeted with more fervor. Florence, rich enough to pay for them, stuffed spices into its dishes at the end of the Middle Ages, and especially in the Renaissance, with such enthusiasm that from time to time alarmed governments enacted sumptuary legislation to impose sobriety on eating habits, with the lack of success characteristic always and everywhere of measures of this sort. A seasoner which appealed especially to Florence was saffron, which used it, together with almonds, in a cream soup, and, together with pine nuts and pistachio nuts, in an asparagus soup. In Modena it colored the famous Royal Golden Soup served in the household of the Duke of Este—consommé enriched with egg yolks and flavored, not only with saffron, but also with almonds, crushed shells and all, orange juice, grapes, verjuice, rose water, sugar, and cinnamon.

In England as in Florence, saffron was one of the early favorites. It was the *raison d'être* of saffron soup, whose recipe is given in *The Forme of Cury*, a cookbook produced by the chefs of Richard II in 1378, and it went also into Three-Colored Soup, a fish chowder which resembled today's Mediterranean *bouillabaisse*. It did not appear in vegetable marrow soup, also described in *The Forme of Cury*, but its absence was hardly noticeable in the compensating presence of cinnamon, nutmeg, and ginger. One sort of ginger might seem enough for any single dish today, but it did not suffice to satisfy the aroused taste buds of the fourteenth century. Appraylere (dressed pork, a name adapted from the French *appareillé*) called for lean boiled pork chopped up together with well-aged cheese, breadcrumbs, salt, saffron, cin-

namon, and two kinds of ginger–ginger proper and galingale. As though this were not sufficient, galingale (this time without ginger) turned up a second time in the same dish as a seasoner of the batter which was poured over it as it cooked. The taste of those times does not appear to have been subtle; whenever there was a choice between two closely related flavors, it was usually the coarser, harsher, and stronger which was preferred: mace instead of nutmeg, cassia instead of cinnamon, oregano instead of sweet marjoram.

The popularity of strong seasoning which had been provoked by the advent of Asiatic spices was accompanied in England by a parallel phenomenon, an increase of interest in home-grown herbs. They became more and more important, reaching something of a climax in the time of the Tudors, a flamboyant period which demanded a flamboyant cuisine. No English manor house from the sixteenth to the nineteenth century was without its well-furnished herb garden. Thomas Tusser wrote in 1557 that the kitchen garden was not worthy of the name unless it was able to provide more than forty different herbs. Across the Channel the cultivation of herbs was developed under the aegis of Olivier de Serres, agronomist to Henry IV, in the sixteenth century, and Jean de La Quintinie, creator

of the royal kitchen gardens of Versailles for Louis XIV, in the seventeenth.

The owner of the Tudor manor house still had to buy his imported spices from the grocer (in France today "grocer" is still *épicier,* spice merchant), and he bought a good many of them. A single day's entry (for 1 April 1549) in the household accounts of Sir William Petre, a former secretary of state to Henry VIII, noted the purchase of "provisions of spice" including "½ lb mace, ½ lb cloves, 1 oz saffron, 20 lb currants, 4 lb dates, 1 lb ginger, ½ lb cinnamon, 6 lb pepper, 1 lb box biscuits, 1 lb carraway, 6 lb almonds, ¾ hundreth great raisins, 3 lb rice."

Sir William lasted into Elizabethan times and so did the vogue for heavy seasoning; we may suppose that the Queen found her food well seasoned when she was the guest of Sir William. She was accustomed to starting her day with a potion described by its French name, *bouillon de santé,* which was chicken consommé flavored, according to Sir Kenelm Digby, with "a handful of Parsley, a sprig of Thyme, three of Spear-minth, a little balm, half a great Onion, a little Pepper & a Clove."

Robert May, writing in the seventeenth century about salad ingredients, advised: "Take all manner of knots of

On 7 October 1571, the navies of the West and of Islam clashed off the coast of Greece in the last great sea fight in which both sides used oared vessels, the Battle of Lepanto (Granaday Castello's painting from Spain's Escorial). The West there won mastery of the sea lanes.

Bottom: Saffron is pictured in the Juliana Codex (A.D. 512) transcribed from the *De Materia Medica* of Dioscorides (first century A.D.)

> "Hast thou ought in they purs?"
> "I have peper and piones (peonies) and a pound garlike. A ferthyngworth of fenel seed for fasting days."
>
> *The Vision of William Concerning Piers Plowman*
> (late fourteenth century)

buds of sallet herbs, buds of pot-herbs, or any green herb, as sage, mint, balm, burnet, violet-leaves, red coleworts streaked of divers fine colours, lettice, any flowers, blanched almonds, blue figs, raisins of the sun, currans, capers, olives; then dish the sallet in a hep or pile, being mixed with some of the fruits, and all finely washed and swung in a napkin, then about the centre lay first sliced figs, next capers and currans, and lastly either jagged beats, jagged lemons, hagged [sic] cucumbers, or cabbidge lettice in quarters, good oyl and wine vinegar, sugar or none."

John Evelyn, another expert on salads, listed 73 herbs and plants suitable for flavoring them, but ruled one firmly out—garlic. "We absolutely forbid its entrance into our *Salleting*," he wrote, "by reasons of its intolerable rankness, and which made it so detested of old, that the eating of it was (as we read) part of the punishment for such as had committed the horrid'st crimes."

It was under Elizabeth that the British East India Company was launched, perpetuating the English interest in strong Oriental seasonings. Like the Roman soldiers of antiquity and the Crusaders of the Middle Ages, the British soldiers and administrators in India were captivated by the spices of the East. They pay tribute to them to this day, less in the form of the pure spices themselves, but in that of dishes developed from them—curries, chutneys, kedgeree (from the India khichri, lentils and rice with ginger, cloves, allspice, white peppercorns, and cardamom seeds, among other ingredients, to which the English added fish to make it an acceptable breakfast dainty), and gallimaufry (chicken with a sauce containing mustard, ginger, vinegar, stock, and verjuice), which a Member of Parliament complained

21

Roger Williams (d. 1683) landing in the New World, where he founded the colony of Rhode Island. American Indians introduced Europeans to tobacco, of which Charles Kingsley said: "There's no herb like unto it under the canopy of heaven." More pertinently for us, the Indians discovered by Columbus also gave the world one of its most important spices, red pepper, as well as allspice, vanilla, and chocolate.

Opposite: An eighteenth-century view of a wharf of the British East India Company, where the spices of the Orient were landed for England.

only a few years ago was being unjustly neglected by the dining room of the House of Commons.

When the first English-speaking colonists reached the New World, they found themselves deprived of the high seasoning to which they had been accustomed in the Old. America is poor in native seasoners, and the few which did originate there (vanilla and chilies, for example) grew in the subtropical and tropical regions where Spanish and Portuguese became the adopted languages. It is even possible that English-speaking America, in the beginning, even lagged behind Nahuatl-speaking America in its use of seasoners. Bernal Diaz, chronicler of Cortez's conquest of Mexico, who as a Spaniard must have been familiar with a cuisine made heady by the aromatic essences introduced into Spain by the Moors, was impressed by the number of "medicinal and useful herbs" he saw in Montezuma's garden. Some of the Mexican seasoners, notably chilies, did push northward to enter the diet of the Indians of what was destined to become the southwestern United States, but the Atlantic seaboard was almost devoid of them. The Eastern Indians contented themselves with the natural tastes of their foods, except when they had recourse to the genus *Allium* (wild onions and wild garlic existed in North America). One might also except the hickory nut, from which a seasoning "milk" was extracted, and maple syrup, a condiment today when it is poured over griddlecakes or used to flavor ice cream; but both were limited in their applications. The new settlers quickly planted European herbs in their new home, with such success that many of them escaped from home gardens and became naturalized as wild plants in America, and imported spices from Asia in such quantity that for a time the busiest spice port in the world was Salem, Massachusetts. The traditions of Tudor and Elizabethan England had been transplanted in America, where they persisted until the Civil War.

Eliza Leslie, in her *Directions for Cookery,* first published before 1830, gave instructions for drying herbs and prescribed them freely in her recipes. Great quantities of cloves went into sausage meat. Milk soup sounds simple, but it was complicated at the period by the addition of cinnamon and both sweet and bitter almonds. Domestic rabbit is less flavorful than wild rabbit, so it

Right: Tudor England grew herbs in lush profusion, protected by the calm of national unity, symbolized, in this frontispiece of a collection of motets in honor of Henry VIII, by the white rose of York and the red rose of Lancaster growing together from the stem of the crowned Tudor rose. Also shown are the emblems of England, Wales, and Spain—for Henry had not yet divorced Catherine of Aragon.

was cooked with parsley, basil, sweet marjoram, celery, cloves, and mace. Boiled beef was garnished with capers or "nasturtian" seeds, boiled *corned* beef was served with mustard made by the housewife herself from "the very best mustard powder," wrote Miss Leslie, plus tarragon vinegar and garlic. Mutton was seasoned with a bouquet garni, cloves, and mace.

Early American cookbooks offered many recipes for curries and other gastronomic borrowings from India, such as mulligatawny soup, a great favorite in those days, which was flavored with turmeric, cassia, coriander, black pepper, and cayenne pepper. The housewife made her own artificial condiments, such as vinegars (whose flavorings included chilies, horseradish, shallots, tarragon, basil, and burnet) and "catchups" (lobster, anchovy, oyster, walnut, mushroom, lemon, "tomata," and sea catchup, designed to keep during long ocean voyages, for which Miss Leslie's recipe begins: "Take a gallon of stale strong beer, a pound of anchovies washed from the pickle, a pound of peeled shalots or small onions, half an ounce of mace, half an ounce of cloves, a quarter of an ounce of whole pepper, three or four large pieces of ginger, and two quarts of large mushroom-flaps rubbed to pieces"). Sauces used a variety of seasoners: mint, capers, nasturtiums, celery, onions, parsley. The family beverages were also made at home and also employed seasoners, in ginger, spruce, and sassafras beers, elderberry wine, and anise-flavored cordials.

In 1861 the Civil War upset the American economy, interrupted communications, and incidentally depleted the stocks of seasoners in the cupboards. They would never be so well filled again.

A FLIGHT FROM FLAVOR?

If the spice cupboard of the United States in the twentieth century is less well stocked than was that of the nineteenth century, this is surely not an American phenomenon alone, nor did it begin only in the nineteenth century. If any consistent trend can be discerned at all in the history of the use of seasoners in the Occidental world (the Oriental world is another story), it has been in the direction of the diminution of their numbers. After the four hundred herbs of Hippocrates, the long but imprecise list of Apicius, the seventy-three of John Evelyn, and the forty-plus of Thomas Tusser, we find Alexandre Dumas writing in the nineteenth century that only twenty-eight herbs were then being used in French cooking. Elizabeth David in her *Italian Food* devotes a chapter to "The Italian Store

Cupboard," in which fourteen herbs are listed. In her *Spices, Salt and Aromatics in the English Kitchen* she names sixteen as in current use (counting thyme and lemon thyme as two). The American housewife today would probably consider her pantry well stocked with herbs if it contained basil, bay leaves, chervil, mint, oregano (or sweet marjoram), parsley, sage, thyme, and watercress (fresh, one hopes), to which can be added, if they are in the form of foliage (in the form of seeds they are spices), celery, coriander, dill, and fennel—thirteen in all. The number of spices in common use has diminished also, though perhaps in lesser proportion. What has happened?

First of all—first in time and first in importance—the arrival in the West of cane sugar.

"As soon as there was plenty of sugar available," Reay Tannahill wrote in *Food in History,* "sugar became popular.... Competition over sugar brought to an end that phase of imperialism which had begun with competition over spices." It also brought to an end the popularity of some of the spices. As the use of sugar increased, the use of other seasoners decreased.

The process was slow. It took several centuries for sugar to drive out the others. It could not exercise a preponderant influence over eating habits until it became a common food; and this was for a long period out of the question because it was too expensive. "Sugar never hurt anybody" (a debatable opinion), went an old French saying, "except in the pocketbook." Even in the United States, where sugar was just next door in the great plantations which had arisen in the West Indies, sugar did not become the principal sweetener until the middle of the nineteenth century, for few persons could afford it. Maple sugar and molasses, the cheaper by-product of the cane, were used instead.

Sugar was also inconvenient until the latter part of the nineteenth century. It came in large blocks or cones (the sugar loaf), often so hard that they had to be broken into pieces of manageable size with a hammer or reduced to powder in a mortar. When granulated cane sugar appeared (and was joined later by beet sugar), its use increased mightily. It was now the easiest sweetener to combine with foods in cooking or to sprinkle over them; and in the form of syrup it pre-

served fruits which had formerly been conserved in spices.

Sugar, a bully among seasoners, began its conquest of the domain of flavor by driving out rival sweeteners with sheer brute force, overpowering their more subtle savors with an impact on the taste buds which stunned them into submission. Up to that time the principal sweetener had been honey. Honey is delicate and variable, capable of innumerable delicious variations; bee-hives are frequently placed in apple orchards, or near patches of wild thyme, or elsewhere where their bees will gather nectar from particularly desirable sources. Every type of honey is different; the palates of those who sweetened their food with it were educated to make fine distinctions among closely related tastes. Sugar, with its blanketing overwhelming strength, almost devoid of gradations, corrupted the taste buds and robbed them of the ability to distinguish between one savor and another, to discriminate, for example, between oregano and marjoram, or between ginger and galingale. Seasoners whose flavors did not differ markedly from those of their fellows became unrecognizable and consequently obsolescent. At the same time sugar entered more largely into cuisines in general; in the United States it was even added to salad dressing! Cooking dominated by sugar became incompatible with the sharp, tart, or acid flavors of many herbs and spices which had formerly been prized. They began to disappear.

Fewer seasoners, however, does not necessarily mean

maintaining its quality, before the onslaught of supermarkets interested first of all in sales and their quantity. It has become increasingly profitable to concentrate on a few standardized products in wide demand, and increasingly costly to deal in a wide variety of items of which many are necessarily in slight demand. Seasoners, usually sold in the smallest of units, are particularly prone to become victims of this situation.

Seasoners are also vulnerable to the increasing industrialization which is draining from the land into the cities more and more of the persons familiar with the soil and its products, accustomed to and appreciative of native herbs because they have cultivated them or gathered them wild. Urbanization has had a particular impact on seasoners in the United States, where they had never been seriously commercialized except by the Shakers; their consumers were almost exclusively those

Urbanization and industrialization, not to mention the large-scale production and preservation of food, have caused a decline of flavor in most of our diets, while tending to alienate twentieth-century human beings from their natural environment.

This trend, however, has not gone unopposed. Even as land becomes constantly scarcer, people on the outskirts of many major European cities maintain their own tiny plot *(left)* which they cultivate lovingly. Flowers, herbs, and a wide variety of vegetables flourish in these postage-stamp oases, such as the Swiss ''Schrebergarten'' shown here.

inferior seasoning: it is a case of the survival of the fittest. The crucial question is whether what is fittest to survive is measured by gastronomic criteria or is governed by other perhaps contradictory factors. It happens that our society has been evolving for the last century, in other domains than in that of food, as well, in a direction which limits variety of choice and consequently the exercise of the finesse which the art of choosing requires. The pressures of competition and the economies of a large-scale operation discourage the survival of small enterprises in many fields; in that of food it is translated into the disappearance of small grocers, often deeply interested in food itself and jealous of

For centuries after sugarcane reached Europe, sugar remained too expensive for general use; but with the discovery of America, sugar was brought within reach of everybody's purse following the establishment of vast sugar plantations in the West Indies—like this one, pictured in the anonymous *Voyages aux côtes du Guinée et en Amérique,* published in Amsterdam in 1799. Caribbean sugar was cheap because it was produced by slave labor; one of the results of this development was intensification of the slave traffic. Another was a gastronomic revolution, which occurred when the swaggering savor of sugar invaded with ever-increasing success the domains of most of our foods. Many less assertive seasoners, especially spices, fell into relative disuse: they were unable to hold their own against an adversary more heavily armed. The weapon of the subtle seasoners of former times was the fencer's foil; that of sugar was the battle-axe.

who lived in the country, or had close relatives who lived in the country, which meant, not so many years ago, a considerable majority of the population; today a minute fraction of it raises the food for all the rest. Many European cities used to be girdled with garden areas (some of them still are) divided into small individual plots, where city dwellers nostalgic for the land they had left, or simply desirous of enjoying a brief period of liberation from the confinement of cramped apartments, could escape on weekends or after work to grow flowers or food; herbs were particularly popular among these plant potterers because they required so little space. Alas, urban sprawl has now wiped out many of these gardens. Creeping out through their suburbs, the cities have covered them with high-rise apartment buildings; and the expanded perimeters of the municipalities are too far from their centers to make new gardening areas practical.

Is the future of flavor, then, dark and dismal? Perhaps not. There are signs that the decline in the number of seasoners has reached its limit and is about to be reversed. They have been appearing in the very quarter which led the way in banishing marginal flavorers—the United States. If that country is now prepared to lead the way in resuscitating them, its example may very well be followed elsewhere. The return to an interest in seasoners dates already from the middle of the century, since which time, seed merchants and nurserymen report, Americans have been buying more herbal seeds and plants. They start with the commoner kinds, and when they succeed with them, seek new and less familiar fields to conquer. Lesser-known plants, some of them little grown for a century and a half, are making a timid reappearance. Fanciers of flavor are growing herbs indoors, in window boxes, or, when they have access to a little soil, in full-fledged herb gardens outdoors. Books on growing herbs and on cooking with them are in ever increasing demand. Their readers are experimenting with these rediscovered treasures in their own cooking, and they are more knowledgeable about them when they eat in restaurants. We are perhaps on the eve of a renewed impetus in the pursuit of flavor.

Some food writers have been unkind enough to explain this phenomenon as a desperate attempt to return to food the flavor which its processors, in the interests of profit, have only too often eliminated from it. Whatever the motivation, one can only rejoice (with Shakespeare, a product of an herb-conscious age) if the world is returning to the recognition that

"O! mickle is the powerful grace that lies
In herbs, plants, stones, and their true qualities."

26

Wilder feldsaffran.

Choosing your Herbs and Spices

PAULA WOLFERT

Reference Section I

In the chart found on the following pages, the 100 herbs and spices chosen by the authors are listed alphabetically, with appropriate foods and dishes provided for each. The food items under each seasoner are arranged by category: Soups, Sauces and gravies, Salads, Fish, Eggs and cheese, Meats, Poultry and game, Vegetables, Sweets and baking. Many seasoners have a variety of uses in several of these categories; other herbs or spices are more limited in range.

Cross-references to other parts of the book are included. A number accompanies each herb or spice; it refers to the exact location of the seasoner in the Plant Lexicon (pp. 43–71), where the 100 herb and spice plants are illustrated and described (under their Latin botanical names). An asterisk before the name of a dish refers the reader to a complete recipe in Reference Section III (pp. 138–151).

Cooking with herbs and spices is a longstanding tradition in most parts of the world. In olden times, even as now, the cook complemented his own homegrown seasoners with more exotic varieties raised under a hotter sun and shipped to local markets. This woodcut from Hieronymus Bock's *Krëutterbuch* printed in Strasbourg in 1577 shows a late medieval German market scene, with women selecting vegetables and spices.

Left: Wild saffron, a woodcut by Leonardo Fuchs from his herbal published in 1543.

The matching of an herb or spice to a specific food is, basically, a matter of taste. When all is said and done, each cook must depend on his own judgment; each will experiment on his own with herbs and spices, as with so many other elements of cooking. And yet guidelines are useful. The cook, especially the relative newcomer to the realm of seasoners, will find that suggestions and recommendations can save him a good deal of time, wasted ingredients, and heartburn.

The herb and spice chart on the following pages, then, is offered as a series of recommendations rather than hard and fast rules. An effort has been made to pass on to readers the fruits of past experience—the experience of the author herself, Paula Wolfert, as well as the wisdom of past masters she has consulted and the national cuisines that she has studied all over the world.

This reference section aims to help the reader in the selection, and indeed in the identification, of seasoners. Before anyone can decide whether to purchase and cook with a particular herb or spice, or to cultivate it

in his garden, it is logical to ask how it is going to taste, what kind of food it is likely to be used with. Once that information is obtained from Reference Section I, it is possible to follow up a particular seasoner in other sections of the book, where one will find other types of information.

A note on the choice of herbs and spices presented in this book. The number 100, while somewhat arbitrary, is also easily large enough to encompass all the basic seasoners. Most cooks, even the finest, manage a wide variety of dishes with far fewer than 100 seasoners. Thus it is unlikely that the authors of this book, in their selection of these 100 seasoners, will have to atone for any sins of omission. In the choice of the less familiar items, however, controversy is more difficult to avoid. Our authors have braved this risk, in the interests of variety, character, and originality. The result is a list of seasoners that, while covering all the requisites, also offers material for experimentation, a judiciously exotic touch, and, it is hoped, the element of surprise. *—Ed.*

REF. NO.	HERB OR SPICE	SOUPS	SAUCES AND GRAVIES	SALADS	FISH
72	ALLSPICE	Beef broth, tomato, split-pea	Tomato, barbecue, chili raisin sauce (for ham and pork), vinegar-pepper sauce (for oysters), brown gravy, catsup	Aspics, fruit cocktail, pickled carrots	Court-bouillon, shrimp marinade, stuffings, *gumbo
81	ALMOND	*Creamed, white gaspacho	Catalan sauce "Romesco," Greek skordalia with garlic, Toulousian aillade	Green bean, orange (with lettuce and dates), pimiento	Sautéed trout, soft-shell crabs, sole, stuffing
11	ANGELICA				Peeled stems baked
73	ANISE	Snail, Dutch milk soup, Hispanic soups	Vinaigrette	Melon, fresh leaves in salad, fresh fruit salad	Court-bouillon
40	ASAFETIDA		Curries, vegetarian dishes		
57	BALM	Chicken, cream		Fruit salads, vegetable salads	Eel or other oily fish
18	BAMBOO SHOOTS	Oriental		Oriental	Curried shrimp, abalone
	BASIL, see Sweet Basil				
51	BAY LEAF	Stock, beef, vegetable, chicken, fish	Tomato, creole, spaghetti, barbecue, Spanish	Cold rice and pasta, salads, aspics	Court-bouillon, fish stews, *gumbos, poached fish
59	BERGAMOT			Flowers fresh in salads	
77	BLACK PEPPER	Beef, chicken, fish, vegetables, stocks	Salad dressings, brown gravy, cream, barbecue, mignonnette	Meat, chicken, fish, and vegetable salads	All, broiled, baked and fried; croquettes, stuffing oysters; coating for fried fish
20	BORAGE	Eel soup, fish stews	Court-bouillon	Tomato salad, greens, nasturtium salad, cucumber	
74	BURNET			Greens, fish	
93	CACAO		Molé sauce, sweet-and-sour sauces for game		
23	CAPER		Sauce verte, piquant sauces (for fish, boiled meats, poultry), tartare, remoulade, *olive, mayonnaise, hollandaise, white wine, tomato sauce, beef gravy	Mediterranean-style salads, tomato	Tuna, anchovy, broiled fish, grilled trout

* An asterisk before the name refers to recipes in the section "Cooking with Herbs and Spices," pp. 137 ff.

EGGS AND CHEESE	MEATS	POULTRY AND GAME	VEGETABLES	SWEET AND BAKING
Spiced cheese, pickled eggs	Sausages, corned beef, lamb tarts, stuffings, tongue, Swedish meat-balls, pot roast, *chili con carne, beef, lamb, veal, pork	Marinades (for game), stuffings	Tomatoes, spinach, carrots, beets, red cabbage	Mincemeat, fruit pies, spice cakes, plum cakes, pumpkin pie
	Lamb stews	Rabbit, stuffings, chicken with chick peas	Green beans	Tourtes, cakes, pies, custards, peaches, apricots, prunes
				Custards, creams, stewed fruit, jams, Scandinavian pies
Fresh cheese		Moroccan chicken with baby onions	Beets, carrots	*Moroccan bread, Languedoc cookies, candies, spice cake, German Christmas cookies, Swedish apple sauce, Italian cakes
	Meatballs		Beans, lentils, potatoes and cumin, mushrooms and cumin	
Scrambled eggs, fresh cheese	Lamb stews, veal, pork	Chicken, stuffings for turkey	Mushrooms	Custards, jams and jellies, summer drinks
Eggroll	Pork stir-fry, beef stir-fry	Steamed chicken	Mushrooms, cabbage, Buddha's delight	
	Beef stew, potted meats, tongue, lamb stews, veal ragouts, marinades, corned meats, *liver kebab, pork paté	Potted game, marinades, rabbit and wild bird stews, chicken stuffing	Carrots, potatoes, tomatoes, chestnuts	Rice pudding, custards
Cheese	Sausages, veal, pork	Stuffings		
Deviled dips and spreads, rarebits, all egg dishes	Beef, pork, lamb, veal, variety meats	All poultry and game	Tomatoes, carrots, broccoli, artichokes, creamed vegetables, peas-and-onions	*Cookies, mincemeat
Omelets	Pork stews		Sautéed in butter, green beans	Cakes, custards, ices, fruit dishes
Cheese			Tomatoes	Iced drinks
	*Chili con carne	Spanish partridge, Mexican turkey, rabbit and hare		Cakes, custards, pies, ice cream, sauce
Hard-boiled with anchovy	Boiled lamb, beef stew, tongue, *liver	Chicken	Stuffed tomatoes or peppers, onions	

REF. NO.	HERB OR SPICE	SOUPS	SAUCES AND GRAVIES	SALADS	FISH
27	CARAWAY	North African soups (use young leaves in soup)	Tunisian hot pepper sauce	Cucumbers in vinegar, coleslaw, *zucchini, potato	
37	CARDAMOM	Scandinavian fruit soup, pea soup	Curry basting sauce for duck, *spiced mixture for coffee	Orange, Waldorf, fruit	Boiled fish
13	CELERY SEEDS	Stocks, split-pea	Boiled salad dressing, tomato sauce	Potato, coleslaw	Court-bouillon, stuffings, shrimp
13	CELERY LEAVES	Stocks, meat, fish, poultry, potages, scotch broth	Meat, fish, and poultry sauces	Assorted green, tomato	Court-bouillon, marinades stuffings
12	CHERVIL	Cream, cold tomato (with lemon and sorrel), green fish, stock	Salad dressing, tartare, butter, sauce verte, remoulade, white wine, cream	Greens, potato, beet, tomato, coleslaw, chicken, fruit	Boiled fish, court-bouillon, stews, mousses
25	CHILI (CAYENNE)	Cream, bisques, pepper-pot, fish, beef, chicken, vegetables	Creole, cheese, curry, barbecue, tomato, cock-tail, salad dressings, rouille for fish soups, catsup	Oriental chicken, orange-olive, rice, carrot, *tomatoes and green peppers	Any fish (broiled, boiled, poached, creamed, or fried), shellfish, deviled seafood, Mexican and Indian dishes
6	CHIVES	Cream soups, oyster bisque, vichyssoise, cold lemon soup	*Butter sauce, sauce verte, mustard-tarragon sauce, gribiche, tartare, green goddess, sour cream	Shellfish, mixed greens, crab, chicken, tomato, meat, potato, fruit	Poached sole, marinades stuffing, creamed fish
29	CINNAMON	Moroccan Harira, Iranian soups	Chocolate sauce, curries, barbecue sauce, Catalan sauce	Orange-radish, *orange-carrot, fresh fruit	Catalan snails
30	CITRON		Latin American, Mexican, and Catalan sauces	Brazilian salad	
39	CLOVE	Green fish, Swedish pea, Russian crab, bean, beef broth, game	Cream, marinades, chili, curry, fruit, barbecue, catsup, tomato	Fruit salad	Crabcakes, court-bouillor pickled shrimp, baked fis
32	CORIANDER SEED	*Fish, Scandinavian game soup, lentil, pea, chick pea	Curry		Crab, court-bouillon, Portuguese fish stew
32	CORIANDER LEAVES	Oriental soups, beef broth	Moroccan, Mexican	Avocado, egg salad	
53	CRESS	Cream soup, Oriental soups	Green sauce, white butter sauce, mayonnaise, vinaigrette	Chicken salad	
76	CUBEB		In Moroccan mixed spice Ras el Hanout		

EGGS AND CHEESE	MEATS	POULTRY AND GAME	VEGETABLES	SWEET AND BAKING
Munster, deviled eggs, cottage cheese, dips and spreads	Pork, lamb and liver meatballs, goulash		Noodles, sauerkraut, potatoes, cabbage turnips, dumplings	Rye bread, cakes, cookies, salt sticks
	Swedish meatballs, ham, Norwegian meatloaf, hamburgers	Curried chicken, duck	Sweet potato, squash, stuffed cabbage, peas, rice	Apple pie, pumpkin pie, Norwegian waffles, pastries, buns, strawberry-rhubarb pie, gingerbread, cookies, spice bread, Danish pastry
Cheese dips, omelets, scrambled eggs	Corned beef tongue, meatloaf		Braised lettuce, tomatoes, noodles, potatoes, eggplant	Breads, salt sticks, rolls
Dips and spreads, cottage cheese, scrambled eggs	Boiled beef, meatloaf	Boiled chicken, stuffings	Lentils, *pureed celery rib, chestnuts	
Omelet, *scrambled, cheese dips and spreads, soufflés	Stews, stuffing, ground meat, veal, pork	Chicken, rabbit, venison, stuffings, fricassee	Peas, leeks, artichokes, green beans, potatoes, flans, tomatoes	
Deviled eggs, scrambled, cheese dips and spreads, spiced cheese	Pork spareribs, *chili con carne, sausages, lamb ribs, spiced meats, marinades, Mexican and Indian entrees	Chicken, duck, rabbit, squab, game, marinades, Mexican, Indian, and Szechwan entrees	Potatoes, bell peppers, rice, corn, beans, eggplant, chick peas, tomatoes, onions	
Omelet, scrambled eggs, deviled eggs, dips and spreads, cottage cheese	Lamb fricassee	Chicken fricassee, croquettes, rabbit	Creamed onions, artichoke ragout	
	Greek beef stew, meatloaf pâtés, ham, Portuguese pork	*Moroccan chicken stews		Crêpes and fritters, fruit compote, gingerbread, *cakes, cupcakes, ice cream, mincemeat, apple pie, rice pudding, custards
	Italian veal stew	Duck, rabbit		Marmalade, jams, cakes
Deviled eggs, dips and spreads	Boiled beef, meatloaf, stuffings, corned beef, marinades, lamb stew, glazed ham, *chili con carne, pork stew	Curried chicken, duck pâté	Beets, sweet potatoes tomatoes, baked beans, pickled vegetables, onions, marinated mushrooms, choucroute	Fruit cake, mincemeat, applesauce, pumpkin pie, spice cake, *orange ice
	Meatballs, sausages, *roast lamb	Marinades for game	Marinated vegetables, mushrooms, artichokes, eggplant, *pureed celery	Gingerbread, cookies, pumpkin pie, apple pie
		Moroccan stews	Rice, lentils, falafal	
Stilton and pears, roasted goat cheese			Stuffed vegetables provençale	

REF. NO.	HERB OR SPICE	SOUPS	SAUCES AND GRAVIES	SALADS	FISH
35	CUMIN		Curries, salad dressing, Mexican sauces	*Carrot, *green pepper and tomato, green olives	Baked whole fish, broiled fish
92	DANDELION			With crisp bacon	
10	DILL	*Russian fish soups, borscht, kidney soup	Sauce verte, sour cream, salad dressing, Scandinavian mustard, mayonnaise, hollandaise	Cucumber, chicken, fish, avocado, potato	Fresh salmon, smoked salmon, boiled crayfish, poached fish, stuffing
10	DILL SEED	Fish soups, kidney soup	Salad dressings		Stuffings, court-bouillon, poached fish
86	ELDER, BLACK				
41	FENNEL SEEDS	*Fish soups, Bouillabaisse	Spaghetti, salad dressing	Potato salad, shell-fish salad	Salmon, mackerel, court-bouillon
41	FENNEL LEAVES		Butters, hollandaise, mayonnaise	Mixed greens	Court-bouillon, dried stalks (for grilled fish), baked fish
95	FENUGREEK		Yemeni hot sauce, curries		
8	GALINGALE	Bali chicken soup	*Indonesian spice mixture for meat, poultry, and salads	"Gado-Gado"	
5	GARLIC	Provençal soups, fish, lentil, tomato, Vietnamese sour soup	Creole, Italian mayonnaise, Teriyaki, salad dressing, barbecue, curry, cream	"Chapon" cubed garlic bread, tomato, carrot	*Gumbos, fried fish, shrimps
100	GINGER	Chicken, Bali, stocks	Teriyaki, Moroccan sauces, fruit sauce for ham, curries, fresh tomato sauce	Shrimp avocado, bean sprout, fresh fruit, poached chicken	Indian fish cakes, Oriental dishes, stuffing
28	GOOD-KING-HENRY	Lentil soup		Mixed green salad	Seafood, sausage
33	HAZELNUT	Vegetable soup		German salads	Filet of trout, cod à la biscayenne
42	HERB BENNET			Mixed green salad	
46	HOPS		Flemish dishes		
15	HORSERADISH		Cocktail, mustards, cream sauce, hollandaise, beet	Beet, seafood	Shellfish, smoked fish, coulibiac
47	HYSSOP	Health, fish		Mixed greens, lentil, potato	Eel, stuffing

EGGS AND CHEESE	MEATS	POULTRY AND GAME	VEGETABLES	SWEET AND BAKING
Scrambled eggs, dips and spreads, hot cheese appetizers, deviled eggs	*Chili con carne, marinades for pork and veal, beef stew, kebabs, sausages, Bulgarian ham dish	Chicken stew	Curried: peas, eggplant, lentils, carrots, potatoes, cabbage	Eastern European bread
Scrambled eggs				
Stuffed eggs, cottage cheese	Scandinavian lamb stew, pork stew	Chicken fricassee	Boiled potatoes, beets, cucumbers, tomatoes, green beans	
Cream-cheese dips	Boiled beef		Sauerkraut, cabbage, turnips, green beans, coleslaw, marinades, beets	
			Sautéed leaves, Breton style	Fritters, jams and jellies, blossom pancakes, stewed fruits
	Marinade (for pork), meat loaf, lamb stew, Tuscan sausage	Rabbit stew	Marinated mushrooms, artichokes, and fresh fennel bulb	Bread
Cheese		Smoked duck	Cabbage, turnips, beans	
	Home-cured pastrami	Rabbit stew		North Africa bread, Greek honey and boiled seeds
		Curries, Indonesian chicken dishes		Confectionery
Fresh white soft cheese, mozzarella, curried eggs	Pâtés, beef, pork, lamb, veal, meatloaf, sausages, kebabs, marinades	*Chicken, rabbit, marinades	Eggplant, tomato, Spanish rice, spinach, beans, cabbage, potatoes	
Deviled egg, curried eggs	Sweet-and-sour pork, ham, pot roast, stuffing, steaks, marinades, sautéed calves liver	Oriental dishes, marinades, *Moroccan chicken, *chicken stew	Carrots, rice, onions	Gingerbread, spice bread, mincemeat, pumpkin pie, Christmas pudding, fresh fruit, a dash in chocolate cake
			Sautéed in butter	
		Stuffings	Green beans	*Cookies, cakes, buttercreams
				Cocoa substitute
Scrambled eggs with shoots		Stuffing	Young shoots (boiled or sautéed in butter or napped with fresh cream)	
	Roast beef, steak, smoked meats, boiled meats, smoked sausages	Boiled chicken	Beets	
	Stews, roast veal, roast pork			

REF. NO.	HERB OR SPICE	SOUPS	SAUCES AND GRAVIES	SALADS	FISH
50	JUNIPER	Lamb		Chicken	
52	LAVENDER	Vegetable (leaves)		Green (flowers)	
4	LEEK	Cream, stocks, fish, lentil, vichyssoise	Tomato, white wine, salad dressing	Mixed, composed	Poached, baked stews, court-bouillon, stuffing
55	LEMON VERBENA		Salad dressing		
44	LICORICE				Snail soup
54	LOVAGE (Use sparingly)	Beef broth		Mixed greens	
60	MACE		Spiced sauce for fruit	Fruit salad	
	MARJORAM, see Sweet Marjoram				
22	MARIGOLD	Beef broth, chowder, vegetable, Dutch soup		Mixed greens; buds are substitute for capers	
9	MELEGUETA PEPPER		Steak		
56	MELILOT			Mixed green (flowers)	
17	MUGWORT	Onion, vegetable		Green	Eel, carp
21	MUSTARD		Vinaigrette, hollandaise, barbecue, Lamaze, Robert, *tarragon, cheese	Coleslaw, avocado	Marinated salmon, deviled crab, mussels, stuffing
62	MYRTLE				
96	NASTURTIUM			Tossed salad; seeds as substitute for capers	
60	NUTMEG	Alsatian beer, cream	Béchamel, cream, fruit, wine	Chicken	Marinades, stuffings, croquettes
65	OLIVE	Pumpkin	*Spaghetti	Niçoise, chicken, potato	Baked filets, stuffings, casseroles
2	ONION	Fish, chicken, meat, vegetable	Brown gravy, barbecue, tomato, curry, soubise	Mixed, apple	Baked, marinades, court-bouillon
67	OREGANO	Minestrone, tomato, mushroom, vegetable	Italian salad dressing, spaghetti, mushroom, Spanish	Olives, seafood, *Greek, tomato, potato, *cucumber	Broiled fish steaks, marinade
24	PAPRIKA	Meat, chowder	Sour cream, mayonnaise, barbecue	Potato, egg, *cooked tomato and pepper	Broiled, poached, deviled crab, croquettes

EGGS AND CHEESE	MEATS	POULTRY AND GAME	VEGETABLES	SWEET AND BAKING
	Roast lamb, roast pork, pâtés and mousses, sautéed liver, kidneys	Marinades for game, chicken in beer, duck, rabbit stews, *roast squab	Cabbage, sauerkraut, choucroute	
	Stews (leaves)			Jellies (flowers)
Quiches, flans	Lamb, veal, pork, boiled meats, marinades	Chicken, poached casseroles, marinades, rabbit, stuffing	Mixed vegetables, marinated vegetables, *potato cake	
Omelets	Roast lamb		Asparagus, mushrooms	
				Confectionery, drinks
		Stewed rabbit (seeds)		
			Carrots	*Sweet and sour cherries, custards
			Rice	English country pudding
	Grilled steak			Bread
Sapsago	Marinades, sausage, stuffings	Hare stew		
	Veal stew, roast pork	Roast goose stuffing, duck, game		
Dips and spreads	Cold meats, sausages, ham, lamb, pork chops meatloaf, beef steak	Roast chicken, stewed rabbit	Cabbage, sauerkraut, beets	
	Roasts, stuffing	Pâtés, game		Syrups, fruit compote, sauces
			Pickled in vinegar	Fruit cup
Quiches, rarebits, soufflés	Meatloaf, liver pâté, lamb, veal, sausages	Marinades, stuffings, *Moroccan chicken stew	Broccoli, carrots, potatoes au gratin, cauliflower, Dutch style vegetables, spinach	*Cooked fruit, custards, pumpkin pie, eggnog, fruit pies, cakes, pancakes
Fresh cheese, dips and spreads	Stews, *lamb steak	Chicken, stuffings, casseroles	Rice, stuffing, tomatoes, peppers, eggplant	
Eggs à la tripe, omelet, quiche	Meat stews, marinades, meatloaf, *meat pies	Chicken, duck, rabbit, goose, squab, game, marinades	Beans, eggplant, mushrooms, lentils, peppers, artichokes, marinated vegetables, fried rice, potatoes	
Feta, omelets	Meatloaf, canneloni, pork, lamb, beef, veal, *chili con carne	Chicken, rabbit, casseroles, stuffing	Potatoes, mushrooms, marinated vegetables, artichokes, peppers, beans, tomatoes, eggplant, zucchini	Pizza
Scrambled eggs, deviled eggs, rarebit	Goulash, beef, lamb, veal, spareribs, Mexican entrees	*Fried chicken	Stuffed cabbage, potatoes, cauliflower, rice	

REF. NO.	HERB OR SPICE	SOUPS	SAUCES AND GRAVIES	SALADS	FISH
70	PARSLEY	Game, fish, chicken, meat, vegetable soups, garnish	Salad dressings, tartare, herb butter, barbecue, spaghetti, brown gravy, garnish, *gremolata	Mixed greens, seafood, vegetable, potato, marinated vegetables, tomato, chicken, ham, garnish	Broiled, *fried, poached, marinades, stuffings, baked, casseroles, croquettes, court-bouillon, garnish or seasoning for all fish and shellfish
14	PEANUT		Indonesian kebab sauce, Indonesian salad dressing		Shrimp
58	PEPPERMINT	Cold yogurt-garlic soup, Senegalese	Paloise	Fruit, mixed greens, chicken, Waldorf, *Tunisian mixed	Garnish for shellfish
75	PINE NUT		*Pesto and primavera sauces for pasta		Catalan entrees
78	PISTACHIO			Mixed greens	
71	POKE			Mixed green	
68	POPPY		Fruit salad dressing	Fresh fruit	
79	PURSLANE	Cream		*Purslane-olive, winter salads	
7	ROCAMBOLE	Cream	Brown gravy		Court-bouillon, stuffing
38	ROCKET	Use sparingly in vegetable soups		Mixed greens	
82	ROSEMARY	Vegetable, chicken, turtle	Brown gravy, Spanish, cream		Broiled steaks
84	RUE			Use sparingly	
26	SAFFLOWER	Fish, corn	Curry, butter		Grilled steaks
34	SAFFRON	Fish, chicken, corn, Moroccan Harira	Curry, cream, butter		Boiled seafood, bouillabaisse
85	SAGE	Lentil, garlic, vegetable, beef broth, consommé, minestrone	Paprika-butter sauce for pasta		Grilled fresh tuna
80	SALAD BURNET			Fish, mixed greens, tomato slices	
87	SAVORY (Summer and Winter)	Fresh pea, Crimean fish, cream, chowders, vegetable, lentil	Barbecue, salad dressing	Cucumber, mixed greens	Broiled, stuffing, baked
3	SCALLION	Green bean, *Oriental	Salad dressing	Mixed greens	Baked, poached, *Chinese steamed

EGGS AND CHEESE	MEATS	POULTRY AND GAME	VEGETABLES	SWEET AND BAKING
Cream, cheese, herb quiche, omelet, scrambled eggs	Beef, lamb, pork, veal, meatloaf, variety meats, casseroles, *stews, marinades, stuffings, garnish	*Chicken, squab, game, duck, goose, rabbit, chicken livers, casseroles, stews, stuffings, garnish	Potatoes, carrots, noodles, tomatoes, eggplant, zucchini, artichokes, turnips, parsnips, celery, mushrooms, rice, peas, cauliflower, lentils, asparagus, onions, leeks, marinated vegetables	
	Fried wonton	West African chicken stew	Chinese noodles	Candies, cookies, chocolate
Fresh cheese	Lamb stew	Stuffing	Rhubarb, peas, carrots, potatoes, beans, zucchini and eggplant fritters	Chocolate, fruit salad, candy, sherbets
	Ground lamb tarts, sausages		Stuffed grape leaves, *stuffed tomatoes, spinach, rice	Mexican custard cookies
	Pâtés, mortadella, pork roll	Chicken ballotine, duck pâté	Rice	Greek and Italian sweets
			Garnish (leaves); eaten like asparagus (stalks)	
Dips and spreads			Noodles	Apple tart, strudel, Egyptian desserts, cakes, rolls, breads, coffee cake
Omelet	Stews			
			Spinach, rice	
Deviled eggs, goat cheese marinade	Roast lamb, pork, or veal, *beef rib steak	Grilled chicken or rabbit, roast duck, wild boar	Mushrooms, peas, potatoes	Italian chestnut pie
Cheeses (use sparingly)				
	Lamb curry	Chicken curry		
Scrambled eggs	Lamb curry (also pork and beef)	Chicken curry, rabbit	Rice: *Paella, risotto	Swedish cakes, bread
Cream cheese	Ossobuco, *liver, German ham, Saltimbocca, roast pork	Stuffing, poultry liver spread	Fritters, tomatoes, onions, leeks, peas, eggplant	
				In cool drinks
Deviled, goat cheese, marinade, omelets, *flan	Pork, lamb, meat pies, smoked meats	Chicken livers, rabbit	Beans, lima, onions, string beans, peas, carrots, chick peas, oyster plant, lentils	
Scrambled, dips and spreads	Pork, lamb, veal, variety meats, beef stir-fry	Chicken, rabbit, chicken livers	Rice, potatoes, string beans, lentils, carrots, peas, *artichoke hearts	

REF. NO.	HERB OR SPICE	SOUPS	SAUCES AND GRAVIES	SALADS	FISH
69	SCENTED GERANIUM			Fruit	
31	SCURVY GRASS	Cream soup	Used like cress	In winter salads	
89	SESAME		Yogurt, cream	Garnish	Baked, poached, grilled
1	SHALLOT	Billibi, bisques, game, sea urchin, mushroom, oyster	Bercy, bordelaise, *white butter sauce, salad dressing, butters	Mixed greens, tomato	Gratin, sautés, mousse, *potted salmon
83	SORREL	Cream, lentil, Germiny	Sauce verte, mayonnaise, hollandaise		Shellfish, *sausage, salmon, shad
43	SOYBEAN	Oriental soups	Soy sauce, Teriyaki	Bean sprout	Sweet-and-sour shrimp
48	STAR ANISE				Oriental shrimp
88	STONECROP			Green (young shoots, leaves)	
45	SUNFLOWER			Garnish	
64	SWEET BASIL	Cream, vegetable, chowder, turtle, minestrone	Butter, *pesto, tomato, spaghetti, *cream	Chicken, mixed green, tomato	All kinds poached and creamed, broiled fish and shellfish
61	SWEET CICELY	Cream	Cream	Fruit, mixed	
66	SWEET MARJORAM	Lentil, Crimean fish, Italian Easter lamb	Tomato	Zucchini, cucumber, chicken, mixed greens	Baked halibut, creamed clams, grilled tuna
90	TAMARIND	*Sour fish soup, chicken broth	Curry		Indian and Indonesian dishes
91	TANSY		Butter spread		
16	TARRAGON	Cream, consommé, vegetable	*Béarnaise, tartare, remoulade, mayonnaise, *mustard, salad dressing	Mixed, potato, chicken, tuna, shrimp, lobster, coleslaw, eggs	Broiled salmon, shellfish
94	THYME	Lettuce, chowder, vegetable, minestrone, scotch broth	Spaghetti, tomato, butter, barbecue, creole	*Cucumber, coleslaw, chicken, tomato, pimiento	*Gumbo, broiled, poached, baked
97	TRUFFLE	Consommé	Périgourdine, Bagna Cauda	Mixed greens, potato	Sole, lobster
36	TURMERIC	Senegalese	Curry, mayonnaise, chow chow	Céléri remoulade	Shellfish, pilaf
98	VANILLA	A drop in chicken soup		Fruit	
99	VIOLET			Garnish	
49	WALNUT	Yogurt-garlic	*Pesto, Turkish	Mixed greens, potato	Snails, trout
63	WATERCRESS	Cream	Butter, cream, mayonnaise, herb	Mixed greens	Poached, fish, *baked scallops
19	WINTER CRESS	Vegetable		Mixed greens	Substitute for watercress

EGGS AND CHEESE	MEATS	POULTRY AND GAME	VEGETABLES	SWEET AND BAKING
				Jelly, custard
		Stuffed		
	Lamb with prunes	Coating for *fried chicken	Tomato jam, chick peas, eggplant, noodles	Italian bread, Halvah
Deviled, scrambled eggs, quiche	Beef, veal, pork, pâté	Chicken livers, pâtés, mousse	Mushrooms, green beans	
Quiche, scrambled eggs		Stuffing		
Egg foo yung	Oriental stir-fry	Oriental stir-fry	Watercress, broccoli, Buddha's delight	
	Oriental pork, *beef, and spareribs			
Dips and spreads			Green beans	
Scrambled eggs, omelets, spreads, mozzarella	Lamb, pork, veal, liver	Chicken, duck, rabbit, squab	Tomatoes, potatoes, onions	
			Turnips, carrots	Fruit cups, apple pie
Omelets	Meatloaf, *lamb stew, shish kebab, roast pork, sausage, stuffing	Grilled chicken, stuffing, duck, rabbit	Zucchini, cucumber, carrots, marinated mushrooms	
	Lamb	Chicken	Mixed vegetable curry	
		Turkey stuffing		Pudding, cakes
Scrambled eggs, omelet, stuffed eggs, fresh cheese	Lamb, veal, pork, casserole, variety meats	Grilled chicken, pâtés, mousses, duck, squab, rabbit	Tomatoes, marinated: leeks, carrots, potatoes, mushrooms	
Omelet, deviled eggs, dips and spreads	Pork, lamb, veal, beef, meatloaf, stuffing, sausages, pâtés	Chicken, rabbit, duck, stuffing	Tomatoes, beans, potatoes, mushrooms, eggplant, zucchini	Figs in red wine, bread
Omelet, scrambled eggs, Brie	Lamb, beef, pâté	Chicken, duck and goose livers, pâtés	Potatoes, pasta, risotto	
Deviled eggs	Indian curried lamb, pork, beef, lamb stew	Indian curried chicken, *Moroccan chicken	Rice, Paella	
				Custard, cake, rice pudding, cookies, pies
				Cakes, sherbet, jellies, garnish
Roquefort	Stews (lamb, veal, and beef), beef stir-fry	Chicken, coating for frying, stir-fry	Green beans, potatoes, zucchini, peas	Ice cream, *cakes, pies, soufflés
Scrambled	Hunan beef stir-fry	Chicken	Potatoes	

Plant Lexicon

ROY GENDERS

INDEX AND KEY TO THE PLANT LEXICON

Each of the 100 herbs and spices presented in this book is derived from a plant. The following section, the Plant Lexicon, constitutes an illustrated guide to the botanical properties of these plants. The reader will find here detailed information on the appearance, dimensions, location, and habits of the 100 herb and spice plants.

The heading of each text includes the following details: Latin name, English name, plant family, plant number, and references to the geographical distribution of the plant. The distribution is indicated in two lines. The first line gives the plant's original habitat or place of provenance; the second, in italics, indicates areas in which the plant has been introduced by man and grows either wild or cultivated.

Because English common names of herbs and spices are unstandardized and variable, the 100 herbs and spices of the lexicon have been arranged in alphabetical order according to their standard *Latin names* and each plant has been assigned a number from 1 to 100. To locate a plant in the Lexicon, it is necessary to know its Latin name, or else to obtain its *reference number* by looking up its English name in the list printed at right.

Allgood	28	Elder	86	Mugwort	17
Allspice	72	Estragon	16	Mustard	21
Almond	81	Fat hen	28	Myrrh	61
American cress	19	Felon herb	17	Myrtle	62
Angelica	11	Fennel	41	Nasturtium	96
Anise	73	Fenugreek	95	Nutmeg	60
Aniseed tree	48	Field poppy	68	Nut Pine	75
Asafetida	40	Filbert	33	Olive	65
Balm	57	Food of the gods	40	Onion	2
Bamboo	18	French sorrel	83	Oregano	67
Basil	64	Galanga	8	Oswego tea	59
Bay leaf	51	Galingale	8	Paprika	24
Bee balm	59	Garden cress	53	Parsley	70
Bergamot	59	Garlic	5	Peanut	14
Bird pepper	25	Ginger	100	Pepper	77
Black caraway	74	Golden-buttons	91	Peppermint	58
Black elder	86	Goober	14	Pigeon berry	71
Black mustard	21	Good-King-Henry	28	Pine (nut)	75
Black pepper	77	Goosefoot	28	Pinyon	75
Blowballs	92	Grains of paradise	9	Pistachio	78
Borage	20	Green almond	78	Poke	71
Burnet	74	Green pepper	24	Poke weed	71
Cacao	93	Groundnut	14	Poppy	68
Caper	23	Hazel	33	Porret	4
Caraway	27	Herb bennet	42	Pot marigold	22
Cardamom	37	Herb-of-grace	84	Purslane	79
Cayenne pepper	25	Hop	46	Red poppy	68
Celery	13	Horseradish	15	Rocambole	7
Chervil	12	Hyssop	47	Rocket	38
Chili	25	Indian cress	96	Rosemary	82
Chinese parsley	32	Juniper	50	Rue	84
Chives	6	King's clover	56	Rugula	38
Ciboule	3	Laurel	51	Safflower	26
Cinnamon	29	Lavender	52	Saffron	34
Citron	30	Leek	4	Sage	85
Cive	6	Lemon balm	57	Salad burnet	80
Clove	39	Lemon verbena	55	Sand leek	7
Cloveroot	42	Licorice	44	Savory	87
Cobnut	33	Lovage	54	Scallion	3
Cole	15	Mace	60	Scented-leaf	
Coriander	32	Madeira nut	40	geranium	69
Corn poppy	68	Malabar cardamom	37	Scurvy grass	31
Cress	53	Marigold	22	Sesame	89
Cubeb	76	Marjoram	66	Shallot	1
Cumin	35	Melegueta pepper	9	Skoke	71
Dandelion	92	Melilot	56	Soja bean	43
Dill	10	Mercury	28	Sorrel	83
Dragon plant	16	Mirasol	45	Soybean	43
Dyer's saffron	26	Monkey nut	14	Spearmint	58

Spoonwort	31
Star anise	48
Stonecrop	88
Summer savory	87
Sunflower	45
Sweet basil	64
Sweet bay	51
Sweet ciceley	61
Sweet fern	61
Sweet marjoram	66
Sweet pepper	24
Sweet violet	99
Sweetwood	44
Tabasco	25
Talewort	20
Tamarind	90
Tansy	91
Tarragon	16
Thyme	94
Truffle	97
Turmeric	36
Vanilla	98
Violet	99
Walnut	49
Watercress	63
Welsh onion	3
White mustard	21
Wild parsnip	11
Wild spinach	28
Winter cress	19
Winter rocket	19
Winter savory	87
Wood avens	42
Zedoary	36

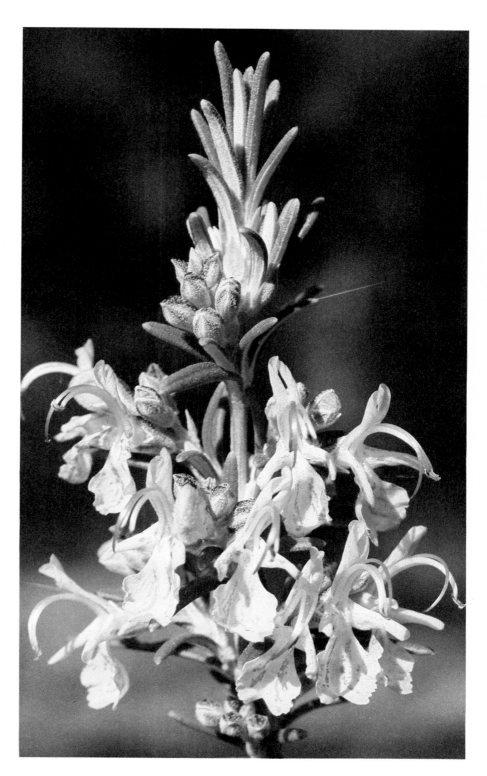

An enlarged close-up of a tiny sprig of rosemary in blossom. It is one of the most aromatic flavoring plants because of the location of its essential oil immediately beneath the surface of the leaf's underside. Its well-known, distinctive flavor, though not universally loved, is often used in combination with roast lamb and other meats, as well as with poultry and several different vegetables.

ALLIUM ASCALONICUM	ALLIUM CEPA	ALLIUM FISTULOSUM
SHALLOT	ONION	SCALLION, WELSH ONION
Liliaceae	Liliaceae	Liliaceae
1 C Asia *Warm Temperate Zones*	2 S Eur, C Asia *Warm Temperate Zones*	3 N Eur, N Asia

A large bulbous plant which takes its name from the Latin *cepa*, a head, for the bunched florets are borne in heads at the end of a hollow 18 in. (45 cm) stem. The bulbs, which are covered with a light brown tunic or skin, can with good culture grow to enormous size, each weighing up to 2 pounds (1 kilo) or more. When grown in a warm climate, they are sweet and juicy; elsewhere they are strong smelling and when cut cause the eyes to water. The name onion is derived from union, single or one, denoting that the bulbs do not form offsets. Onions are raised from seed sown in gentle heat in a greenhouse or frame; or in a warm cli-

mate, in shallow drills outdoors early in spring. Plant out the seedlings into a rich soil in early summer. In cooler climates, sets are grown. These are tiny bulbs which have been retarded and stored under refrigeration. In spring they are pressed into the surface of the soil like shallots and will make rapid growth. Allow 6 in. (15 cm) between the bulbs and 10 in. (25 cm) between the rows. In autumn, when the foliage dies down, the bulbs are lifted, dried, and stored for winter use. Spring or salad onions which make only a small bulb are pulled "green" to use in summer salads and are of the White Lisbon variety.

A bulbous perennial, with a small rounded pear-shaped bulb 1 in. (about 3 cm) in circumference and tapering to a point, with fleshy hollow leaves which grow 16 in. (40 cm) long. There are two forms, one whose bulbs have a silver skin; others with a reddish-brown skin. The small onion-like bulbs form close together about the parent bulb. Propagation is by planting the bulbs on the surface of a well-nourished soil. This is done early in spring by pressing the bulbs into the soil which has been made firm on the surface. Plant in rows 6 in. (15 cm) apart and allow 10 in. (25 cm) between the rows. The tops of the bulbs (the necks) should stick out of the soil. Late in summer, the leaves should be bent over at the neck of the bulbs to encourage ripening. Early in autumn when the leaves turn yellow, lift the clumps and separate the bulbs. Dry them on trays in an airy room and use through winter, replanting leftovers.

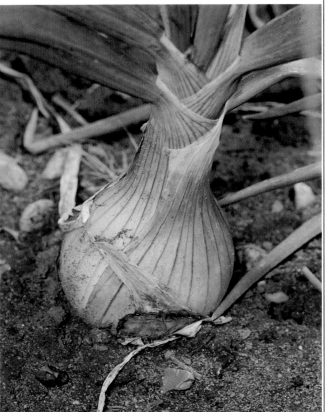

A perennial of the extreme north of Europe and Asia, it takes its second name, Welsh onion, from its being grown in the coldest regions of that country. The plant resembles chives in that it forms no bulb in the accepted sense, its leaves being the part used to impart their mild onion flavor. Like chives, the plant forms dense fibrous roots and has thin hollow stems which grow 6 in. (15 cm) tall. They remain green all winter. Propagation is by division every 3 or 4 years (as for chives), and by seed sown in autumn or in spring in shallow drills 6 in. (15 cm) apart. The grass-like foliage is cut 1 in. (2.5 cm) above soil level, and thus the plants will continue to increase. The plants will be ready to use 3—4 months after sowing and will remain green all year no matter how severe the winter. Like chives, this is a suitable plant for edging. It may be grown in a window box or tub and grows well in ordinary soil.

ALLIUM PORRUM

LEEK, PORRET

Liliaceae

4 N Eur, N Asia

ALLIUM SATIVUM

GARLIC

Liliaceae

5 C Asia
Warm Temperate Zones

An annual or biennial of extreme hardiness, grown for the lower blanched portion of the stem which is the leaves. These arise tightly clasped together from a flat underground plate which forms the base of the leaves. Leeks require a rich soil and a long season to mature, and copious water. Seed is sown in autumn in a frame or greenhouse. Seedlings are planted out in spring in ground trenched to a depth of 10 in. (25 cm), with humus material placed at the base to retain summer moisture. To plant, make a hole 2 in. (5 cm) deep with a piece of cane and drop in the base of the plant. Do not firm or cover with soil. Plant 6 in. (15 cm) apart in a double row the same distance apart. After planting, water in. Well-grown leeks will grow 16—18 in. (40—45 cm) tall and 3 in. (7.5 cm) in circumference. As the plants make growth, draw up the soil at the base to blanch (whiten) the stems. No frost will harm them.

Garlic may well be the most pungent of the 325 species of the genus *Allium*. It is at least the strongest of those commonly used, sufficiently potent so that persons who have not recently eaten it are apt to avoid persons who have. Yet it can be tamed in cooking to an extent which brings out its basic sweetness and makes it inoffensive on the breath. Its great versatility—it can be a subtle whisper in a leg of lamb or an aggressive assault on the taste buds in a green salad—has made it one of the most frequently used seasoners throughout the world.

Garlic is a perennial with irregular shaped bulbs, around which grow small bulblets called cloves. The broad, flat, strap-like leaves taper to a point and arise from an elongated sheath which encloses the bulb. The flowers, whitish-mauve with paper-like bracts, are borne in capitate heads. Rich in alkaline salts and sulfur compounds, garlic is a blood purifier and is used in the kitchen to impart its unique flavor to many savory foods. For the cloves to ripen well (as they do in the Near East), they require a light sandy soil and an open sunny position. It is one of the few plants to enjoy a loose soil which was well manured for a previous crop, or with a little decayed manure worked in before planting. This is done in autumn where winter frosts are not troublesome, or in spring. Propagation is by the cloves or bulblets, since seed is not produced in the cultivated plants. Plant in rows 2 in. (5 cm) deep and 6 in. (15 cm) apart, with 10 in. (25 cm) between the rows. Cloves planted in autumn will be ready to lift late the following summer; those planted in spring are lifted in autumn when the leaves turn yellow. A related species, bear's garlic or ramsons *(A. ursinum),* is sometimes found growing in the humus-enriched soil of deciduous forests and river valleys. Its elliptical, lance-shaped basal leaves are used to impart bright color and a light garlic flavor to spring salads. A flowering stalk appears later, bearing an umbel of many snowy-white 6-petaled blooms. Small black seeds—rather than cloves—are produced for propagation.

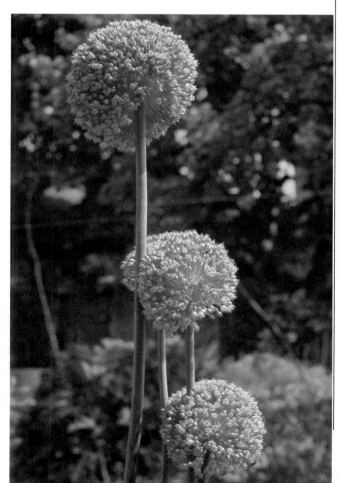

ALLIUM SCHOENOPRASUM

CHIVE

Liliaceae

6 N Eur, Asia
Temperate Zones

ALLIUM SCORODOPRASUM

ROCAMBOLE, SAND LEEK

Liliaceae

7 N Eur, N + W Asia

ALPINIA OFFICINARUM

GALINGALE, GALANGA

Zingiberaceae

8 SE Asia

AMOMUM MELEGUETA

MELEGUETA PEPPER, GRAINS OF PARADISE

Zingiberaceae

9 Tropical W Af
Tropical Af, India, Guiana

Widespread on cliffs and mountainous slopes. An evergreen perennial with round, hollow, rush-like leaves, tapering to a point and bearing, on 8 in. (20 cm) stems, small globular flowers of deep mauve-pink, with paper-like bracts. In bloom July—September, the plants form a clump of small bulbs, like spring onions, and are heavily rooted. They are readily propagated by division. This is done at almost any time of year except when the soil is frost-hard. Plant the offsets 6 in. (15 cm) apart, the bulbous part just below soil level. They require a soil containing humus, to retain moisture in dry weather when the plants will continue to increase through the year. The rush-like leaves are cut away just above the bulbous part and are chopped into small pieces. The plants make a neat edging to the herb garden and they may be planted to good effect in window boxes or tubs.

It takes its name from the Danish *rockenbolle,* a wild onion. A perennial, it resembles garlic in that it forms cloves or small bulbs around the parent bulb. From the bulb, with its elongated tunic which protects the thin base of the flat-toothed strap-like leaves, arises the flower stem which grows 2 ft (60 cm) tall. The brilliant purple flowers like those of chives are borne May—August. The plant requires a light loose soil, like the garlic, and the cloves are planted in spring 6 in. (15 cm) apart in drills made 2 in. (5 cm) deep. Lift in autumn when the leaves turn yellow, shake off surplus soil, and separate cloves.

Native of the tropics, the plant takes its name from the Arabic *khalanjan,* mild ginger. It is grown for its thick tuberous roots which are used in confectionery and medicine as a substitute for ginger. From the roots the flower stem arises to a height of 3—4 ft (1 m) and is enclosed by the leaf sheaths. The leaves are about 12 in. (30 cm) long and are lanceolate but not stalked. They are of shining bright green. The flowers, borne in terminal spikes, are white with veins of dark red. When the plants are several years old, they are lifted and the roots dried in the sun. They are then cut into cylindrical pieces about 3 in. (7.5 cm) long and are about 1 in. (2 cm) thick, marked by rings which are the lower leaf scales. The roots are reddish-brown and have many uses. Arabs ground them to take as snuff and use them to flavor wine and beer. Hindus include them in perfumes and in the preparation of curries.

It is native to Liberia and the Gold Coast, that part of tropical western Africa known as the pepper coast, and it is a herbaceous perennial with a long slender rhizomatous root covered with sheathing leaf bracts. The flower stems arise to a height of 6 ft (2 m) and are enclosed by leaf-sheaths. The leaves are ca. 8 in. (20 cm) long with prominent veins; the handsome wax-like flowers are large and cylindrical. The fruit is a cylindrical yellow capsule, spotted with red, the thick fleshy pericarp enclosing a colorless pulp that contains the shining, hard, round, reddish-brown seeds which have an aromatic taste but no smell and are used as a condiment and to flavor spirits and liqueurs. The pungent principle contained in the seeds or grains is paradol. The name *melegueta* is from an Indian word meaning pepper. When the seed pods, which attain the size of large almonds, are harvested, the seeds are removed.

ANETHUM GRAVEOLENS

DILL

Umbelliferae

 10 SE Eur, SW Asia
Temperate Zones

ANGELICA ARCHANGELICA

ANGELICA, WILD PARSNIP

Umbelliferae

 11 N + E Eur, N Asia
N Am

ANTHRISCUS CEREFOLIUM

CHERVIL, SWEET CHERVIL

Umbelliferae

 12 C Eur, C Asia
N Am

A hardy annual which takes its name from the Saxon *dil-la,* to lull (because the water in which the seeds were immersed for several hours was rubbed on nursing women's breasts to lull children to sleep after feeding). It grows 2 ft (60cm) tall with smooth stems and linear leaves which have sheathing footstalks. The small yellow flowers are borne June—July in a terminal umbel and are followed by oval seeds which are flatter than those of caraway and have a warm, aromatic taste. Seed is sown early spring in drills 10 in. (25cm) apart, the plants being thinned to 8 in. (20cm) in the rows. The fern-like leaves are used in summer to make sauces to serve with fish, and the seeds to make vinegar for pickling. The seeds ripen early in autumn, when the heads are removed and placed on trays in an airy room to complete their drying. An open, sunny position is always necessary for the seed to ripen in cooler climes. Dill is believed to be the aneth of antiquity, which imparted strength to gladiators, and in some countries today it is still called aneth. Dill is particularly appreciated in central and northern Europe, especially in Poland and in Scandinavia. One of its commonest uses is for pickling cucumbers.

One of the hardiest of plants, distributed as far north as Lapland and Iceland. A perennial, it is often given biennial treatment but it will not usually flower until its second year. To be long living, it should not be allowed to flower, though if seed is required for flavoring, the plants can be left to flower in July—August and the seed is harvested late in summer. Also, if one or two seed heads are left on, the plants will seed themselves each year. It has smooth un-furrowed stems which grow 6—7 ft (2m) tall, with leaves 2 ft (60cm) across, with decurrent segments and toothed margins. The greenish-white flowers appear in August in rayed umbels and are visited by bees and other insects for nectar. All parts have a musk-like scent, the roots being used to make vermouth, the seeds to flavor liqueurs. The stems impart a musky flavor to fruit pies. Set the plants 3—4 ft (1 m) apart at the back of a border.

A pubescent annual growing 16 in. (40cm) tall, its hollow stems covered in silky hairs. The leaves are 3-pinnate, pubescent on the underside, and emit a sweet aniseed scent when pressed. If a sowing is made each month from early spring until late summer, there will be a continuous supply of young leaves. Like parsley, sow fresh seed or it will not germinate well. Sow in shallow drills 8 in. (20cm) apart and thin the seedlings to 6 in. (15cm) in the rows. Begin using the leaves when the plants are 6 in. (15cm) tall and the plants will become all the bushier. The white flowers are borne in sessile umbels early in summer.

APIUM GRAVEOLENS	ARACHIS HYPOGAEA	ARMORACIA RUSTICANA	ARTEMISIA DRACUNCULUS
CELERY	PEANUT	HORSERADISH	TARRAGON, DRAGON PLANT, ESTRAGON
Umbelliferae	Leguminosae	Cruciferae	Compositae
13 Eur, W Asia, N + S Af *Warm Temperate Zones*	**14** S Am *Tropical Zones*	**15** Eur, Asia *Temperate Zones*	**16** S + N Eur, N Asia *Warm Temperate Zones*

There are two forms of this hardy perennial. First is French tarragon, native of southern France and Spain, a plant with smooth dark green lance-shaped leaves which is not as hardy as the second variety. This second form is Russian tarragon, *A. redowskii,* which has rougher leaves of paler green. The French tarragon, of much more piquant flavor, is that most often grown for making vinegars, an essential ingredient of sauce tartare. The plants bear drooping white flowers in flat heads, but French tarragon does not set seed in northern parts. Tarragon is a corruption of the Latin *dracunculus,* a little dragon,

An annual or biennial all parts of which have an unusual pungent flavor. Wild celery is found by the wayside, usually in damp places. It grows 2 ft (60 cm) tall with a grooved stem and lobed leaves, the lower stalked, the upper sessile. The small greenish-white flowers are borne in terminal umbels and are followed by light brown ovoid seeds. For garden culture, celery requires a long growing season and fresh seed is sown in gentle heat early in the year, the seedlings being transplanted and grown on in a frame until ready to plant out early in summer. It requires a rich soil and is best grown in trenches. Plant 10 in. (25 cm) apart in a double row and keep the plants watered in summer or the stems will be woody. Begin earthing up the stems toward the end of summer to blanch them. Plants can remain in the ground all winter, lifting as required. For seed, leave several plants to run to seed.

Native of tropical America but grown commercially in the tropics everywhere, it is one of the few plants *(Trifolium subterranean* is another) which bear fruit underground (geocarpy). The flower stems downward, forcing the seed pods to form beneath the soil where the fruits ripen. *Arachis* grows 16 in. (40 cm) tall, its leaves divided into 4-pinnate oval leaflets with short stalks and prominent ribs. As many as 20—30 fruits are formed below ground and are ripe by the end of summer. The nuts are enclosed in capsules 2 in. (5 cm) long, 2 to each, with one nut at each end of the capsule. After lifting, they are dried in the sun and the nuts are usually marketed in the capsules. The almost round nuts when fully grown have a circumference of about 1 in. (2 cm), and are covered in a thin brown tunic. They are highly nutritious, being 28 percent protein, and contain a valuable oil used as an alternative to olive oil.

A perennial growing 2 ft (60 cm) tall with a stout cylindrical rootstock which may grow down to a depth of 2 ft (60 cm). Once planted, it is difficult to eradicate, for the smallest piece of root broken off when lifting will grow again. A plant of extreme hardiness, it has large dark green root leaves with 12 in. (30 cm) footstalks and toothed margins, while the small white flowers are borne in loose terminal spikes. Horseradish sauce made from fresh root will bring tears to the eyes if consumed in too large amounts but helps the digestion of rich meats as an alternative to mustard. Grow it in an out-of-the-way corner, in a rich, deeply dug soil, planting the thongs or roots in autumn or winter, 18 in. (45 cm) apart; or sow seed in spring and plant out at the same distance late in summer. The plants should not be lifted until 3 years old, when the roots are of reasonable size. It will grow in semishade.

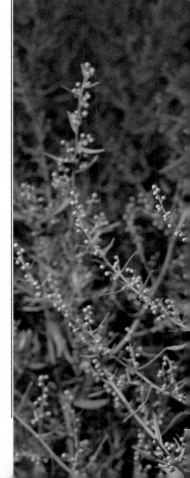

from its serpent-like roots. Both forms are perennial and grow 2 ft (60 cm) tall. Plant 20 in. (50 cm) apart in autumn or spring and in ordinary well-drained soil. The French tarragon requires a sunny, sheltered situation. The leaves are used fresh or are cut and dried in late summer and can be frozen in ice cubes, or after blanching in boiling water for a few seconds, placed in plastic bags in the deep freezer. They will keep fresh for one year. Tarragon vinegar can be made at home using fresh tarragon picked just before it flowers. The herb is placed in a bottle, which is then filled with white wine vinegar and stored.

An erect perennial growing 3—4 ft (1 m) tall with grooved stems and 1—2-pinnate dark green leaves, with the leaflets toothed and slightly downy on the underside. The small fluffy flowers are yellowish-brown or red and are borne in panicles or spikes during late summer. It is a common plant of the wayside. The leaves contain the bitter principle absinthe. The plant is hardy and grows well in ordinary soil. It is propagated from offsets removed in autumn and planted 2 ft (60 cm) apart; or from seed sown in spring.
A. abrotanum, southernwood or lad's love, makes a bushy plant 3—4 ft (1 m), its gray-green leaves being twice pinnately dissected. A perennial but which may lose its leaves in a cold winter, the leaves are lemon-scented and used in stuffings. The plant is native to southern Europe and was introduced early into America, being mentioned in John Gent's *New England's Rarities Discovered* (1672).

A shrubby grass of perennial habit with woody culms which may reach a height of 100 ft (30 m) under natural conditions. The cylindrical stems are bright green and hollow and are grooved with short internodes. The bright green leaves arise in a tuft from the root and are about 30 in. (75 cm) long, being sharply serrated on both edges, terminating to a point and with the leaf surface rough. The fruit is a nut. Under garden culture, the flower stems reach a height of 6—7 ft (2 m), terminating in a large silver inflorescence which will retain its beauty for years when dried. The young shoots are used in salads and are boiled and served with butter. The seeds (nuts) also have culinary uses. The plants require an open situation and a deep, moist soil. Otherwise they suffer from summer drought. Propagation is by division in autumn or spring. There is a form with handsome pink inflorescences, called *Bambusa roseum.*

A perennial with glossy, deep green leaves and angled, furrowed stems, the leaves on the upper part being undivided. The flowers are bright yellow, borne in terminal cymes. It is present throughout the Northern Hemisphere and is completely hardy. Where there is no running water, it may be grown as a substitute for watercress to which it is closely related. A bed made up in semishade and in a soil containing humus will be productive for several years and the plants may be used all year. Like watercress, it is rich in iron and sulfur. Seed is sown in spring in a frame or in shallow drills, and germination takes about 3 weeks if the soil is kept moist. When the seedlings are large enough to handle, move to a prepared bed and plant 8 in. (20 cm) apart. The first green will be ready to cut in late autumn. To keep the plants growing in cold weather, surround half the bed with 12 in. (30 cm) boards; cover in plastic.

BORAGO OFFICINALIS

BORAGE, TALEWORT

Boraginaceae

20 | W Asia
Eur, N Am

An annual or biennial growing 20 in. (50 cm) tall, all parts being covered in bulbous hairs. The oval leaves are gray-green and the flowers which are borne in forked cymes June—August are brilliant blue with purple-black anthers which meet cone-like and dehisce slowly, allowing pollen to fall onto the cone which encloses style and stigmas. When a bee thrusts its proboscis between the stamens, the anthers are displaced and the cone opens to allow pollen to fall on to the stigmas. The flowers are included in salads and the leaves and stems in summer drinks, to which they impart a cucumber-like flavor and give the drinkers a sense of exhilaration. This is due to potassium salts present in the mucilage. Borage is best used freshly picked, since its leaves do not keep very well. For a continuous supply, make a sowing under glass (in a cold frame) in July and set out the plants in spring 20 in. (50 cm) apart. Make another sowing in spring where the plants are to mature. One or two plants should be let seed themselves each year. The plant is named from the Latin *borra*, hair, though the Greeks named it *euphrosynon*, meaning a "sense of well-being." It is present on waste ground, growing in sandy soil.

BRASSICA NIGRA, SINAPIS ALBA

BLACK MUSTARD, WHITE MUSTARD

Cruciferae

21 | S Eur, N Af, W Asia
Temperate Zones

21

Brassica nigra, black mustard, is an annual growing 3—4 ft (1 m) tall with a branching stem, the lower leaves pinnate with rounded terminal lobes, the upper leaves narrow and pointed. The flowers, borne June—August, are bright yellow, followed by quadrangular shortly beaked pods, the seeds providing the condiment mustard. A plant of cornfields and hedgerows, it has been grown commercially in many parts of Europe and Asia since the sixteenth century, to accompany meats to aid their digestion. The finest mustard is grown and made at Dijon in France, in recognition of which Philip the Bold granted armorial bearings to the town in 1382. Dijon mustard is made with tarragon vinegar, anchovies, and capers. It was not until the end of the eighteenth century that Mrs. Clements of Durham, England, invented the modern method of dressing mustard with flour. The green pods form along the upper half of the stem and remain upright, each pod containing 4—8 black seeds. Under field culture seed is sown in drills 12 in. (30 cm) apart in spring, and at the end of summer, the crop is cut and the seed threshed and dried.

White mustard is *Sinapis alba*, an erect annual growing 12 in. (30 cm) tall with pinnate leaves and yellow flowers followed by horizontal seed pods containing 4—5 round pale yellow seeds (hence its name to distinguish it from the black). It is grown "green" for salads, sowing the seed thickly in boxes of shallow soil or on wet flannel in a kitchen window. It is ready to cut in 3 weeks and is grown all the year.

Persons acquainted with the often fiery nature of commercial mustards may be surprised if someone offers them mustard seeds to chew. They have a nutty flavor, are pleasant to eat thus directly, and acquire heat only when processed.

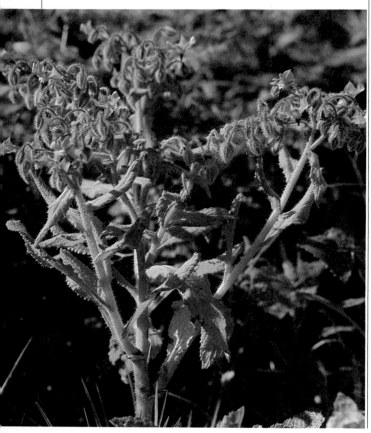

CALENDULA OFFICINALIS

MARIGOLD, POT MARIGOLD

Compositae

22 S Eur, N Af, W Asia
Temperate Zones

CAPPARIS SPINOSA

CAPER

Capparidaceae

23 S Eur, W Asia
Warm Temperate Zones

CAPSICUM ANNUUM

PAPRIKA, SWEET PEPPER, GREEN PEPPER

Solanaceae

24 C + S Am
Torrid + Warm Temperate Zones

CAPSICUM FRUTESCENS

CHILI, CAYENNE PEPPER, TABASCO PEPPER

Solanaceae

25 C + S Am
Torrid + Warm Temperate Zones

A shrubby branched perennial arising from a large taproot and growing to 3—4 ft (1 m), with short-stemmed opposite dark green leaves terminating to a point and small purple-white flowers borne in the leaf axils. The fruit is a large rectangular fleshy berry, the seeds being enclosed in pulp, with the outer case thick and fleshy. Fruits may measure 3 by 2 in. (about 8 by 5 cm), each of 3 or 4 unequal lobes. They can be used green or ripe, when they will have turned bright red (like tomatoes of the same family) and are rich in vitamin C. Hybrid varieties have recently been raised which are resistant to mosaic disease.

A pungent-smelling annual or biennial of easy culture, which grows well in any soil and in the colder regions of the world. Growing 12 in. (30 cm) tall, with a succulent stem and pale green oblong sessile leaves, the flowers are borne with freedom all summer and autumn and are about 2 in. (5 cm) across with orange or yellow ray florets and disk florets of black or brown. The flowers are dried (and are also used fresh) to include in soups and stews, to impart their pungency, hence its old name, pot marigold. The flower heads are cut when dry and spread out in an airy room to complete their drying; then the ray petals are pulled from the disk which is discarded. It readily transplants and seed is sown in pots or boxes in early spring and the seedlings set out 12 in. (30 cm) apart when large enough to handle. Or alternatively the seed can be sown where the plants are to bloom.

A shrubby perennial with slender stems spreading to 3—4 ft (1 m) in length. The alternate simple leaves are fleshy. They are oval with twin reflexed spines formed at the base of the leaves which replace the stipules. The large 4-petaled flowers are borne solitary and are about 2 in. (5 cm) across with the stamens protruding beyond the corolla. They bloom May—June and are followed by large berries 2 in. (5 cm) long containing the kidney-shaped seeds, but it is the unopened flower buds that are removed for pickling and used to flavor vinegars and sauces. They are known as capers and are harvested in early summer. The plant is present on rocks and cliffs around the Mediterranean. The variety *C. inermis* has large, dark green fleshy leaves with straight spines and more pendulous branches. It is present on old walls and mountainous slopes and also provides the capers of commerce.

Chili (Cayenne) can be either *C. frutescens* or *C. minimum*, each of which is a perennial plant of similar habit and botanical characteristics to the sweet pepper. It bears larger numbers of fruits, which are smaller and cylindrical, usually growing 2—6 in. (5—15 cm) long and tapering to a blunt point. Each contains 10—30 small seeds embedded in the pulp and protected by the outer flesh which turns from bright green to red or orange as the fruit ripens. The fruits are "hot" and spicy, hence the name "hot" pepper, and are used for making pickles and chutneys. The seed when dried and ground provides the cayenne pepper of commerce, the plants being grown in those parts of the New World close to the equator. In northern Europe the plants are treated as annual and are grown under glass, as they are less hardy than sweet peppers. Seed is sown early in March in a temperature of 65 °F (18 °C), the seedling replanted.

CARTHAMUS TINCTORIUS	CARUM CARVI	CHENOPODIUM BONUS-HENRICUS	CINNAMOMUM ZEYLANICUM
SAFFLOWER, DYER'S SAFFRON	CARAWAY	GOOD-KING-HENRY	CINNAMON
Compositae	Umbelliferae	Chenopodiaceae	Lauraceae
26 S Eur, C + S Asia, Af	**27** N Eur, Asia *N Am*	**28** Eur, W Asia *Temperate Zones*	**29** SE Asia *S Am*

Native of tropical Southeast Asia including Ceylon, Malaysia, and Indonesia, it is an evergreen tree which grows in sandy soil and requires a high rainfall for its cultivation. It will reach a height of 35 ft (10 m). The large leathery leaves are glossy and pale green above, white on the underside. The flowers are white and borne in panicles. They are followed by small, oval blue berries. The bark, smooth and ash-gray, is removed from the branches when the tree is about 6 years old. The younger branches yield the finest

The genus, with about 20 species, is native of the Canary Islands and the Mediterranean region as far as Central Asia. *C. tinctorius* is believed to have come from Eurasia. It is an annual growing about 30 in. (75 cm) tall with a branching stem and with spiny oval stem-clasping leaves. The rayed flowers have yellow outer petals and a central boss of red petals which, in the East, are used to dye silk red, hence its second popular name "dyer's saffron." The dried outer petals yield the safflower of curry powder when dry; it is also used as a substitute for saffron, or added to saffron as a less expensive adulterant. The flowers are mixed into bread and some other foods in Eastern Europe. The almost white fruits are rectangular and yield an essential oil used as a substitute for olive oil; safflower is among the salad oils lowest in cholesterol content. When ground, the seeds are used for flavoring food.

A glabrous biennial growing 2 ft (60 cm) tall with hollow stems and a parsnip-like root running deep into the ground. It has an aromatic smell like that of parsnip and the 2-pinnate leaves resemble those of parsley. During its first year, the plant forms a rosette of leaves and in its second year the flower stem arises, at the end of which are borne umbels of small white flowers. They are followed by the carpels (the fruit) which are oblong and boat-shaped with small ridges. When dry they divide and emit a powerful scent. The value of the seed depends on the amount of carvol present and the extent of its purity. Besides its use to flavor cakes and bread in most northern European countries, its seed gives a special flavor to the liqueur kummel. In northern climes it will ripen its seed only in a dry, hot summer. Seed is sown in shallow drills in July where the plants will mature.

A hardy perennial growing 2–3 ft (60–90 cm) tall with long stalked arrow-shaped leaves of dark green which are thick and fleshy and are as if frosted on the underside. The flowers are green, without petals and borne on leafless spikes in midsummer. It is a common plant of the wayside and seashore, for all members of the family are maritime plants. It is named after Henri IV of France who discovered its culinary properties. The young shoots are earthed up in spring and when 6–8 in. (about 20 cm) long are cut, peeled, and steamed to serve with melted butter. Later in the year, the leaves are used as a substitute for spinach. Seed is sown in spring in shallow drills and when large enough to move, the young plants are set out 12 in. (30 cm) apart in well-prepared soil. Established plants may be lifted and divided in spring in alternate years. The plant has had a great number of popular names.

CITRUS MEDICA	COCHLEARIA OFFICINALIS	CORIANDRUM SATIVUM
CITRON	SCURVY GRASS, SPOONWORT	CORIANDER
Rutaceae	Cruciferae	Umbelliferae
30 E India *Warm Temperate Zones*	**31** N Eur, N Asia, N-N Am	**32** S Eur, Asia, N Af *Temperate Zones*

bark. It is removed throughout the year by making an incision lengthwise on each side of the branch, so that the bark comes away as a hollow cylindrical section. It is tied into bundles, each weighing 2 pounds (1 kilo). The inner bark is the best. It is sold in the markets of the East for drying, then ground and shipped to all parts as cinnamon powder. It is one of the world's oldest commodities, having been imported into Egypt and Judea by the Phoenicians, the caravans meeting at Babylon on the Euphrates. Oil is obtained from the berries.

Those bits of candied peel which you come upon in fruit cakes and puddings, and take for lemon, are in all probability not lemon *(C. limonia),* but *C. medica,* though lemon is used in this way too, as is lime *(C. aurantifolia)* and bitter orange *(C. aurantium).* The citron is the *etrog,* one of the four species of foods involved in the celebration of the Hebrew Succoth. It is sometimes held to be the forbidden fruit of the Garden of Eden. Citron, a thorny shrub or small tree, can grow to 10 ft (3 m), with oblong leaflets 4–7 in. (10–17 cm) long. It bears clustered flowers that are purplish in bud and usually remain pale purple on the outside. The oblong yellow fruit, 6–10 in. (15–25 cm) long——and more elongated than lemon——has a thick, rough rind, which is candied. The citron, like the orange, lemon, lime, and other trees of this genus, is propagated by seeds and then by grafting stock on seedlings.

One of the earth's hardiest and most health-giving plants, it is not a grass but closely related to watercress and, like that plant, its fleshy leaves are rich in iron and sulfur. An annual or biennial growing 12 in. (30 cm) tall with angular stems, it is present near seashores and on cliffs. It has heart-shaped root leaves which are stalked and spoon-shaped stem leaves. The small white flowers are borne in corymbs from a multi-branched stem. Before it was known that citrus fruits had a high vitamin C content, scurvy grass was eaten by sailors at sea to prevent scurvy disease. It too is rich in vitamin C. It can be included in salads instead of the cresses, to which it imparts the same pleasant bitter taste. To have a supply in the garden, seed is sown in spring and again in June, in shallow drills in ordinary soil, thinning the plants to 8 in. (20 cm) apart. If a few plants are covered with cloches, it can be cut all the year.

An annual growing 8–12 in. (20–30 cm) tall with solid branching stems which are ridged and with 2-pinnate dark green leaves, the lower divided into deeply cut segments. The white or pale pink flowers are borne in 5–8-rayed umbels and are followed by pale yellow fruits of peppercorn size and shape with 2 oil ducts in each half. The whole plant and the unripe seed has the offensive smell of bugs, and takes its name from the Greek *koros,* a bug. But when the seed is fully ripe it assumes the sweet smell of orange, and the longer the seeds are kept, the stronger the orange smell becomes. The seed is included in most curry powders and imparts its delicious flavor to junket and blancmange. The leaves, known as Chinese parsley, are sometimes used as an herb. Seed is sown in spring in shallow drills, in an open sunny situation. Thin the plants to 6 in. (15 cm) apart and harvest the seed in early autumn.

CORYLUS AVELLANA	CROCUS SATIVUS	CUMINUM CYMINUM
HAZEL, FILBERT	SAFFRON	CUMIN
Betulaceae	Iridaceae	Umbelliferae

33 C + S Eur, W Asia *Temperate Zones*

34 S Eur, W Asia

35 S Eur, W Asia, N Af

Believed to be the Karkom of the Song of Solomon, it takes its name from the Persian *karkum,* yellow, from the dried grains (powder) collected from the stigma. It is from *karkum* that the genus takes its name; and saffron is from the Arabic *sahafarn,* a thread, from the thread-like stigma. To the ancients, it was the most important of all plants, and in the time of Alexander the Great, merchants distributed it to all parts of Europe. A late-flowering crocus, it produces its narrow gray-green leaves in early summer and its purple-red chalice-like flowers in autumn. They open flat and do not close up again so that where grown commercially, a dry climate is essential. Also, to be free flowering, the corms must be baked in the sun during summer. The oval corms are planted 2 in. (5 cm) deep and 4 in. (10 cm) apart, in well-drained soil in June and the stigmas are removed in early autumn when dry. When they are then put under pressure by heavy boards, the stigmas will form a solid mass. The yield increases for 5 years; then the corms are lifted, divided, and replanted. It takes 70,000 blooms to produce 1 lb (½ kilo) of saffron grains (powder); yet a century ago, 50,000 lb (25,000 kilos) were imported each year into Britain from Spain.

Small trees or shrubs growing 16 ft (5 m) tall with heart-shaped saw-edged leaves, broad at the base, pointed at the apex. The trees are present in open woodlands and a hazel coppice is a valuable part of the economy of the countryside. The stakes are used to make hurdles for sheep enclosures and for fencing and windbreaks; also for basket making, while the nuts (fruits) are an economic crop, gathered when ripe in autumn, when the husks and nuts have turned dark brown. The female flowers are borne on the old wood and rely on wind for their fertilization, which carries pollen from the drooping golden-yellow catkins which are the males. The flowers appear early in spring and rely on dry weather for their successful pollination and a heavy crop. For satisfactory pollination, plant 3 varieties together. Plant 12 ft (3—4 m) apart. It will take a tree 5 years to come into bearing, at about 5 ft (1.5 m) tall.

An annual cultivated in Egypt, Syria, and Malta for its many uses in curry powders, pickles, and Indian chutneys to which it imparts a hot spicy taste. In Germany, it is put into bread and cakes and the Dutch use it to flavor cheese. It grows about 16 in. (40 cm) tall, with branching slender stems and fern-like leaves biternately dissected. The tiny flowers which appear in late summer, are white or blush-pink and are borne in 4—6-rayed umbles. They are followed by large elongated seeds, ½ in. (1 cm) long, light brown and straight, whereas caraway seeds are curved. The taste is more bitter than that of caraway but the flavor is aromatic and spicy. In northern Europe, it will ripen its seed in a sunny garden only in a hot dry summer. Sow in shallow drills early in spring and thin to 6 in. (15 cm) apart. Ordinary soil is suitable. Tithes were paid in aromatic seeds in Biblical times.

CURCUMA LONGA, CURCUMA ZEDOARIA	ELETTARIA CARDAMOMUM	ERUCA VESICARIA SUBSP. SATIVA	EUGENIA CARYOPHYLLATA
TURMERIC, ZEDOARY	**CARDAMOM**	**ROCKET, RUGULA**	**CLOVE**
Zingiberaceae	Zingiberaceae	Cruciferae	Myrtaceae
36 S Asia *Torrid Zones*	**37** SE Asia *India, Ceylon, Guatemala*	**38** S Eur, W Asia, N Af *Temperate Zones*	**39** SE Asia, Madagascar *Tropical Zones*

Curcuma longa produces the turmeric used in curry powders, the best coming from Malabar and Java. A perennial with a multi-rhizomatous rootstock each of which is cylindrical and varies in size from 2 to 3 in. (5 to 7 cm), tapering at each end. When dried and ground the orange-colored powder has a "hot" aromatic peppery taste. In habit, the plant resembles ginger, the dark green erect leaves being enclosed in a sheath while the cylindrical flowers are borne in an erect spine and are deep yellow. It is propagated by small pieces of root planted 4 in. (10 cm) deep and 12 in. (30 cm) apart. *C. zedoaria,* zedoary, is also grown for its rhizomatous roots and has a more camphor-like odor. Its roots are also yellow and covered in rings, the marks of the old leaves. The flower stems consist of the leaf sheaths which are covered in down. The flower spike arises to a height of 16 in. (40 cm) and the flowers are scented.

Known in commerce as Malabar cardamom, it grows on the coast by spontaneous germination. This is done by felling a number of older trees and shaking up the soil. In a month, seedlings appear and produce a crop in 4 years. It forms a thick rhizome-like root from which arises a stem 6—7 ft (2 m) tall, enclosed by the spongy sheath of the leaves which grow 2 ft (60 cm) long and terminate in a point. The flowers and branches alternate. The plant needs an annual rainfall of more than 100 in. (250 cm) to flourish. The fruits, called Malabar "shorts" in the trade, are about 1 in. (2 cm) long, being smooth and pale yellow and containing 3 valves each of 16 small seeds.

This subspecies of *E. vesicaria* is cultivated as a flavorer for salads, its leaves being quite strong in taste. It is a half-hardy annual, which branches to a height of 2—3 ft (60—90 cm). The plant bears erect siliques at least 1 in. (2.5 cm) long. The flowers, white to cream colored, have purplish veins. The sepals are early-deciduous. Because of its pronounced flavor verging on pepperiness, the leaves are best if used when young and tender. Keep them well trimmed back to stimulate fresh growth. Running quickly to seed in summer, the plant is best used in spring or autumn. Sow in open ground in early spring; first leaves should be ready within 2 months. Rocket is used primarily in England, Greece, Turkey, and Italy; its strong peppery flavor is particularly appreciated in Rome, where rockets are the basis of the mixed salad which is the local favorite, *misticanza.*

Native to Indonesia (Moluccas) and introduced into Mauritius by the French in 1770, and later to Zanzibar where it flourishes in the yellow clay subsoil as nowhere else. Long before then, cloves were imported into Britain and northern Europe for flavoring food. Shakespeare mentions the custom of sticking cloves into dried oranges to hang from the waist, to be inhaled to counteract unpleasant smells. They became known as pomanders. It is an evergreen tree growing to a height of 60—65 ft (18—20 m) with smooth gray bark; its lance-shaped leaves covered with oil glands which release the aromatic clove smell when pressed. The crimson-purple flowers are borne in cymes at the ends of the branchlets, and it is the dried flower buds that yield the cloves of commerce. A tree begins to yield when 6 years old and continues for 100 years. The season lasts from August until November.

53

FERULA ASSAFOETIDA	FOENICULUM VULGARE	GEUM URBANUM	GLYCINE MAX, GLYCINE SOJA
ASAFETIDA, FOOD OF THE GODS	**FENNEL**	**HERB BENNET, CLOVE-ROOT, WOOD AVENS**	**SOYBEAN**
Umbelliferae	Umbelliferae	Rosaceae	Leguminosae
40 C Asia *Iran, Afghanistan, India*	**41** S + E Eur, N Af, W Asia *Temperate Zones*	**42** Eur, N Af, Asia *N Am, Aus*	**43** SE Asia *US, Brazil, SE Asia*

A hardy perennial growing up to 10 ft (3 m) tall and up to 4000 ft (1200 m) above sea level, with large cabbage-like heads which are edible. From the woody root of the plants when 3—4 years old, a milky resinous juice is obtained which coagulates upon exposure to air. Soil is pulled away to expose the roots and a deep incision is made in them. After 4—5 weeks, the hardened juice, now reddish-brown after exposure to air, is collected by scraping it from the roots. The soil is then replaced. The gum resin acts as a stimulant and with its garlic-like flavor has culinary uses. The Romans used it to rub onto the gridiron on which meat was to be cooked. It quickens the appetite and improves the digestion. John Evelyn tells that in ancient Greece it was so highly esteemed that it was dedicated to Apollo at Delphi, hence its name "food of the gods." The center "bud" or head also contains the aromatic juice.

An erect perennial growing 5—6 ft (1.5 m) tall, its 3—4 pinnate leaves divided into numerous narrow segments, with the whole plant taking on a bluish appearance. The small yellow flowers are borne in compound terminal umbels and are followed by narrow ovoid fruits with blunt ends and with 8 longitudinal ribs. The seed, believed to allay the pangs of hunger, was eaten by the poor and for the same reason was included in bread and cakes to which it imparted an aromatic flavor. From the fresh leaves is made a sauce to serve with fish. The Romans named it *Foeniculum* because of its hay-like smell when dried. The plant grows best in a chalk or limestone soil and seed is sown in summer where it is to mature, but it transplants easily. Plant 2—3 ft (60—90 cm) apart and in a sunny position or the seeds will not ripen. The plant is present on waste ground and cliff tops, usually in calcareous soil.

An erect hairy perennial growing 16—20 in. (40—50 cm) tall, its radical leaves pinnate; its cauline leaves ternate. It has reddish stems and bears golden-yellow scentless flowers about 2 cm across. Self-fertilization of the flowers occurs in the absence of insects. It is present in open woodlands and by the wayside, preferring shade and moisture about its roots which are clove-scented and when dried were placed among clothes and vestments to impart an aromatic perfume. The clean and washed roots may be included in apple pies instead of cloves. Plants are raised from seed sown in pots or boxes in spring and set out 12 in. (30 cm) apart when large enough to handle. The water avens, *G. rivale*, is present in ditches and by streams and bears drooping flowers of reddish-orange nearly 1 in. (2.5 cm) across. In North America, the dark brown roots when dry are used as a substitute for cocoa and to make a beer.

Closely related to the dwarf or bush bean, it makes a low bush 16 in. (40 cm) tall with trifoliolate leaves with long stipules and pea-like flowers borne in the leaf axils. In some regions it grows erect to 6 ft (2 m) high. The white beans are borne 3—4 to a pod, which are formed in threes or fours. They are similar to broad beans, though shorter. Like all beans, they have a high protein content and are rich in Vitamin B; indeed soybeans are the richest protein vegetable food known. They also yield soya flour, which is sold in health food stores, and a valuable oil which has many seasoning uses (including value as a substitute for olive oil). Soybean can be cultivated under very diverse soil and moisture conditions, and for this reason as well as its high protein content, it has become an increasingly frequent crop, particularly as a food crop in overpopulated developing countries. Seeds cannot be sown until all risk of frost is past.

GLYCYRRHIZA GLABRA

LICORICE

Leguminosae

44 SE Eur, SW Asia
SW Eur, N Af, C Am

HELIANTHUS ANNUUS

SUNFLOWER

Compositae

45 Mexico, Peru
Temperate Zones

HUMULUS LUPULUS

HOP

Moraceae

46 Eur, Asia
Temperate Zones

Native of Mexico and Peru whose peoples adopted it as the emblem of the sun god (hence its name from *helios,* the sun) and carved it on the walls of Aztec temples. The Spaniards introduced it into Europe. An annual, it sends up its thick hairy stem to a height of 10ft (3m) and has large heart-shaped leaves. If seed is sown in spring, plants will grow about 3ft (1m) during each month of summer, the stem terminating in a flower 12in. (30cm) across and of brilliant gold, with the center "like some curious cloth wrought with a needle," this being in reference to the many tubular florets which form a cushion-like boss. It is grown commercially in southern Europe and Asia, its leaves for cattle food; its seed to make into cooking fats and margarines, for sunflower seed oil is low in cholesterol and is now recognized as a valuable health food. The oil is pale yellow and equal to olive oil for table use. The seeds yield 50 percent high-quality oil. With commercial plantations, seed is sown singly 10in. (25cm) apart in drills made 3ft (90cm) apart, but for garden culture, seed is sown under glass early in spring, one seed to a small pot, and the plants set out without root disturbance, early in summer. The stems need support as they will grow tall.

A plant of the Mediterranean and Near East, it is perennial, increasing by underground stolons or runners while the roots penetrate to a depth of 3—4ft (1m). It grows 4—5ft (1.5m) high with dark green leaves divided into pairs of narrow leaflets. From the leaf axils in midsummer arise the flower spikes, pea-like and purple-blue. Long pencil-like roots are required by the trade so it is given a deeply worked soil. It grows well in volcanic ash and in sandy soil. The roots are cut into 4in. (10cm) long, each with 2 "buds" or eyes, and they are planted early in spring 16in. (40cm) apart in the rows and just below the surface. The rows are made 3—4ft (1m) apart. The plants are undisturbed for 3—4 years; then they are lifted early in autumn. The soil is scooped away to enable the entire plant to be removed. They are washed and the juice extracted while fresh. The best licorice root is said to come from Spain.

A hardy perennial growing 16ft (5m) tall. The 3—5-lobed leaves, cordate at the base, are serrated and have a petiole as long as the blade. The flowers are greenish-yellow, the males borne in a catkin-like inflorescence, the females in the axils of the bracts to form a cylindrical spike, like a pine cone. The bracteoles bear glandular hairs which yield the gold dust lupulin, the chief ingredient in brewing beer. Plants are raised by sowing seed in a frame or in the open in shallow drills in spring. When large enough to move, plant them 3—4ft (1m) apart, in autumn; or propagate by root division in spring or autumn. A rich humus-laden soil is needed. Poles about 18ft long (5m) are placed close to the plants in spring and the plants will begin to yield heavily from their third year. The hop canes (strobiles) are picked late in summer when they turn dark brown. Commercially, they are dried in kilns before using.

HYSSOPUS OFFICINALIS

HYSSOP

Labiatae

 47 S Eur, SW Asia
Temperate Zones

ILLICIUM VERUM

STAR ANISE, BADIAN

Magnoliaceae

 48 SE Asia
Warm Temperate Zones

JUGLANS REGIA

WALNUT

Juglandaceae

49 SE Eur, SW Asia
Temperate Zones

JUNIPERUS COMMUNIS

JUNIPER

Cupressaceae

 50 Eur, NW Af, Asia, N Am
Temperate Zones

It is a plant primarily of the Holy Land and was mentioned so often in the Bible that it was named *azob,* holy herb, from the Hebrew. An evergreen, it makes a dense bush 16 in. (40 cm) high and is hardy in all but the coldest regions but needs a sunny aspect and a light, well-drained soil. It has square stems and linear leaves and during summer bears pink, white, or purple flowers in racemes. They are attractive to bees. All parts of the plant are aromatic, but the tops of the stems contain the most flavor and perfume and this is the part used. In northern Europe it has become naturalized on old buildings. In the garden it is planted 2 ft (60 cm) apart and is propagated by seed or from cuttings removed with a "heel" in summer and rooted in sandy compost. Set out the plants the following spring. The flowers and leaves are used in soups and stews, to which they impart a sharp, aromatic taste. The leaves are also used in stuffings.

A genus of 6 trees or shrubs, native of China and Japan and the warmer parts of America. *I. verum* is evergreen with broad elliptic leaves which are poisonous; it grows 30 ft (9 m) tall. The tree bears spice-fragrant creamy-yellow red-tinted flowers in clusters, which gives the tree its name *Illicium,* meaning "allurement." They are followed by flat star-like fruits, with 8-rayed boat-shaped carpels arranged around a central disk, in appearance like a starfish. Since early times the seeds have been exported from the Chinese province of Kuang-si to use in cooking, for they are cinnamon-scented. *I. griffithii* is native of the Khansia Hills of Bengal, the seed pods having 15-rayed carpels. *I. floridanum* of the United States has lance-shaped leaves and bears purple-red flowers.

Deciduous nut-bearing trees, *J. regia* grow to 100 ft (30 m) with a trunk 9–10 ft (3 m) in circumference, covered by smooth gray bark and with dark green stalked leaves 16 in. (40 cm) long, divided into 7–11 opposite pairs. The male flowers are borne in long, drooping catkins; the female or pistillate flowers in small clusters at the end of the shoots. The walnut is not self-fertile and 2 trees must be planted together (though not too close) for reliable pollination. Walnuts take 10 years to bear fruit; of irregular shape, the nut is enclosed in a woody brown shell which is covered by an oval green husk divided longitudinally into 4 sections. The nuts will fall when ripe in autumn, when the shells are removed from the husks. The shells divide to expose a nut in each half. Plant trees not more than 3 years old, unless grown in pots, for older trees resent transplanting. Do not prune them or they will "bleed."

An evergreen tree growing 40 ft (10 m) high and of great hardiness and adaptability. It requires a chalk-laden soil to attain tree proportions, and in mountainous regions and in peaty moorland soil, grows dwarf and bushy. The small spiky awl-shaped leaves enable it to tolerate considerable warmth or intense cold, for there is a minimum of moisture loss through transpiration. All parts are fragrant. The tiny white flowers are followed by fleshy pea-like berries (fruits), really cones, and are first green, ripening to deep purple, which takes 2 years. They are used to impart their unique perfume to gin which takes its name from the plant. The tree has attractive red bark, which flakes off like that of yew, and the wood is also scented when burnt. In Scotland it is used to impart its flavor to smoked salmon. In *The Anatomy of Melancholy,* Robert Burton tells that it was used at Oxford on open fires, to sweeten the air of student's rooms.

LAURUS NOBILIS

BAY, SWEET BAY

Lauraceae
51 S Eur, NW Af, SW Asia

LAVANDULA SPICA

LAVENDER

Labiatae
52 S Eur, NW Af

LEPIDIUM SATIVUM

CRESS, GARDEN CRESS

Cruciferae
53 S Eur, W Asia
Warm Temperate Zones

The Romans named it from *laudare*, to praise, for it was thought to be worthy of the highest honors and they crowned their victorious leaders and poets with chaplets made of the leaves. Its name bay is from the Anglo-Saxon meaning a crown or chaplet. An evergreen with glossy dark green lance-shaped leaves, it forms a multi-branched tree or shrub with smooth bark and grows about 20 ft (6 m) tall. The leaves emit a sweet balsamic scent when bruised and are an important part of the *bouquet garni*. The inconspicuous yellow flowers are followed by cherry-sized berries (fruits) which turn from green to black as they ripen.

Though adaptable to wide climatic variations, it is not fully hardy in colder regions where it should be grown in a tub of convenient size for moving indoors before winter, to be kept in a frost-free room or greenhouse. The plant is attractive when grown on a single stem and the head clipped into ball or square shapes. The plants are lifted outdoors in early summer when frost has vanished. In this way the fresh leaves are available all year. "Bitter and aromatic, with something of both vanilla and nutmeg" according to the description by Elizabeth David, the bay leaf imparts a fragrance more like that of a spice than an herb.

A shrubby perennial growing 2—4 ft (1 m) tall with opposite entire oblong leaves terminating to a point and downy on both sides which gives them a silver-gray appearance. The flowers, blue or violet, occasionally white or pink, are borne 6—10 in an erect spike early in summer. The flowers have a 2-lobed upper lip and a 3-lobed lower lip. *L. spica* is the Old English lavender and grows 4 ft (1 m) tall and the same across. The Grappenhall variety bears flowers of deepest lavender. *L. nana compacta* makes a dwarf hedge 12 in. (30 cm) tall and bears mauve flowers; and *alba*, a variety, bears white flowers. The twickle purple variety bears dark violet flowers and is of similar habit. These lavenders are hardy in northern Europe but *L. stoechas* is not and needs a warmer climate. The flowers have purple (instead of green) bracts which intensifies their color. Lavenders require an open, sunny situation and well-drained soil.

A quick-growing annual, native of Persia and the Near East, and cultivated all the year in most parts of the world to provide "green" for salads, especially in winter. It grows 16 in. (40 cm) tall with much-divided leaves, though for salads it is cut (as white mustard and rape) when only 3 in. (7.5 cm) tall. There is a plain-leaf variety which is of milder flavor and is more popular for salads and for garnishing. When allowed to develop, the plants bear white flowers. Seed is sown thickly outdoors in spring and summer or in a frame or a sunny window in winter. Sow in shallow boxes containing 1 in. (2.5 cm) of soil and do not cover the seeds. Or sow on flannel without soil. In a temperature of 48 °F (9 °C) cress will be ready to cut within 3 weeks of sowing. If grown with mustard, sow the cress 4—5 days earlier so that both will be ready together. (If sown on flannel, cress must be used quickly.)

LEVISTICUM OFFICINALE	LIPPIA CITRIODORA, ALOYSIA CITRIODORA	MELILOTUS OFFICINALIS	MELISSA OFFICINALIS
LOVAGE	LEMON VERBENA	MELILOT, SWEET CLOVER, KING'S CLOVER	BALM, LEMON BALM
Umbelliferae	Verbenaceae	Leguminosae	Labiatae
54 S Eur *Temperate Zones*	**55** C + S Am *Warm Temperate Zones*	**56** Eur, Asia *Temperate Zones*	**57** S Eur, SW Asia, N + W Af *Temperate Zones*

An erect branched biennial growing 2–3 ft (60–90 cm) tall with pale green tri-foliolate leaves and yellow pea-like flowers borne in one-sided racemes, the keel shorter than the wings and standard. In bloom through-out summer, the flowers are sweetly scented and the leaves and stems contain coumarin. As they dry they release the refreshing scent of new-mown hay. The flow-ers are followed by black one-sided hairy seed pods, containing black seeds which are also scented when dry. Seed is sown in late summer in shallow drills for the plants to bloom the following year. Thin to 16 in. (40 cm) apart.

A hairless perennial growing 3–4 ft (1 m) tall with hollow purple stems and bright green glossy leaves with broadly toothed leaflets, like those of celery and with a similar pungent smell. The yellow flowers are borne in umbels and are followed by yellow fruits, curved like those of caraway and with much of the celery flavor. The plant forms a taproot about 6 in. (15 cm) long which is also pungently scented. It grows on cliffs by the sea but under garden culture requires a rich moist soil. It is propagated from seed (which must be fresh) sown in shallow drills in spring, thinning the plants to 16 in. (40 cm) apart; or by di-vision of the offsets in au-tumn. The fresh leaves are included in salads and the stems when blanched are used like celery in summer. The seeds are also used for flavoring and the plant has numerous medicinal virtues. It will die down in winter but comes into fresh growth in spring each year.

A shrubby deciduous peren-nial growing 6–7 ft (2 m) high and bearing its leaves in whorls of 3, the pale green narrow leaflets being 2 in. (5 cm) long and pointed. The pale lilac flowers are borne in slender spikes. In northern Europe the plant requires a warm wall to survive an aver-age winter and even then may be cut down by frost. A light, sandy soil is necessary for its long life. Or the plants can be grown in tubs during summer and lifted indoors before winter. The crinkled leaves are harvested in late summer and after drying are rubbed down to impart their lemon flavor to stuffings. The powdered leaves may also be included in pot pour-ris and talcum powders. It is propagated by young shoots removed late in summer and rooted under glass. Plant out from small pots in spring. This plant is suitable to growing in a greenhouse, at a temperature of 55 °F (13 °C); the pots are then planted outside in summer.

A perennial plant of the Mediterranean countries but long naturalized in Britain and northern France, where it may have been brought by the Romans. It is present in hedgerows and open wood-lands and grows 2 ft (60 cm) tall with hairy upright stems and stalked ovate leaves, deeply wrinkled and serrate, and of palest green. The flowers which appear late in summer are blush-white and borne in short-stalked axil-lary whorls from the upper part of the stem and leaf joints, with the calyx cover-ed in long white hairs. All parts of the plant are de-liciously lemon-scented when handled. The sweet-ness of balm was proverbial in olden times and all parts were used. The plant re-quires a cool, moist soil and is propagated from seed sown in summer in a frame, setting out the plants the fol-lowing spring; or from cut-tings removed in July and rooted in a sandy compost. The plant takes its name from the Latin for honey.

MENTHA PIPERITA

PEPPERMINT

Labiatae

58 S Eur
Temperate Zones

MONARDA DIDYMA

BERGAMOT, OSWEGO TEA, BEE BALM

Labiatae

59 E-N Am
Temperate Zones

MYRISTICA FRAGRANS

NUTMEG, MACE

Myristiceae

60 SE Asia
Tropical + Warm Zones

It grows naturally in western New Guinea and in the Molucca and Banda Isles, the "Nutmeg" Isles of Indonesia, in volcanic ash and where it enjoys great humidity. It was introduced into Bourbon and Zanzibar and several West Indian islands, especially Jamaica. An evergreen tree growing to 30ft (10m) high with an undivided trunk, the large leaves are deep green and glossy and highly aromatic. The small, fragrant white flowers cluster in the axils of the leaves and are followed by golden-yellow pear-shaped fruits with a longitudinal groove on one side (like a peach) which when ripe burst open into 2 parts. The seed is enclosed by a red fleshy part known as the aril, which is the substance called mace. The seed has a thick outer shell which encloses the nutmeg which, because of the intense pressure of the aril, is deeply wrinkled. A mature female tree will bear about 2000 nuts and will bloom and ripen its fruit the whole year. It will be productive for at least 80 years. One male tree will fertilize 20 female trees. The leaves, on distillation, yield a colorless oil with a nutmeg-like odor. Oil of mace has a similar perfume.

Possibly a natural hybrid between *M. aquatica*, the water mint, and *M. spicata*, spearmint, peppermint grows 16 in. (40cm) tall with opposite lanceolate leaves, serrated at the edges and purple flowers borne in a blunt terminal inflorescence. The stems are reddish-purple, and in dry weather the plant takes on a similar hue. It is widespread in ditches throughout Europe but not Scandinavia. Oil of peppermint is extracted from the plant. *M. spicata* (syn. *M. viridis*) is spearmint, the best for mint sauce. It is a hairless erect perennial growing 12 in. (30cm) tall with brilliant green lanceolate leaves, unequally serrate, and lilac flowers borne in a spire-like inflorescence, hence its name should be spiremint.
M. aquatica grows 3ft (90cm) tall, its ovate leaves downy on both sides and releasing a fruity scent when pressed. Its reddish flowers are borne in terminal whorls.

A hardy perennial growing 2–3 ft (60–90cm) tall with square deeply grooved stems branching at the top and lance-shaped leaves with serrated edges, slightly hairy on both surfaces. The white, pink, or crimson flowers are borne in whorls at the end of the stems and have green bracts, the reflexed petals being long and narrow. They appear throughout summer. The plant takes its botanical name from that of Dr. Monardes of Seville, who published his herbal on the flora of America in 1569; and its popular name is from the scent of its foliage, which was likened to that of the bergamot orange of Spain. The plant was first collected at Oswego, near Lake Ontario, in 1744 by John Bartram, who sent seed to England. The plant requires a moist soil and increases by underground stems. It is propagated by division in winter; or from cuttings; also by seed.

MYRRHIS ODORATA	MYRTUS, COMMUNIS	NASTURTIUM OFFICINALE	OCIMUM BASILICUM
SWEET CICELY, SWEET FERN	MYRTLE, COMMON MYRTLE	WATERCRESS	SWEET BASIL
Umbelliferae	Myrtaceae	Cruciferae	Labiatae
61 Eur, Asia	**62** S Eur, N Af *Warm Temperate Zones*	**63** Temperate Zones	**64** Asia *Temperate Zones*

In the East it is sacred to the Hindu gods, Krishna and Vishnu, and is grown in pots in most homes, worshipped by the household. In the cooler west, it is also grown in small pots indoors for it is frost-tender. To accompany tomato dishes, it has no equal; it is grown in Italy in large quantities for this purpose. From the leaves, the French make a sauce to accompany fish, and in England the plant gave its unique sweet spicy smell to the once famous "Fetter Lane" (London) sausages. In northern Italy basil leaves, crushed or ground with fresh garlic, form the basis of *pesto* sauce.

Sweet basil is a much-

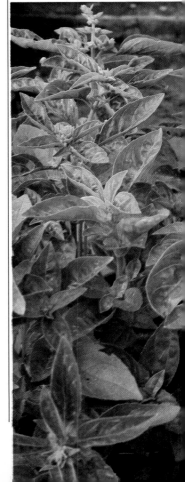

A hardy pubescent perennial growing 4–6 ft (1.5 m) tall, its stem hollowed and furrowed and with large downy pinnate leaves of palest green. The white flowers are borne in terminal umbels and are scented as are all parts of the plant, resembling myrrh. The leaves when included in salads, though spicy, taste as if they have been steeped in sugar, hence its popular names. The seeds reach 1 in. (2.5 cm) in length and have 5 prominent ribs. The unripe seeds are used in salads, and, when ripe and after being ground, to flavor cakes. From the leaves a sauce is made to accompany fish, and the candied roots are eaten as a sweetmeat. They have a warm aniseed taste. The plant requires a rich, well-drained soil and is best raised by sowing seed in spring where it is to grow, at the back of a border. In its second year, thin to 2 ft (60 cm) apart and begin using the leaves when young.

To the ancient Greeks and Romans, no plant was more highly prized, for the berries (fruits) have a pleasant aromatic taste and were used to flavor food as they are today. Pliny said that the best myrtles grew in Egypt and their gum exudations resembled myrrh, hence the plant's name. It forms a large bush 6–8 ft (2–2.5 m) tall with shining evergreen box-like leaves and in July bears pure white flowers of powerful scent in the axils of the leaves. They have protruding golden stamens. The leaves, too, are scented and retain their fragrance when dried. The essential oil is contained in pelludic dots (cells) embedded in the leaf. From the leaves and flowers is distilled a perfumed water, eau d'Ange. The fruits are yellow and large and are harvested at the end of summer. Like the flowers, they have a sweet, aromatic taste. The wood is also fragrant. There is a pretty small-leaf form called Jenny Reitenbach.

A hardy aquatic perennial growing about 8 in. (20 cm) tall with hollow stems and bright green pinnate leaves. The small white flowers which appear throughout summer are followed by cylindrical seed pods, and the plant increases by underground stems. It has been appreciated by man since earliest times. It is so rich in iron that the leaves and stems turn purple-brown if exposed to the air for too long before consuming. It is a blood purifier as well as having many culinary uses. It requires slow-running water to grow and the plants are set out 4 in. (10 cm) apart. They need 4 in. (10 cm) of water over them. Use rooted offsets to make up a bed; early summer is the correct time to do so. The plants will then become established before winter. The beds will crop all year in a mild winter climate; otherwise cover the beds with polythene frames placed 12 in. (30 cm) above the plants to exclude frost.

OLEA EUROPAEA	ORIGANUM MAJORANA	ORIGANUM VULGARE
OLIVE	SWEET MARJORAM, KNOTTED MARJORAM	OREGANO, WILD MARJORAM
Oleaceae	Labiatae	Labiatae
65 S Eur, N Af, SW Asia *S Af, W-N Am, Aus*	**66** S Eur, W Asia, N Af *Warm Temperate Zones*	**67** Eur, C + N Asia *N Am*

branched annual growing 16 in. (40 cm) tall with reddish-green ovate leaves obscurely toothed and bearing small white flowers in leafy clusters. The variety dark opal has bronze leaves. *O. minimum* is the bush basil which makes a small bushy plant 6 in. (15 cm) tall and if grown outdoors is used as an edging to the herb garden. Its taste is practically identical with that of the larger plant. Seed is sown under glass early in spring, the seedlings being moved to small pots in which they are grown or planted outside early in summer. Allow 10 in. (25 cm) between plants of sweet basil; 6 in. (15 cm) between bush basil.

A small evergreen tree growing about 20 ft (6 m) tall with twiggy branches clothed in lanceolate leaves about 2 in. (5 cm) long, pale green above, silver on the underside. The small creamy-white flowers appear in the leaf axils and are followed by olive-green drupes (the fruits) which change to reddish-purple as they ripen. The fruits contain a single seed. The flesh of the drupe contains the oil which is extracted by pressure of the ripe fruit. The trees begin to crop in their second year and continue to grow slowly for 200 or more years, the weight of crop increasing each year. The finest oil, greenish-yellow, known as "virginal oil," is that obtained from the first crushing of the fruits. Further crushings follow, to produce oil of inferior quality. The unripe fruits are also used. The trees have pale gray bark and the wood can be polished so that it is used in cabinet making.

A perennial which in northerly climes is treated as a biennial, seed being sown in boxes in April, for it is long in germinating and the plants are wintered under glass to be set out the following spring 8 in. (20 cm) apart in a sunny position. The plant grows about 16 in. (40 cm) tall with downy oblong ovate leaves. Early in summer it bears white or purple flowers in terminal spikes. In hot dry weather, the plants secrete an essential oil from the stems which leaves on them a deposit of crystalline matter with a camphor-like smell. The flowering tips of the young plants are the most fragrant and make an ideal seasoning for sausage meat and for stuffings. The plant also has valuable medicinal qualities. Pot marjoram is *Origanum onites*. It is a perennial undershrub, growing 12 in. (30 cm) tall, and is propagated by cuttings. Its ovate serrate leaves are unstalked; its white flowers borne in terminal clusters.

A hardy perennial growing 16–20 in. (40–50 cm) tall with square stems and broadly ovate, short-stalked opposite leaves, covered in down and with oil glands. The rosy-mauve flowers are borne in crowded terminal cymes. They have reddish bracts which are longer than the calyx and appear late in summer. It is present on hilly pastures (downland) growing in calcareous soils. Its name is from the Greek words *oros* and *ganos*, "joy of the mountain." There is a variety with variegated leaves and one with golden leaves. The flowering tops are used fresh or dry (oregano) for stuffings and seasonings while the leaves are included in salads. Bees visit the flowers of all the marjorams during summer. Plants are raised from seed or from cuttings, removed in summer, and rooted in sandy compost. When rooted, move to small pots and plant out the following spring. They require a well-drained calcareous soil.

61

PAPAVER RHOEAS

POPPY, CORN
POPPY, FIELD POPPY

Papaveraceae

68 C + S Eur, C Asia
Temperate Zones

PELARGONIUM CAPITATUM

SCENTED-LEAF GERANIUM

Geraniaceae

69 S Af
Warm Temperate Zones

PETROSELINUM CRISPUM

PARSLEY

Umbelliferae

70 C + S Eur, N Af, SW Asia
Temperate Zones

70

An annual of cornfields and waste ground, growing to 20 in. (50 cm) tall with branched hairy stems and 1—2-pinnately cut leaves, the ascending lobes having a bristle at the tips. The brilliant red flowers, about 3 in. (7.5 cm) across, are shaded with purple at the base and appear throughout summer. They are followed by large globular fruits (capsules) which open by means of small valves, to release the seeds. The small seeds are blackish-purple; dried, they are used in baking and for their oil. Seed is sown thinly in spring in shallow drills or in circles where the plants are to bloom, and the seed capsules are removed.

A branched woody subshrub with alternate bright green 3—5-lobed leaves, cordate at the base and toothed at the margins, the peduncles longer than the leaves and pink flowers veined with purple borne on short pedicels. The stems and leaves are covered in glandular hairs and when pressed release a rose-like perfume which provides a basis for rose geranium, an adulterant of the expensive attar of rose. There are numerous scented-leaf varieties.
P. clorinda has leaves smelling of eucalyptus and bears large flowers of orange-pink; *P. tomentosum* is peppermint-scented and makes a delicious mint sauce. Its stems and leaves are densely covered in hairs as protection against strong sunlight and transpiration of moisture. These geraniums make admirable pot plants, being always in leaf and bloom and are attractive when used for summer bedding. They require a sunny situation and a light porous soil.

A biennial with perennial tendencies, it takes its botanical name from *petra*, a rock, for this is where it grows naturally but in the garden it requires a rich deep loam. It grows 10—12 in. (25—30 cm) tall with a long taproot and bright green 3-pinnate leaves which form a rosette. One variety of parsley is plain-leaved; it is the more flavorful. The curly-leaved is more favored for decorative garnishing. There are three other principal varieties which are seldom found on the market today. These crimped leaves retain their color and freshness for several days after cutting. If seed is sown in spring in

shallow drills and the young plants thinned to 6 in. (15 cm) apart, the leaves will be ready to cut in winter through which they remain green. In their second season a flower stem will arise, but if removed early, the plants will remain green for at least another year. If seed is required for flavoring (in Europe it is much in demand to flavor cheese), allow a few plants to flower and ripen seed. Several can be left to seed themselves. The pale gray seeds are produced in a small capsule and are curved, like caraway. They soon lose their pungency. Parsley seed is slow to germinate and must be sown fresh. The whole plant has a clean, pungent smell and is the richest source of vitamin A of all the vegetable kingdom and one of the richest sources of iron. Champion moss curled is the best variety with its fern-like leaves and for pots or a window box grow clivi, of neat habit with curled leaves.

PHYTOLACCA AMERICANA

POKE, POKE WEED

Phytolaccaceae

71 SE-N Am
Warm Temperate Zones

PIMENTA OFFICINALIS

ALLSPICE

Myrtaceae

72 S Am, West Indies
*Tropical Zones
of the New World*

PIMPINELLA ANISUM

ANISE, ANISEED

Umbelliferae

73 SW Asia, N Af
Warm Temperate Zones

PIMPINELLA SAXIFRAGA

BURNET, BURNET SAXI-FRAGE, BLACK CARAWAY

Umbelliferae

74 S Eur, C + W Asia
N Am

It should not be confused with the salad burnet which is of the Rosaceae order, though the burnet saxifrage has similar uses. It grows 20 in. (45 cm) tall, usually in dry chalky pastures, and is a branched perennial with solid ridged stems and leaves arising from the base which are divided into 5 or more pairs of toothed un-stalked 2-pinnate leaflets. The white flowers, in terminal umbels, appear in mid-summer and are followed by small, black shiny round fruits. The thick root grows to 8 in. (20 cm) in length. The leaves are mild and used in salads. Seed is sown in April and the young plants moved in autumn.

A hardy perennial growing to 10 ft (3 m) high with large fleshy poisonous roots and erect purple hollow stems branching at the top. The stems are removed in spring when 6 in. (15 cm) tall and cooked and served with melted butter. The stalked leaves are about 6 in. (15 cm) long with a prom-inent midrib and waved edges and appear first dark green, changing to purple late in summer. The flowers, which have 10 stamens and no corolla, are borne in ter-minal spikes on leafless stems and are followed by large purple fruits, like black-berries, made up of 10 unit-ed carpels and filled with red-dish-purple juice. They are eaten by poultry and pigeons but, like the roots, contain purgatives and may cause death if eaten in quantity. The plants, which should be set 3 ft (90 cm) apart, grow well in deep loam and in par-tial shade and are propagat-ed by root division in au-tumn.

Its warm, aromatic flavor and scent are due to eugenol, also the principal ingredient of cloves, and it is to the New World as the clove tree is to the Old. Its odor, however, is more a mixture of clove, cinnamon, and nutmeg, hence its name allspice. An evergreen tree, it grows 35 ft (10 m) tall, its slender trunk covered in gray aromatic bark and with op-posite shortly stalked leaves like those of bay laurel. They are dark green with a prom-inent midrib and with glan-dular dots (cells) on the underside which release an aromatic perfume when pressed. The greenish-white flowers are produced in panicles at the ends of the branches, their fragrance being almost overpowering. The fruit is a shining suc-culent berry, first green, then ripening to dark purple and containing 2 flat pea-size seeds. They are gather-ed by hand and dried until the seeds rattle in the ber-ries.

An annual, only half-hardy in northern Europe and North America, where it is grown for flavoring liqueurs but re-quires long hours of sun-shine to ripen its seeds. The best anise comes from Egypt and the Near East. It grows 16—20 in. (40—50 cm) tall with finely serrated upper leaves and long stalked heart-shaped lower leaves. The flowers are white, borne in large rayed double um-bels. The fruit is small and round, with the peculiar sweet aniseed smell. This is due to the presence of anisic aldehyde and is also present in the leaves. The plant is mentioned in St. Matthew's Gospel, for it was included in the Mosaic Law concern-ing tithes. A single seed was enclosed in layers of hard sugar which took an hour or more to suck through. Seed is sown in spring in shallow drills where the plants are to mature, thinning to 10 in. (25 cm) apart. An open situ-ation is necessary.

PINUS EDULIS	PIPER CUBEBA	PIPER NIGRUM
NUT PINE, PINYON	CUBEB	BLACK PEPPER
Pinaceae	Piperaceae	Piperaceae
75 W-N Am	**76** SE Asia *Tropical Zones*	**77** SE Asia

A perennial climbing plant which will attain a height of about 20ft (6m) where growing in open forests; in commercial plantations, growth is restricted to about half that height. The plant has a woody stem and dark green ovate leaves with short footstalks. The small white flowers are bisexual and arranged in short spikes. They are followed by red globular berries which first form when the plants are 4 years old; they continue to crop for about 10 years. The red berries are removed when almost ripe and dried on mats in the sun. They are then ground down, the "hot" aromatic powder being dark brown. Malabar and Penang produce the best pepper, which was known to the Greeks of ancient Athens and highly prized as a condiment. White pepper is obtained from the same plant and is produced by immersing the berries in water for several weeks before drying. It is less pungent than black pepper. The natives make use of the old roots to extract a tonic drink as with the roots of *P. methysticum,* a species native to Polynesia known as Kava bush.

Native of California where it is found at altitudes of up to 4000ft (1200m) and grows 90—100ft (30m) tall with a diameter of 3—4ft (1m). Widely branching, it has glaucous-blue twisted leaves 10in. (25cm) long and coffee-brown cones 6—8in. (15—20cm) long. The seeds (nuts) from the cones are sweet and juicy and since early times were prized by the native Indian peoples for their nutritional value. It is necessary to roast the cones over a low fire before they open and release the nuts. *P. sylvestris* is the European counterpart of *P. edulis.* Known as the Scots pine, it grows 80—90ft (almost 30m) tall with reddish-brown bark and twisted dark green leaves. The small stalked cones are borne in clusters and have square ridged scales. Completely hardy, the Scots pine is present almost to the Arctic Circle and grows in rocky ground often almost devoid of soil.

A perennial of climbing habit, bearing its flowers in symbodial spikes of 20 or more. The dark green leaves with short stipules have prominent veins and are about 2in. (5cm) long, terminating to a point. The fruit, a small round drupe or berry containing up to 20 percent volatile oil, is harvested not quite fully ripe and dried and ground so that it resembles allspice. The plant is native of Malaya and the East Indies and is grown in coffee and coconut plantations, usually against the trees for support because it enjoys semishaded conditions. *Piper methysticum,* of Southeast Asia and Polynesia, is also used for flavoring, but in this case it is the dried root that is used. Known as kava bush, the plant is perennial and makes a dense bush about 10—12 ft (3—4 m) tall.

PISTACIA VERA	PORTULACA OLERACEA	POTERIUM SANGUISORBA	PRUNUS AMYGDALUS
PISTACHIO, GREEN ALMOND	PURSLANE	SALAD BURNET	ALMOND
Anarcardiaceae	Portulacae	Rosaceae	Rosaceae
78 S Eur, W Asia *Warm Temperate Zones*	**79** S Asia *Warm Temperate Zones*	**80** N Eur, N Asia *Temperate Zones*	**81** C Asia, N Af *Warm Temperate Zones*

A large genus of deciduous trees which includes cherry, plum, peach, and apricot. The almond is of the sub-genus *Amygdalus* and grows 20ft (6m) tall with smooth bark and broad lanceolate saw-edged leaves. The pink flowers appear early in spring before the leaves and on wood formed the previous year. The oval plum-like fruits are pale green tinted with red and contain a single deeply pitted yellow shell (the endocarp) which encloses the nut. When the fruit ripens, the outer covering opens to release the nut which is pointed at one end, round at the other, and covered in a thin brown tunic.

A genus of some 10 mostly deciduous trees native to the Canary Isles, islands of the Mediterranean, and the southwestern United States, growing in sandy soil close to the sea. Several species yield resins and oils, while *Pistacia vera* is grown for its edible seeds. It is a spreading, deciduous tree which attains a height and spread of 20—25ft (6—8m). Leaflets grow in 1—5 pairs, with pinnately compound leaves. A reddish-shelled fruit is borne containing a green or yellow edible seed. Long, hot, relatively dry summers are favorable, with rather cold winters for necessary chilling. Propagation is by budding on seedling rootstocks. It will require 4—5 years for the trees to bear fruit. The plant can be pruned to keep it small in the garden. The pistachio kernels, which contain 20 percent protein and 40 percent oil, are valuable foods. The nuts are removed, dehusked, placed in water, and left in the sun for drying.

An annual growing 6in. (15cm) tall, native of India and only half-hardy in cooler climes. A smooth spreading, fleshy herb with nearly opposite oblong leaves and bearing almost stalkless golden-yellow flowers with 4—6 petals which appear in mid-summer. It reached Britain and northern Europe early in the fifteenth century. The leaves are a welcome addition to summer salads, after removal of the stalks; with sorrel, they impart a sharp taste to broths and stews. Giles Rose, cook to Charles II of England, always included the leaves in salads he prepared for the king. The plant is used as an edging, seed being sown in spring and the plants thinned to 4in. (10cm) apart. Or sow in boxes indoors and plant out early in summer in a sunny position and in a well-drained soil. Golden purslane has yellowish-green leaves. In northern Europe, the young leaves are pickled to serve with cold meats.

An erect perennial growing 16in. (40cm) tall, the pinnate leaves divided into 4—12 opposite oval leaflets, serrate at the edges, and with a mild cucumber taste and smell. William Turner in the *New Herbal* (1543) described the leaves as "like the wings of little birds, setteth out when they intended to fly." The tiny purple-green flowers are borne in a capitate cyme. The upper female flowers forming red brush-like stigmas and the lower males their yellow stamens. Pollination is by wind agency. The flower heads have prickly wings to the calyx tube. The plant is present on downlands, growing in calcareous soils, and remains green all winter, being a valuable winter food for sheep. Seed is sown in boxes in spring, and the young plants are set out in summer in a well-drained soil. Begin to use the leaves in their second year. The lesser burnet is an umbellifer and in no way connected with this plant.

ROSMARINUS OFFICINALIS

ROSEMARY

Labiatae

82 S Eur, SW Asia, N Af
Warm Temperate Zones

RUMEX ACETOSA, RUMEX SCUTATUS

SORREL, FRENCH SORREL

Polygonaceae

83 Eur, Asia
Temperate Zones

RUTA GRAVEOLENS

RUE, HERB-OF-GRACE

Rutaceae

84 S Eur
Warm Temperate Zones

An evergreen shrubby perennial; though native of the Mediterranean coastline and its islands, it possesses sufficient hardiness to survive the intense cold of a northern winter. It grows 6—7 ft (2 m) tall and enjoys a sunny wall. It has stalkless linear leaves, hoary on the underside, and its aromatic essential oil is stored in goblet-shaped cells immediately below the surface so that the scent is released with the slightest breeze or by one's clothes brushing against it. When there was no dry cleaning, rosemary bushes were grown near the entrance door of most houses so that all who entered would brush against the plant. The oil is used today in making perfume. The pale blue flowers appear in short axillary cymes early in spring and are much visited by bees. It takes its name from *ros marinus,* dew of the sea, for it grows best near the sea, in light calcareous soils and in full sun. The flavor of rosemary, which suggests incense to some, is fairly strong; discretion is advisable in its use for flavoring. The flowers make a pleasant addition to early salads, and a sprig (shoot) stuck into meat for roasting will impart its aromatic flavor. The plant has numerous medicinal uses and is propagated from seed or by cuttings. Plant in spring 3—4 ft (1 m) apart.

A tufted hardy perennial growing 12—16 in. (30—40 cm) tall with arrow-shaped leaves, the lower shortly stalked, the upper stem-clasping. The flowers are borne in spikes and are reddish-green, resembling those of the closely related rhubarb and dock. They are followed by hard, flat fruits. The plant is widespread on mountainous slopes and on wasteland and has been used in salads and as a substitute for spinach since early times. John Evelyn thought "it gave so grateful a quickness to a salad that it should never be omitted." The French sorrel, *R. scutatus,* is the best form. From the leaves a "green" sauce is made to serve with duck. But the leaves contain oxalic acid and should be used sparingly. Seed is sown in spring in shallow drills, thinning the plants to 6 in. (15 cm) apart. If not allowed to seed, the plants will remain productive for many years.

A glaucous aromatic woody perennial growing 2 ft (60 cm) tall and present on limestone cliffs. Its leaves, of metallic blue-green, are divided into oblong obovate segments. The flowers are greenish-yellow with curved petals. It is a plant of considerable hardiness, retaining its leaves through winter in northern Europe and Asia. The leaves are rich in mineral salts and contain oil glands. When pressed, they release a pungent smell but with undertones of orange, for it is of the same plant order. Rue enjoys a calcareous soil and an open, sunny position. It is readily raised from seed sown in spring in shallow drills, thinning or planting out the seedlings to 20 in. (50 cm) apart; or propagate by cuttings of the half-ripened wood removed in summer and inserted in sandy compost. There is an attractive variegated leaf form and the variety Jackman's blue has the bluest foliage of all plants.

SALVIA OFFICINALIS

SAGE

Labiatae

85 S Eur
Temperate Zones

SAMBUCUS NIGRA

ELDER, BLACK ELDER

Caprifoliaceae

86 Eur
W Asia, N Am

SATUREJA HORTENSIS, SATUREJA MONTANA

SUMMER SAVORY, WINTER SAVORY

Labiatae

87 S Eur
Warm Temperate Zones

Summer savory, *S. horten-sis*, is an annual growing about 8 in. (20 cm) tall with branching stems and downy oblong linear leaves with short stalks; its pale lilac flowers are borne in clusters. It is present on cliffs and downlands, growing in calcareous soils, and is readily raised from seed sown in spring in shallow drills. Thin to 6 in. (15 cm) apart. If the plants are cut back in mid-summer and the stems hung up to dry, there will be another cutting to make in autumn. The first growth will be ready to accompany broad beans, to which it imparts an aromatic flavor. *S. montanta* is the winter savory, a perennial of spread-ing habit, growing 12 in. (30 cm) tall, its oblong leaves terminating to a point and bearing purple-pink flowers in loose racemes. The dried leaves are used with sage and thyme to make stuffings and used fresh to make a "butter" to serve with meat or fish. The plant remains green through winter and makes a pleasing edging to the herb garden. Propagate from cuttings or by root division in spring, planting 10 in. (25 cm) apart in sandy soil and in an open situation. If the plant is kept cut back, new growth will continually appear. There is not a great deal of difference in the taste of summer savory and winter savory.

An evergreen of shrubby habit growing to 20 in. (50 cm) tall, with square stems as if covered in down and wrinkled oval gray-green leaves. The plant has, since earliest times, been reputed to give long life to those who ate it and takes its name from *salvia*, salvation. The purple irregular 2-lipped flowers appear in the axils of the leaves during late summer. The red-stemmed variety, *purpurea* is a handsome garden plant, the leaves also being shot with crimson; and *aurea* has golden leaves. *S. rutilans*, the pineapple sage, is more tender but is one of the most delicious of all herbs, its leaves having the smell and taste of ripe pineapples. It is propagated by cuttings but *S. officinalis* will also grow readily from seed sown in spring. Set out the plants 2 ft (60 cm) apart in a sunny position and in a well-drained calcareous soil. The plants may lose their leaves in a cold winter but will grow them again in spring.

A deciduous shrub of considerable hardiness with which there are more superstitions and more uses than any other plant. It grows in any soil, in hedgerows, and on waste ground, reaching a height of 12—15 ft (4 m) with deeply furrowed pale gray bark that has a rather sharp smell. The dark green leaves have the same unpleasant smell. They are divided into 5 leaflets with saw-like, but not sharp, edges. The small creamy-white flowers are borne in flat-topped cymes and, when newly open (before fertilization) and warmed by the sun, emit a powerful musky smell which is retained after cutting. Pear growers in France place the fruits on layers of elder flowers to complete their ripening so that the fruits take on a muscatel perfume. The plant has hollow stems which were used to make musical instruments. The small juicy berries are first green, then red, before turning jet black when they are gathered for flavoring.

SEDUM REFLEXUM	SESAMUM INDICUM	TAMARINDUS INDICA	TANACETUM VULGARE
STONECROP, SEDUM	SESAME	TAMARIND	TANSY
Crassulaceae	Pedaliaceae	Leguminosae	Compositae
88 C + S Eur, W Asia	**89** S Asia, C Af *Tropical Zones of the Old World*	**90** S Asia, C Af *Tropical Zones*	**91** Eur, W Asia *N Am*

A succulent evergreen with trailing stems and leaves arranged in 6—7 rows which are awl-shaped and swollen at the base. From the trailing stems, shoots arising to a height of about 10 in. (25 cm) bear the flowers. They are bright yellow with reflexed petals and are borne in terminal cymes. The stem leaves also have reflexed tips. It is a plant of rocky outcrops and is found on old walls; hence both its botanical and popular names are from the Latin, *sedere*, to sit on. The stonecrops require a sunny situation and a well-drained soil. Propagation is from pieces of the root. Other varieties include *S. cristatum*, coxcomb sedum.

An annual herb growing 3—4 ft (1 m) tall with spirally arranged lance-shaped leaves and pinkish-white flowers borne in the leaf axils. The fruit is a capsule provided with hooks, the wedge-shaped seed being surrounded with endosperm. The seeds contain oil and are whitish-brown and shiny. They have a nutty flavor and are widely used in countries of southeastern Europe and the Near East, to sprinkle over bread after baking. Ground sesame seeds are the basis of *halva*, a popular Near Eastern candy, and of *tahina*, a creamy paste used to flavor certain dishes and as a kind of dip. The seeds were exported from central Africa in early times and may have reached Europe following the Roman occupation of North Africa, for sesame seed was in great demand in ancient Rome. The oil extracted from the seed also has culinary uses and is an ingredient in the production of margarine.

A deciduous tree growing to 35 ft (10 m) high with pale gray bark and alternate leaves divided into 12—15 pairs of pale green leaflets. The scented reddish-purple pea-like flowers are borne in terminal racemes, the upper sepals and the 3 fertile stamens united. The seeds are borne in pendulous curved pods and are encased in pulp. The East Indian tamarinds number 6—12 seeds to a pod and are black after removal of the smooth brown tunic, which is done before the seed is dried and marketed. West Indian tamarinds have shorter pods containing 3—4 seeds. The ground seed is used in curry powders and to make chutneys, while the leaves yield a yellow dye. The pulp of the seed pods is used in cases of dysentery.

An erect hardy perennial growing 3—4 ft (1 m) tall with branched angular stems and dark green fern-like leaves divided into numerous pinnatifid leaflets with serrate edges which release a powerful balsamic smell when handled. This is due to the essential oil stored in minute glandular cells in the leaves. The tiny button-like flowers, which appear late in summer, have yellow disk florets and are borne in flat-topped terminal heads. Ray florets are absent. It takes its name from the Greek *athanasia*, immortality (for it remains long in bloom). The plant has a creeping rootstock and is propagated by lifting and dividing the roots in winter. It requires a well-drained soil and sunny position. Plant 20 in. (50 cm) apart. It is also grown from seed. The form *T. foliis crispis* is an attractive garden plant of dwarf bushy habit, used for summer bedding in Victorian times, its fern-like leaves for garnishing.

TARAXACUM OFFICINALE	THEOBROMA CACAO	THYMUS VULGARIS
DANDELION, BLOWBALL	CACAO, COCOA, CHOCOLATE	THYME, GARDEN THYME
Compositae	Steruliaceae	Labiatae
92 Temperate Zones	93 S Am, Jamaica *Tropical Zones of the New World*	94 S Eur *Warm Temperate Zones*

A hardy perennial common everywhere, but an obnoxious garden weed unless controlled and so its culture should be confined to waste ground. The dark green lobed leaves arise from the long, fleshy root and have the lobes or teeth pointing backward. The flower stalks are hollow and leafless while the flowers are borne singly and are of brilliant gold. To make plenty of leaf, grow the plants in rich soil. In spring, sow seed singly, 2 in. (5 cm) apart in circles of 16 in. (40 cm) diameter, and 1 year later cover the plants with a large earthenware pot when they begin to make growth; this will blanch the leaves, reducing bitterness.

Its name means "food of the gods" and its seeds provide cocoa and chocolate. The tree grows 12—14 ft (4 m) tall with dark brown bark and lanceolate pale green leaves. The red flowers are produced all year, as are the fruits that follow them. The large reddish-yellow fruits are divided into 5 chambers, each of which contains a double row of large flattish seeds (beans) pointed at one end. It is usual to harvest the crop 3 or 4 times a year; the pods are then opened and the seeds left to dry in the sun. The beans contain about 50 percent of fat which is removed. The beans are mixed with sugar, roasted, and then ground to produce cocoa. When the fat is retained, the product is chocolate. The trees grow better in semishade and are usually under-planted as companions to taller trees grown for their commercial crop, thus obtaining two crops from the same ground.

An evergreen shrublet known as garden thyme, it grows 10 in. (25 cm) tall, with small oblong ovate leaves, dark green above, gray on the underside, and purple flowers borne in conical clusters. It is a plant of mountainous slopes and has been appreciated for its medicinal and culinary qualities since earliest times, being in demand for stuffing the richer meats. Thyme grows in light calcareous soil and in dry, sunny conditions, and there are many well-known varieties. The silver posie variety has rose-pink stems and leaves splashed with silver, while *aureum* has golden leaves. *T. citriodorus* is the lemon-scented thyme, the one most frequently cultivated and used in cooking, after *T. vulgaris*, while *T. nitidus* has narrower foliage and a pungent incense-like scent. *T. herba barona* is the baron-of-beef thyme for it was used to accompany beef when roasting, to which it imparts a distinctive

caraway flavor. *T. serpyllum* is the mountain thyme, a plant of almost prostrate habit found as far north as the Arctic Circle of which there are several varieties. It forms a mat of crimson flowers, borne in terminal heads. This wild thyme differs enough from the cultivated variety so that the French, who call the latter *thym*, give wild thyme a separate name, *serpolet*, in recognition of the difference. Its flavor has been described as "more concentrated and zestful" than that of its tamed cousin. The variety *alba* bears white flowers and *lanuginosa* is entirely covered in white hairs as if frosted. *T. fragrantissimus* has orange-scented leaves and its hybrid, lemon curd, is lemon-scented. These thymes are propagated from cuttings removed in summer and rooted in sandy com-

post. Move to small pots when rooted and plant out in spring in a well-drained soil. Thymes resent root disturbance and should be planted from pots.

TRIGONELLA FOENUM-GRAECUM

FENUGREEK, BIRD'S-FOOT

Leguminosae

| 95 | SW Asia *Warm Temperate Zones* |

TROPAEOLUM MAJUS

NASTURTIUM, INDIAN CRESS

Cruciferae

| 96 | S Am *Torrid + Temperate Zones* |

TUBER MELANOSPORUM

TRUFFLE

| 97 | C Eur |

A hairless annual growing 6 in. (15 cm) tall with stalked trefoil leaves, the leaflets spoon-shaped and pungent when handled. The pale pink pea-like flowers are borne June—July in the leaf axils and are followed by curved pods containing small brown oblong seeds. The seeds and leaves give off a celery-like smell. The seeds are sprouted in water or grown on damp flannel and, when 4 in. (10 cm) high, are cut and included in salads. The dried and ground seeds are included in curry powders and used to make condition powders for cattle. From its smell of newly mown hay, due to the presence of coumarin, the ancients named it *foenum-graecum* and would mix it with grass to dry for winter keep. The plant also has numerous medicinal uses. Seed is sown in shallow drills in spring, thinning the plants to 4 in. (10 cm) apart. It requires a well-drained soil and an open situation.

Of the same family as watercress, its leaves are equally rich in iron and sulfur and both leaves and flowers give a pleasant bitterness to salads. Native of Chile and Peru, it takes its botanical name from *tropaeolum*, a trophy, from the resemblance of the leaves to a shield and of the long spurred flowers to a Greek warrior's helmet. A trailing annual with round peltate leaves and bearing showy flowers of yellow, red, or orange. The 5 sepals unite at the base with the upper, forming a long free spur. In bloom throughout summer and autumn, the flowers are followed by large succulent deeply grooved seeds which are used as a substitute for capers. The plant requires an open, sunny situation but will grow in any soil and is decorative in a window box or hanging basket. Seed is sown in pots or boxes in spring, the plants being set out early in summer; or sow outdoors 10 in. (25 cm) apart.

Forms of *T. melanosporum* are among the most expensive and gastronomically appreciated members of the vegetable kingdom and grow underground in total darkness. Because of this, it is necessary for trained dogs to seek them out, drawn to them by their unusual smell. They are found mostly in deciduous woodlands of central Europe, and around the Piedmont district of northern Italy. The collection of truffles has often been in the same family for generations and even pigs have been trained to seek them out, burrowing into the leafy ground with their snouts and unearthing them. In Ireland, they are known as pignuts, the knobbly tubers often being uncovered when bogland is plowed. Strictly speaking, the species cited above is the black truffle or Périgord truffle, universally conceded to be the best, but the black truffles of Umbria, Italy, can give them a close race; it seems probable that they belong to the same species. *T. brumale*, the winter truffle, is a notch below, and *T. aestivus*, the summer truffle, found in Great Britain, several notches below. Several species of truffle are found in the United States, but they are hardly worth eating. The white truffle of Italy's Piedmont, *T. magnotum*, is very different.

VANILLA PLANIFOLIA

VANILLA

Orchidaceae

98 S Am
Tropical Zones

VIOLA ODORATA

VIOLET, SWEET VIOLET

Violaceae

99 S Eur
Temperate Zones

ZINGIBER OFFICINALIS

GINGER

Zingiberaceae

100 S Asia
Torrid Zones

Native of China, India, and Southeast Asia, it is also cultivated in Jamaica and Queensland. It has a creeping rhizomatous rootstock from which arise 4—5ft leafy stems (1.5m) tall, the stems being enclosed in the leaf sheaths. The flowers are yellow and borne in a cone-like spike. Pieces of root about 2in. (5cm) long are planted in March, 4in. (10cm) deep and 10in. (25cm) apart. The stems die back the following March and the roots are lifted before they put out new shoots. They are then soft and succulent. One acre will yield about 4000 pounds (2000kilos). The roots are washed and scraped and then dried in the sun. This is known as "white" or "uncoated" ginger. One root will produce about 8 tubers. As Shakespeare said, a piece of dried ginger was and still is known as a "race." The pale yellow Jamaican product is considered the best, for the roots have been scraped of their epidermis. Chinese ginger is usually the tuberous root of *Lapinia officinale*. If ginger is left too long in the ground it becomes fibrous, which is detrimental to its quality. The best ginger cuts clean and bright when it reaches the kitchen. Although some of the finest ginger is produced in Jamaica, the New World has no native varieties.

A climbing epiphytic perennial of tropical forests where the plants pull themselves up tall trees by their aerial roots to reach the sunlight. Commercially, they are grown against posts and their climbing is restricted. The leaves are thick and fleshy and grow 10in. (25cm) long, while the yellowish-green flowers are borne in a dense inflorescence. They are followed by pods about 8in. (20cm) long which contain the beans from which vanilla extract is obtained by fermentation. Much used in perfumery and cooking, the odoriferous principle is vanillin. The fragrance is a stimulant to the mental system and was first used as a perfume by François Coty in his L'Aimant perfume. The pods resemble those of pole beans and are imported in bundles of 50 or more. A plant will begin to bear pods in its fourth year and continue to do so for 50 years. They are gathered in autumn just before fully ripe.

A perennial and the only species with scented flowers. It has a short rootstock and forms long runners (underground stems) which root at the leaf nodes. They can be detached and replanted into moist soil to make a new bed. The stalked leaves are heart-shaped with glandular stipules; the flowers, white or purple-blue, are borne on leafless stems. The flowers are spurred, with 4 upper oblong petals and 2 side petals with or without a tuft of hairs. In bloom in spring, violet grows in open woodlands and in hedgerows, in semishade and in a moist soil. The plant was so highly regarded by the ancient Greeks that it became the symbol of Athens. The flowers are candied and used for sweetening, and are included in salads. They have numerous medicinal uses too. The plants were grown in pots on window sills in the shade, for their perfume counteracted the musty smells of medieval houses.

From the Garden to the Kitchen

ROY GENDERS

This Victorian painting depicting a cottage herb garden gives some idea of the informal habit of the plants and their various leaf hues. In the picture can be seen cotton lavender, meadowsweet, wormwood, and lamb's tails *(Statice lanata)* to the front right.

All the herbs seen gathered in this bouquet (they include rosemary, rue, balm, sage, fennel, marjoram, and thyme) can be used fresh or dried. They are gathered late in summer to dry for winter use.

Right: The final step in the process of raising herbs and spices: the seasoner, harvested, dried, and stored, is ready for the cooking pot. This photograph brings together several different forms in which ginger can be stored and used.

Herbs and spices reach our table by the most various routes. Spices are likely to have the longest journey, often from points far to the south or east, and to arrive dried or ground or preserved, in a state quite unlike their natural condition on a living plant. But with herbs (and even with a few spices or other condiments), as is shown in the present chapter, it is possible to shorten the interval from plant to food and to partake of seasoners in a fresher, more natural state—by growing one's own. Whether you have several acres of arable land, or just a window box, you can create an herb garden, grow and process or store your own favorite herbs, and enjoy the aesthetic pleasure to be derived from the presence of natural plants in your environment.

In this chapter we discuss the planning of a garden; the choice of herbal plants for various functions and different types of soils; planting and cultivation indoors and out; propagation methods; and finally harvesting and storage. We begin by looking at some of the earliest herb gardens.

Herbs were first planted in gardens attached to the monasteries of medieval Europe during the Middle Ages, for the monks were then the only people with the knowledge of how to use herbs and only the monastic gardens were protected by walls built of the same stone used to erect the religious houses. The herbarium was under the care of the sacristan, who provided the monks with herbs for culinary purposes, usually to hide the often unpleasant taste of meat which had become tainted by long keeping; and also for medicinal purposes, because the monks administered to those who sought their help for all manner of illnesses. Herb gardens later came to be attached to all religious foundations and to castle and manor, where large quantities of herbs were grown for strewing on earthen floors and to counteract the musty atmosphere created in buildings that had no damp course.

In Britain and Europe, herbs of all kinds first came to be planted in cottage gardens during the latter years of the fourteenth century, when more settled times prevailed following the wars between France and England. With more gracious living, large quantities of herbs were required for making washing waters for personal cleanliness and for washing clothes. As methods of communication became easier with better roads, people were able to move from one

place to another, visiting friends and relations, and they dressed in better clothes for the purpose. The clothes were kept sweet smelling and clean by washing in scented waters. There was also a continual advancement of the culinary arts as people began to travel abroad to all parts of Europe and to the Near East. Later came a two-way exchange of plants between Europe and America, all of which had a considerable impact on the mode of living.

CLIMATIC CONSIDERATIONS

Useful herbs grow in all parts of the world. In the cold northerly climes, in North America, northern Europe, and Asia, the plants possess great hardiness and are mostly perennial, dying back in winter with new stems arising in spring. This enables the plant to survive intense cold. In the warmer parts of southern Europe, the Near East, and North Africa, the plants are

Temperatures prevailing in various parts of the world determine where herbs and spices can be grown. While some spices are native to the Old World, they may be grown with equal success in the New World provided conditions are similar. For example, coffee is native to Arabia and eastern Africa but for years has been the most important commercial crop of Brazil; ginger grows equally well in Queensland as in Jamaica.

tween 50 °F (10 °C) and 80 °F (27 °C) are fairly consistent. Over this entire area, one can find, growing naturally and also in gardens, hardy herbs such as leeks and chives, angelica and chervil, tansy and tarragon, chicory, Good-King-Henry, fennel, licorice, lovage, and watercress as well as the various mints, violet and cowslip, parsley, sorrel, nasturtium, and mustard. Each of these plants enjoys a temperate climate and a soil able to retain moisture in summer.

Central. One or two degrees north and south of latitude 40° N, which takes in the

Northern zone:
40° N to 55° N

Among the perennial herbs that grow in this zone are tarragon and angelica *(above)*, plus balm *(right)* and bergamot.

mostly of shrubby habit, with the leaves often covered with hairs to protect them from strong sunlight while there is no cold weather to damage the stems. Here and in Asia also grow herbs whose seeds are used for flavoring. On the equator grow those plants, mostly trees, requiring intense heat to ripen the fruit. Many spices are obtained from the tropics where they grow in the rain forests, in the semi-shade cast by the trees of other commercial crops.

We can distinguish three principal areas in which the commonest herb and spice plants naturally grow.

North. Most of the plants grown for their leaves which are used fresh or dried are native to the Northern Hemisphere, to northern Europe and Asia, and to the northern United States and Canada where they grow between latitudes 40° N and 55° N. In addition to large areas of the New World, this takes in the British Isles, France, Germany, and Central Europe, the most southerly parts of the USSR, and north China where summer temperatures of be-

Mediterranean regions and the Near East, will be found those aromatic shrubby herbs, the rosemary and lavender; and also sage and thyme, growing in their natural state, usually on calcareous outcrops. Here, too, grows saffron, along the North African coast and in the Near East, and it can also be raised commercially in East Anglia which is the driest and warmest part of the British Isles. Saffron can also be grown in Spain and southern Italy, where conditions more nearly resemble those of the Near East.

In those countries bordering the Mediter-

And lucent syrups, tinct with cinnamon;
manna and dates, in argosy transferred
from Fez: and spiced dainties,
from silken Samarkand to cedared Lebanon.

John Keats, "The Eve of Saint Agnes"

ranean are grown commercial crops of caraway, cumin, anise, and dill and a number of the spices grown for their seeds. For although they can be grown in Britain and northern Europe (in a hot summer), they will ripen better south of latitude 40° N. The hotter and drier the summer, the better the seed ripens and the more essential oil is present in the seed when harvested. This enables the seeds to retain their flavor and aroma for as long as two years or

The southern United States and Mexico—where today we find okra, chili pepper, and cacao—lie between the Tropic of Cancer and latitude 40° N where temperatures are not quite so high.

Close to the Equator, in the countries of the Old World, cinnamon and cardamom are produced, and in southern India, Ceylon and Malaysia, and in Haiti and Indonesia, turmeric and zedoary. Nutmeg and mace come from Indonesia and the West Indies; cloves from Zanzibar; ginger from India, Queensland and Jamaica; grains of paradise

Central zone: around 40° N

Shrubby aromatic herbs such as rosemary and marjoram (above) and bay (right).

Southern zone: 20° S to 20° N

Spices, including pepper and cardamon (above), nutmeg and vanilla (below).

There is of course some overlap between zones, so that the shrubby herbs such as rosemary and marjoram, with their highly aromatic foliage, can be grown, under certain circumstances, north of 40° N latitude. But for the most part the gardener must keep climatic considerations in mind in his particular area. Warm-weather or "Mediterranean" herbs, for instance, might have to be kept indoors in pots. Where the spices are concerned, climatic considerations are not easily overcome. Vanilla, for example, must have not only warmth but also the damp conditions of the tropical rain forests.

more after they are harvested and their drying is completed.

South. South of the Tropic of Cancer (about 20° N and S of the Equator) are grown those spices requiring high temperatures and no frost to bring them to maturity. Frost, which occurs occasionally, may seriously damage the crops. Between the Equator and latitude 40° N are to be found most of the spice-growing areas of the world, including India and Ceylon; Malaysia, Indonesia, and the Philippine Islands; Central Africa; Brazil and the Amazon; and the islands of the West Indies.

(melegueta pepper) from Liberia and the Gold Coast. Here, too, is grown cola, so much used in beverages, and white and black pepper. From Cuba and the West Indies comes allspice; and from tropical South America, cocoa and vanilla, both in demand for confectionery all over the world. The gardener will do well to take note of geography and climate in deciding which herbs and spices to plant in his own area. In North America and northern Europe some plants would not survive the winter, and are grown only in the warmer parts.

Overleaf: An herb garden of beauty and intelligent planting, the herbs being set out in groups of herbs to be used for different purposes. Those of taller habit are placed to the back, those of dwarf habit to the front, so that the sun rays can reach every plant in the garden. This particular garden contains seventy different herb species.

MONASTERIUM PRINCIPALE S.GALLI

What greater delight is there
than to behold the earth apparelled with plants,
as with a robe of embroidered worke,
set with Orient pearles
and garnished with great diversitie of rare
and costly jewels? ...
But these delights are in the outward senses:
the principal delight
is in the mind, singularly
enriched with the knowledge of these visible things,
setting forth to us
the invisible wisdome and admirable workmanship
of Almighty God.

John Gerard, 1597

The monasteries were the first to make intelligent use of herbs for culinary and medicinal purposes. One of the earliest herb gardens was that of the Abbey of St. Gallen on the shores of Lake Constance, shown here in a copper engraving from 1702.

The rose "Zéphirine Drouhin" can be grown as a hedge to enclose an herb garden; it will also cover a wall to a height of 12 ft (360 cm). The rose, with silver-pink, powerfully scented flowers, will grow in any type of soil. Several hundred years old, it may be "the rose without a thorn" used to describe Queen Elizabeth I of England.

THE HERB GARDEN

One of the earliest plans of a herb garden, that of the monastery of St. Gall on the shores of Lake Constance, a plan designed by its Abbot, Walfred Strabo, in the ninth century, shows the monastic garden divided into two parts. In the orchard apples and pears, medlars and figs, walnuts and almonds were grown; in the kitchen garden grew vegetables and herbs. The abbot tells that here grew sage "of good scent" and rue with its blue-green leaves, "so placed that the sun and air can reach all its parts." This is the key to successful herb growing: providing the plants (or most of them) with an open, sunny situation, in Abbot Strabo's words, where both sun and air can reach all their parts. In the fifteenth century "Le Livre de Rustican," written in French and now in the British Museum, London, provided a delightful picture of a herb garden of the time. It is situated in a small town of France and the garden is surrounded by a stone wall which, compared to the figures tending the garden, would seem to be about 7 ft (2 meters) high. The garden is divided into numerous small beds, each about 6 ft (nearly 2 m) by 4 ft (1.25 m) with paths of sand or gravel between each bed. The ground looks like a patchwork quilt and the plants growing in the beds are entirely open to the sun.

Today, a small area of garden could be used in a similar way, surrounded by a fence, perhaps of wattle hurdles (osiers) or interwoven fencing, to protect the herbs against strong winds; or by a hedge of the sweet-scented rose Zéphirine Drouhin, which sends out long graceful shoots several yards (meters) long and entirely thornless. Train them along strong galvanized wires fastened to posts which have been fixed in the ground at regular intervals, about 6 ft (2 m) above ground. This rose comes early into bloom and its powerfully scented flowers will perfume the air all around. There should be an archway, possibly of rustic woodwork, to give access to the herb garden, and over this hops may be grown. They will die back in winter but come again in early summer and will quickly cover the arch again.

Or one could surround the herb garden with a hedge of Lawson's cypress or the faster growing Cupressus leylandii; or plant the evergreen honeysuckle, Lonicera nitida, with its dense growth and tiny leaves of darkest green. Its golden counterpart, Baggeson's gold, is the brightest plant of the garden in winter and possesses extreme hardiness. The evergreen honeysuckles can be kept in trim by clipping.

Another plant which makes a compact evergreen hedge is Pittosporum tenuifolium mayi and its silver-gray form, silver queen.

Native of New Zealand, it is planted in southern Europe and the warm westerly parts of the British Isles to provide the markets with its long, elegant stems of glossy pale green leaves, crinkled at the edges, which are most decorative. Each of these hedging plants should be kept well clipped back each spring. Whichever form of wind protection is given, make sure that it does not obscure the sunlight from the herbs.

Francis Bacon, writing in the early seventeenth century, said that the herb garden "is best to be square, encompassed on all four sides by a stately hedge." Indeed, most herb gardens were thus made, divided into small square beds, or the beds were made in the shape of a heart or circle, enclosed by a low box hedge which was hardy and evergreen. A hedge was sometimes made of sweet marjoram, which was also known as the knotted marjoram and so named because it was widely used to make the "knot" gardens of the sixteenth century, in which small beds planted with herbs were joined together by low hedges. Other plants used were hyssop,

Francis Bacon *(left)*, whose essay "Of Gardens" has been read by every English gardener since it appeared in 1625, wrote that "the herb garden is best square, encompassed on all four sides by a stately hedge." It is thought that he wrote this following a visit to Hatfield House in Hartfordshire, England, then a royal palace, now home of

Herbs like vegetables, require an open, sunny situation; few will grow well in shade. If there is room at one end of the garden to grow both herbs and vegetables, you could divide the area into two equal parts, separating each by a fence or hedge. In the herb garden, you could also plant those herbs which have medicinal uses, those which lend their delicious fragrance in potpourris or have other uses such as moth deterrents when placed among clothes and linen. Herbs and spices can also be used in cleaning and dyeing.

winter savory, and the upright thymes. Golden hyssop was also used to give color variation, a purpose also served at times by one of the dwarf lavenders. The plants, set 6 in. (15 cm) apart, were often made into the most intricate designs, which gave the herb garden a laced effect. Chives may also be used as an edging; like the other plants recommended. These small hedges should not be allowed to grow more than 6 in. (15 cm) tall and in autumn should be clipped along the top so that they are always neat and tidy.

We now go on to consider a type of garden arrangement that is particularly well suited to herbal plants, the scented path.

the Marquis of Salisbury. Its herb garden remains much as it did in Bacon's time, divided into small beds, each joined together by low hedges of evergreen herbs like strings knotted together. Each small bed was usually filled with a single herb of compact habit such as cowslips and primroses, marigolds, violets, and pinks; the herbs used to make the "knots" or low hedges were marjoram, thyme, winter savory, and dwarf lavender. Chives were also used as edging for small beds. The beds were often made heart-shaped and later took on more intricate designs which gave rise to the lavish parterre gardens of Versailles.

Above: Another knot garden, New Place, in Stratford-on-Avon, England.

A SCENTED PATH

A herb garden may be divided into two parts, intersected by a path of paving stones between which are planted prostrate herbs such as the creeping thymes, calamint, and chamomile. The path should be made a-

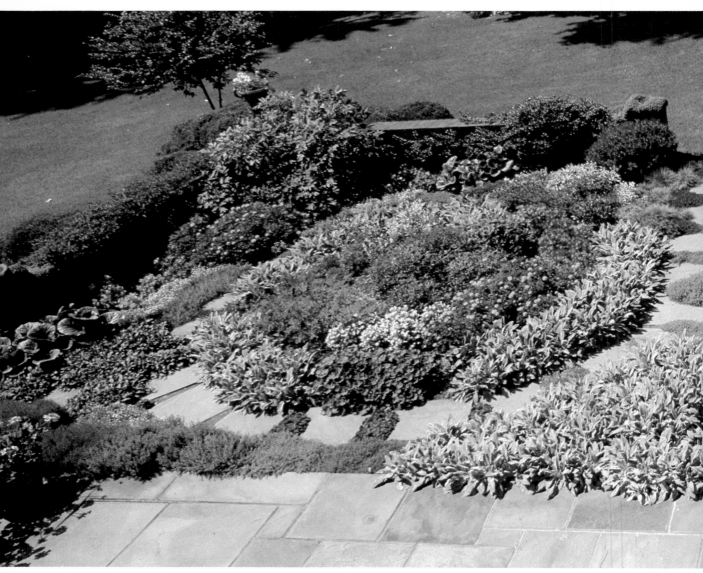

The fragrant path should be in an open sunny position, for the plants to be used are sun lovers. They also like a well-drained soil; hence it is advisable to set the stones on a bed of sand about 3 inches deep and made compact. The plants are set in pockets of soil, but it is preferable to use pot-grown plants and to plant the soil ball intact so that there will be no disturbance of the roots. Pot-grown plants can be set out at any time, but spring is perhaps the best.

bout 2 ft (60 cm) wide, the stone placed on a layer of sand. To make the path, fix boards on either side of where the path is to be made, corresponding to the exact width of the path and held in place by wooden pegs driven into the ground. Then sort out the stones and lay them with the straightest edge along where the boards are fixed so that, when the path is finished, the edges will be in a straight line. Also, wherever possible,

Appropriate to border on a path, as well as being attractive to bees, are the four plants seen here *(from left to right)*: borage, sweet basil, hyssop, and lavender. Rosemary is another plant that provides valuable nectar when few others are in bloom.

A selection of four herbs that offer rich variation in the shape and color of their leaves *(from left to right)*: Tansy has unusual fern-like dark green leaves with serrate edges. Golden marjoram, in sharp contrast to herbal greens, has leaves that turn daffodil yellow in summer. Water mint comes next, with dark green leaves. And finally, silver sage *(Salvia argentea)*, one of the silver-leaf plants.

lay the stones as close together as possible, leaving only a small space here and there large enough to take the soil ball which contains the roots of the plants. The upper surface of the stones should be as level as possible to make for easier walking; it is advisable to use a builder's spirit level to assist in achieving this. If the edging boards are fixed so that the top edge of the board is about 1 in. (2.5 cm) above the sand base, the level can be so placed that it rests on the top edge of the boards and the stones can be kept below it. Set the stones so that they are firmly embedded in the sand by tamping them with a length of strong timber.

After the path has been made, set the plants in the spaces, taking care not to break up the soil ball holding the roots. Most herbs do not like root disturbance and will become

flowers in summer which are of pinkish-mauve and are much visited by bees. "We preserve them with all the care we can in our gardens," wrote John Parkinson, botanist to Charles I of England, "for the sweete and pleasant scents they yield." Wild thyme *(T. serpyllum),* equally suitable for a path, quickly forms a prostrate mat of tiny dark green leaves. The variety *T. coccineus* is covered in blood-red flowers all summer, while *T. alba* is pure white. The form *lanuginosa* has caraway-scented leaves covered in what appears to be white wool but which are really silky hairs, giving the plant a silvered appearance. The basil thyme, *Calamintha acinos,* is also at its best between stones. It has tiny leaves and bears purple and blue flowers in whorls. When walked upon, the plant releases a minty smell.

An herb garden may be divided into sections by making a path of flagstones, brick, or crazy (irregular) paving—there are numerous designs available. Bricks may be used, laid on their side either in straight lines or in herringbone style, omitting one or two here and there for carpeting plants. These are low growing herbs which spread out and partly cover the bricks; or flagstones can be used, omitting a stone in one or two places for carpeting herbs. But perhaps the best

of all paths is made of crazy paving stone which blends admirably with plants such as mountain thyme and Corsican mint. A path should be made as level as possible and to the same width throughout. This is done by fixing in position two lengths of board on either side of where the path is to be made, the boards being the same distance apart at both ends and the stones (or bricks) set accordingly. It is advisable to lay the stones on a firm bed of sand.

established more quickly if the roots are kept intact. There are one or two exceptions such as borage and marigold which will tolerate transplanting at almost any age.

A path may also be made of old weathered red bricks which are placed end to end over a sand base or laid in herringbone fashion, but first make an edging of brick up to the boards to give the path a neat appearance. To make the surface level, use a builder's spirit level as when making a stone path.

There are a number of interesting herbs to grow in a path. Of the prostrate thymes, *Thymus doerfleri,* which is one of the mountain thymes, forms a dense mat of gray-green which has a fruity aroma, while *T. fragrantissimus* smells deliciously of orange and *T. micans* has the resinous scent of pine needles. Each of these plants bears

The Corsican mint, *Mentha requienii,* is a delight when growing between stones forming thick mats of peppermint-scented foliage; in early summer it is studded with tiny spikes of palest mauve. The dainty rock savory, *Satureia rupestris,* native of southern Europe, is also suitable for a path. It makes a spreading mat of dark green peppermint-scented foliage above which it bears, in late summer, dainty spikes of purest white flowers. Chamomile is another good plant to use in a path; its handsome leaves are free from down and emit a powerful fruity scent when trodden upon.

All these plants can be used to make an aromatic "lawn." They can be planted on a sunny bank where the soil is well-drained and hot and where little else will grow—how delightful to lie there in summer and

The sages, one among the most useful plants of the garden, are also attractive in flower and in leaf. The broad-leaf variety shown here is dried and used in stuffings. There is a silver-leaf form *(argentea)* and a golden form *(aurea,)* while *S. purpurea* has reddish-purple stems and leaves shot with red. The sages have purple-blue flowers, but those of pineapple sage are crimson. Bees visit the sages when in bloom.

relax while inhaling their powerful scent. "I know a bank where the wild thyme grows," wrote Shakespeare. To make such

On either side of the path you can plant as wide a variety of herbs as climate and soil permits.

Flagstone paths, as these four examples show, blend admirably with herbs, giving an Old World quality to the garden. They also have more practical uses. A path enables the herbs to be reached and cut if the rest of the garden is wet with rain, while the herbs can be allowed

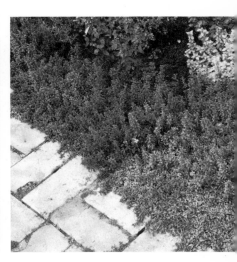

a fragrant bank or a "lawn," set the chamomile 8 in. (20 cm) apart in squares, and if using other creeping plants, plant one at the center of each square. One ounce (28 g) of chamomile seed will produce about 1,000 plants and the seed is sown in spring, in drills made 8 in. (20 cm) apart. The plants will be ready to make into a lawn by early autumn. During the first year, remove all weeds as they appear and keep the plants watered. Roll the lawn in autumn and clip back any long shoots at this time. "Now [October] is the time to beat, roll, and mow carpet walks of chamomile," wrote John Evelyn in the seventeenth century. Do not walk on the plants the first year; let them become established first, when regular walking over the plants will reduce the need for clipping.

PLANTING THE HERB GARDEN

It is suggested that the ground on one side of the path be planted with those herbs of perennial habit, with the annuals and biennials on the other side. Perennials are permanent and the plants may occupy the ground for twenty or thirty years, with the soil occasionally fortified by a dressing of limestone, chalk, or mortar and a little decayed manure. Or alternatively, those plants requiring a dry, well-drained soil (they include the shrubby herbs of southern Europe such as lavender and rosemary) may be planted on one side of the garden, while those requiring a moist, humus-laden soil are placed on the other side.

There are many herbs which prefer a

to grow over the stones, which increases the area of ground under cultivation but causes no harm to the stones (or bricks). Herbs can harm grass if allowed to grow over the edges of a lawn. Much of an herb garden can also be tended from the paths, without constantly treading the soil. Treading causes it to compact and hinders drainage, and most herbs require well-drained soil. A path can be used to divide one part of the herb garden from another or to divide a piece of ground into numerous small beds.

A wonderful selection of herbs growing in a cottage garden and well grouped, with the tall growing bay laurel, elecampane, and fennel to the back; sage, hyssop, and lavender to the front. Leaf colors are well displayed.

1 Bay laurel
2 Elecampane
3 Fennel
4 Pink lavender
5 Thyme
6 Cotton lavender
7 *Santolina neapolitanum*
8 Rue
9 Marjoram
10 Sage
11 Hyssop
12 Burnet

gravelly soil and grow well in soils of a calcareous nature. These are mostly the woody herbs which are found in their natural state growing about the rocky coastline of the Mediterranean. Perennial plants, they may be grown in those gardens where the soil is difficult to bring into suitable condition for growing other plants. Few vegetables and fruits will flourish in such a soil, but many of these herbs will grow and reproduce themselves in a soil which contains 70 percent gravel, shingle, or pure sand and which heats up in summer to a point which could be detrimental to the growing of many other plants. Such a soil will also retain little moisture during the warmer months, but here too, most of the shrubby herbs are able to survive long periods with the minimum of moisture. Where the weather is warm and dry, herbs may be grown in preference to many other plants; for under arid conditions, herbs give off by oxidation a vapor from the oil glands contained in the leaves and surround themselves with an invisible cloud. This protects them from being scorched by the sun and from undue loss of moisture. Indeed, the hotter the conditions become, the more oil do the leaves produce and this adds to the value of the plants when used in potpourris and in cooking.

The essential oil of the leaves is secreted in minute droplets which evaporate on exposure to the air to give off the pleasant scent. The oil is stored in numerous ways. In the bay laurel leaf it is stored as capsules, while in the myrtle the oil is embedded deep inside the leaf tissue and the scent is released only with considerable pressure. In rosemary, the oil is stored just below the leaf surface in oblong cells and its fragrance is released with the slightest pressure such as a light breeze; hence the delicious smell which is perceptible far out at sea when approaching the isle of Corsica with its rocky coastline where the plant abounds. The powerful scent of leaves is due to the presence of alcohols; borneol, the chief one, gives the rosemary its resinous scent as in pine needles. Another alcohol, geraniol, is present in the leaves of the scented-leaf geranium; and menthol is present in the mints.

It is important that the scented-leaf herbs obtain as much sunlight as possible to convert the alcohols in the leaves into sweet-smelling substances. The scent will be more intense if the plants are growing in a dry climate and in a well-drained soil. A dry soil is therefore ideal for the aromatic herbs, and the plants will be even more heavily scented if the soil contains a liberal amount of limestone. As the most important ingredient in their diet, limestone may be given as mortar from old buildings; as ground chalk or limestone; or as hydrated lime obtained from a builder's merchant. This should be worked into the soil before planting, when the weeds are removed. Work the ground as deeply as possible, for most herbs are deep rooting and some may occupy the ground for upward of fifty years. No manure is necessary, but a sprinkling of bone meal or a little well-decayed farmyard manure or old mushroom bed compost can be dug in when the soil is prepared. Do not use artificial manures.

In Calcareous Soil. The herbs listed in the box on page 86 can be grown in gardens where the soil is light and well drained and of a calcareous nature. The best time for planting is spring, when the soil begins to warm. Await for the soil to be clear of frost and is in a friable condition after winter

HYSSOP

Chamomile *(right)*, lavender, rosemary, sage and marjoram are perennial herbs which always grow best in light, sandy soils of a calcareous nature (i.e., chalk or limestone). This brings out their flavor and fragrance to the full.

FOR DRY, CALCAREOUS SOIL

Plant	Height
Anise	18 in.
Bay	3 – 12 ft
Calamint	10 in.
Chamomile	prostrate
Coriander	10 in.
Cotton lavender	2 ft
Cumin	2 ft
Dill	3 ft
Hyssop	2 ft
Lavender	1 – 4 ft
Mountain thyme	prostrate
Mugwort	3 – 4 ft
Rosemary	6 ft
Rue	2 ft
Sage	20 in.
Scented-leaf geranium	16 in.
Southernwood	3 – 4 ft
Summer savory	8 in.
Sweet basil	16 in.
Sweet marjoram	12 in.
Tansy	3 ft
Thyme	10 in.
Winter savory	10 in.
Wormwood	12 in.

DILL

rains. As a general rule of planting, allow the same space between the plants as they will grow tall. Thus plant winter savory 10 in. (25 cm) apart. In order to obtain worthwhile amounts of each herb to use in the kitchen, set out three or four plants of each of the less vigorous herbs, though a single plant of rosemary will provide the home with all that is necessary when the plants are three years old.

At the back plant rosemary; if making the herb border against a wall (or fencing panels), plant the rosemary at the foot of the wall and train it to grow about the wall. Tie in the woody stems as they form, and within three years it will cover a wall to a height of 6–7 ft (1 m). This was the way it used to be grown in Tudor England and in Europe in the seventeenth century, for it will retain its green through the coldest winter and when cut will keep green longer than any other plant. Hence it was used at funerals and weddings as symbolic of life everlasting: "Be't for my bridall or my burial," wrote the poet Herrick, and in *Romeo and Juliet,* Shakespeare refers to the custom of dropping a sprig of rosemary onto the coffin as it is lowered into the grave.

Rosemary blooms in early summer when bees in their hundreds visit the flowers. The plants were accompanied by other tall-growing herbs such as bay laurel, mugwort, and southernwood which also love the protection of a wall. Jasmine and climbing roses (to make potpourris from the flowers) were also planted with them, to make a "wall herber" as they were called. In this way the plants took up little space in the garden and yet they provided the home with much valuable "green" to serve many uses the whole year through. Sir Thomas More, at whose Chelsea home Holbein and Erasmus stayed when in England, wrote: "As for rosemary, I let it run all over my garden walls, not only because my bees love it but because it is the herb sacred to love and remembrance, and therefore to friendship." Every wall should be covered with it,

for no plant has as many uses—as a tonic drink, as a hair conditioner, and in the kitchen.

At the back will be planted those other taller growing plants such as southernwood and the taller lavenders. *Lavendula spica* will eventually grow as wide as it grows tall (1 m), the silver-gray foliage adding beauty to the border during winter. Tansy is another herb which grows to a similar height, and it too is handsome with its dark green fern-like leaves divided into pinnatifid leaflets. They may be shredded and beaten up with eggs and flour and fried in flat cakes, known as "tansy cakes," which are usually served during Lent. The tiny yellow button-like flowers also add their beauty to the herb border. At the back, plant the sunflower which grows 6–7 ft (2 m) tall and may need supporting.

To the front, plant rue, with its handsome leaves of steely blue, which grows about 2 ft (60 cm) tall. It is the bluest plant in the garden. Near it plant the cotton lavender *(Santolina incana)* with its leaves like tiny lamb's tails, of a silvery gray. It is a plant of extreme hardiness, and the contrast between the two plants is remarkable. Another plant with handsome leaves and which bears flowers of pink or mauve is hyssop, which also grows 2 ft (60 cm) tall. The poet Spenser wrote of "sharpe isope," for its leaves impart a sharpness to soups and stews, while the dried flowers and leaves can be included in potpourris. Here, plant the more compact lavenders such as *L. nana compacta;* the sweet marjoram; winter savory; the upright thymes, *T. citriodora* with its lemon-scented leaves and the handsome golden-leaf form *T. aureus* which is not so aromatic. The

As for rosemary, I let it run
over my garden walls,
not only because the bees love it
but because it is the herb
sacred to remembrance, to love, and to friendship.

Sir Thomas More

sages, handsome in flowers and with their foliage of unique sage-green coloring, are suitable companions for the middle of the border: they grow about 20 in. (50 cm) tall. From the Latin name comes the word "salvation," for there is an old saying which asks: "Why should men die whilst sage grows in the garden?" Sage fritters (dipped in batter and fried and served with lemon juice) were served at the end of all medieval banquets to aid the digestion. For stuffings they are indispensable but plant also the delicious pineapple sage, for its leaves really do smell exactly like ripe pineapples.

At the middle of the border, set a few plants of the ancient shrub rose, *Rosa gallica officinalis,* one of the oldest of plants still in cultivation. Its flowers were engraved on the shields of Persian warriors as early as 1000 B.C. and it was introduced into northern Europe by the Romans because its flowers retained their fragrance when dried better than all others. They had so many medicinal and culinary uses that the dried flowers were kept in apothecary's shops, usually in wooden drums and sold all the year round; hence its name the apothecary's rose. When in bloom in the garden, its rich crimson flowers enhance the herb border with their beauty and are especially attractive when planted near the silver foliage of cotton lavender or the gray foliage of the sweet-scented lavender. The plants grow about 2 ft (60 cm) tall and require very little pruning. The flowers are an important ingredient of a dry potpourri.

At the front of the border, set summer savory and coriander, both of which are annuals. Sow them in spring where they are to mature, scattering the seed in circles and later thinning the seedlings to a distance of 4 in. (10 cm) apart. Here too plant calamint and wormwood, and if the winter climate is not too severe, the gorgeous French lavender, *L. stoechas.* Its spikes are the deepest purple of all lavenders, for the flower bracts are also purple, not green as with other lavenders. If you wish, plant one of the thymes as an edging. We have already

mentioned lemon thyme and the golden-leaf variety; the genus is very versatile. Or use chives, which are handsome in flower and are quite happy in a light soil though they like a little humus at the roots.

In a Moist, Humus-Laden Soil. There is an equal number of herbs which prefer a moist, humus-laden soil. (See the list in the box on page 89.) Ordinary loam suits them well and if the soil is light and sandy, some peat, bark fiber, or decayed manure should be incorporated. Leaf mold or material from the garden compost heap is equally suitable. Many of these herbs are plants of hedgerows or damp meadows, native of northern hemispheres, and will survive cooler conditions. They are not happy in calcareous soils

Though native to the Mediterranean islands of Corsica and Sardinia where the climate is hot and dry, rosemary is hardy enough to withstand a winter of intense cold elsewhere. It is a plant that prefers to be grown against a warm wall, where it will reach 6 to 7 ft (2 m) in height, but it also makes a thick bush in the herb garden. It remains green all year and is used fresh from the garden, while its pale blue flowers in spring, much visited by bees, are delicious in salads.

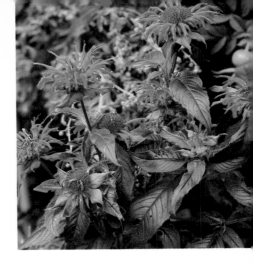

Bergamot is a plant of North America and one of the loveliest of the herb garden. A perennial of great hardiness, it grows 2 to 3 ft (60–90 cm) tall. In summer it bears whorls of red or pink flowers and has lanceolate leaves which when crushed smell deliciously of bergamot orange.

The Gallica rose (sketch at right) is one of the oldest plants known to man which is still grown in gardens. Originating from Persia and the Near East, its flowers are red and retain their perfume when dry long-

er than those of all other roses. In this frieze from Darius' palace in Susa (ca. 500 B.C.), the Persian warrior's garment is decorated with flowers which appear to represent the Gallica rose.

although some will flourish in such a soil provided the plants are given some humus about their roots. These herbs are more tolerant of partial shade—but this does not mean overhanging trees. Less sunshine is better, and they may be planted facing north where they do not receive the maximum amount of sunlight in summer, as they would if growing in a more southerly position. The exception is caraway, which requires a heavy soil to grow well but must have plenty of sunlight to ripen its seed.

In a cold climate and in a moisture-retentive soil, these herbs will give a good account of themselves, though no herbs will

flourish in a badly drained soil. If the soil is of a heavy clay nature, work in some shingle to assist drainage when the humus is dug in. The humus materials will open up a heavy soil and make it more porous, in addition to retaining moisture.

A large number of these plants may be classed as vegetables and are usually grown in the vegetable garden rather than in the herb garden. These include the onion and shallot; parsley; celery; chicory, and dandelion, both of which are blanched in the dark before using; and lamb's lettuce and Good-King-Henry. The plants require a well-nourished soil, capable of holding moisture during dry weather, as do most other vegetables. Onions and shallots are grown for their bulbs, which are lifted at the end of the

growing season and are dried and stored during winter. Celery is also used during winter but is allowed to remain in the ground and is lifted as required.

Many of these plants—such as bergamot and balm, lady's smock and tansy, cowslip and violet—are perennial and more suitable to plant in the herb garden where they will be permanent, to be used each in their season. The annuals and biennials may be included either in the herb or vegetable garden, sown directly into the open ground in spring for they do not easily transplant.

When planning this section of the herb garden, follow the same procedure as described above, setting the taller plants at the back (these include the sunflower, angelica, fennel, and sweet cicely, each of them handsome in leaf). It may be advisable to give them support when they reach 3–4 ft (1 m) in height, for their stems are not as strong as those of other herbs and when wet, the foliage may fall onto nearby plants, depriving them of sunlight. As they grow tall, insert several long canes around each plant and fasten garden twine to each cane, enclosing the plants.

At the middle of the border, plant tarragon, with its pointed lance-shaped leaves. Here will grow borage and chervil; bergamot and balm, among the loveliest plants of the herb garden; bergamot, which bears its red, white, or pink flowers in elegant whorls; while there is no garden plant which bears flowers of more true-blue coloring than borage. The anthers are black and meet in a cone-shaped protrusion. The leaves and stems, when broken, release a cool, mossy scent and are placed in drinks.

To the front of the border set cowslips and violets in small groups, and the various

Though almost all herbs prefer a well-drained sandy soil, there are several which are tolerant of a wet soil and they also grow well in semi-shade. They may thus be planted where few other herbs will grow. Herbs suitable for these conditions are listed in the box at right.

Below: A mid-sixteenth-century woodcut, by Peter Brueghel the Elder, shows the multiple gardening tasks being performed simultaneously, and apparently with a good deal of vigor. The garden typifies the formal, geometric ground plan then very much favored.

mints including the bergamot-scented *Mentha citrata,* also known as Eau-de-Cologne mint or bergamot mint. Its leaves are sometimes attractively variegated and in hot weather take on a purple tint, while the flower spikes are of deeper purple than those of other mints.

Apart from the bergamot mint, whose roots do not spread as vigorously as the others, the mints should be planted in a bed to themselves. They spread rapidly by underground stolens and will choke out other plants growing near them. They require a soil containing some decayed manure or other

all manner of purposes. They die back in winter but begin to grow again early in spring and can be cut when about 4 in. (10 cm) high.

To edge the border, sow parsley, which will remain green all winter for at least two years if sown in well-nourished soil. And at the back of it plant chives, for the thin rush-like stems can be cut all the year. They are in daily use and are handsome in bloom, the globular flowers being almost as large as a golf ball and of brightest pink. Or they can be planted in the vegetable garden, in rows or to surround a bed of salad plants.

FOR MOIST, HUMUS-LADEN SOIL	
Plant	*Height*
Alexanders	3 – 4 ft
Angelica	5 – 6 ft
Apple mint	2 ft
Balm	2 ft
Bergamot	3 ft
Black mustard	2 ft
Borage	2 ft
Caraway	2 ft
Celery	20 in.
Chervil	16 in.
Chicory	10 in.
Chives	8 in.
Clary	12 in.
Cowslip	8 in.
Dandelion	6 in.
Elecampane	4 – 5 ft
Fennel	4 – 5 ft
Garlic	12 in.
Good-King-Henry	2 ft
Herb bennet	18 in.
Horseradish	2 ft
Lamb's lettuce	10 in.
Licorice	18 in
Lovage	3 ft
Nasturtium	trailing
Onion	16 in.
Parsley	8 in.
Peppermint	12 in.
Rocambole	16 in.
Salad burnet	12 in.
Shallot	16 in.
Sorrel	10 in.
Sunflower	6 – 7 ft
Sweet cicely	3 – 4 ft
Tarragon	2 ft
Violet	3 in.

forms of humus to hold moisture, for they are plants of marshy ground and the banks of streams.

The best mint sauce to accompany lamb is made from apple mint, *Mentha rotundifolia,* and spearmint, *M. spicata*. Its flowers are born in handsome spire-like inflorescences; hence its name should really be spiremint. The creeping string-like roots of mint are planted in winter when the ground permits it. They are planted 4 in. (20 cm) deep, and are spreading out like the fingers of a hand. Plant perhaps two roots of each of 5 or 6 species or varieties, setting them 16 in. (40 cm) apart; they will soon spread and provide plenty of sprigs (shoots) to use for

Licorice and horseradish are best planted on their own, in an out-of-the-way corner, for they grow coarse, with large leaves that keep the sunlight off nearby plants while their roots, which is the part used, penetrate to a depth of several feet (perhaps 1 m) and when once established are difficult to eradicate. They are obnoxious plants in the garden but have so many culinary uses and are used all the year round, lifted out as required. Plant them 2 ft (60 cm) apart in deeply dug ground and they will grow well in semishade.

An attractive herb garden can be made with a circular bed at the center of a diameter of perhaps 12 ft (say 4 m) with a sundial or

An All-Herb Garden

With their informal habit and delightful leaf colors and variations, and for their many different fragrances, herbs make a most interesting garden planted entirely to themselves. A labor-saving garden in a small area may be made by using paving stones to form a rectangular garden or to divide up an area by means of a path. Climate must play a part in selecting the plants, but the choice is large even in the coldest gardens. The garden plan sketched below incorporates a sundial (center), and shown at the top, a seat for relaxation amid the cool scents and shades. The paving permits access to all the plants, and a rose hedge forms the perimeter.

bird bath at the center, around which are grouped the more compact lavenders and catmint with a few roots of the clove-scented pink set here and there. Surround the center with a brick path made about 16 in. (40 cm) wide; then make other beds of semicircular shape for low growing herbs and surround these with another circular path. If it is practical to surround the garden with a hedge of roses or of rosemary to be trained against wires or wooden palings, this would allow for the taller growing herbs to be planted in the corners between the hedge and the outer path. It would give the herb garden a degree of privacy and would provide the plants with protection from cold winds. Herbs of all types can be planted, but with space limited, plant those most often used for culinary and medicinal purposes. Possibly a garden seat could be placed at one side so that one could sit and enjoy the beauty of the plants and the wild-life that visits them. (See the sketch directly below.)

An herb garden can be made in autumn or in spring; the latter is the most suitable time if the garden is bleak or is situated in the cooler parts of the world when planting is delayed until the soil begins to warm with the sun's rays. Plant only when the soil is in a friable condition, and wherever possible use pot-grown plants. This will prevent root disturbance and enable the plants to grow away without check. Plant them so that the top of the soil ball is just covered with soil, and make them quite firm.

Where garden space is strictly limited, a herb garden can be made, perhaps in a sunny corner of a lawn, using an old cartwheel set into the turf and planting low-growing herbs in the spaces between the spokes. Or make a simulated wheel of about the same diameter and plant chives for the spokes and one of the upright thymes for the rim of the wheel. Then, in the eight spaces between the spokes, plant sweet marjoram, parsley, hyssop, sorrel, cowslips, clary, salad burnet, and marigolds for a splash of summer color.

Seat

Elecampane · Borage · Angelica · Fennel · Sage · Catmint · Comfrey · Caraway · Balm · Parsley · Sorrel · Feverfew · Mints · Mints · Marigold · White horehead · Hyssop · Coriander · Lovage · Chamomile · Cotton lavender · Chives · Alkanet · Rue · Thyme · Lavender · Marjoram · Salad burnet · Chicory · Nasturtium · Dill · Borage · Rosemary · Chervil · Bergamot

When space is limited, a number of herbs can be grown in large pots or tubs, or in deep boxes placed in sunlight on a terrace, veranda, or the balcony of a house which has no garden at all. Herbs are grown in this way in many of the crowded towns of southern Europe and North Africa. They are tolerant of dry conditions and where water is a scarce commodity, need little.

In the tub shown here, the herbs are arranged in graduated height, in three principal concentric zones: at center, balm, tarragon, and sage; surrounding them, hyssop, sweet marjoram, and winter savory; and on the outer edge parsley, thyme, chives, and a few nasturtiums to lend color and a pleasing overflow effect.

GROWING HERBS IN TUBS, POTS, AND BOXES

Herbs, with their many handsome leaf designs and colors, are admirable plants to grow in a tub, one or more being placed around a sunny courtyard or on a terrace or verandah. An old oak cider cask or vinegar barrel cut into two, with drainage holes drilled in the base, will be most suitable for making an herb garden. First treat the wood inside and outside with preservative and the iron rims with a noncorrosive metal preservative. Do not paint the tubs; they are more attractive in their natural color, and if of oak, will have years of use left in them. If possible, stand the tubs on stones or bricks which will keep the base above ground and so that excess water which may collect at the base will not damage the wood. Also make sure the tubs are secure. Then cover the drainage holes with some old earthenware crocks or pieces of broken brick, and over these place some turves, grass side downward, which will prevent the compost from choking up the drainage holes. The compost should be of fresh turf loam or sterilized garden soil, to which some coarse sand (3 parts soil to 1 part sand) has been mixed. Mix in some lime rubble (mortar) or 1 lb (½ kilo) of hydrated lime to each tub to keep the compost sweet and to provide the herbs with some chalk or limestone in their diet. Fill the tub to the top and allow it several days to settle down before planting. The top of the compost will then be about 2 in. (5 cm) below the top of the tub and this will allow for watering (though with herbs this is rarely a matter of urgency for the plants will go for many days in summer without attention) and for top-dressing each spring. Remember to provide the herbs with the same open, sunny situation, exactly as if they were being planted in the open ground. (See the illustration above.)

At the center, plant balm, tarragon, and sage and around them hyssop, marjoram, and winter savory, graduating the heights and edging the tubs with parsley (from pots), thyme, and chives. To give summer color, insert a few seeds of nasturtium around the edge for them to trail over the sides. There will be a succession of brilliant red, orange, and gold flowers which are allowed to seed, and the seeds can be used as a substitute for capers while the leaves provide a health-giving bitterness to summer salads.

The herbs will be kept under control by their daily use, but if any have grown too large, thin out the shoots in spring and top-dress the tubs at the same time.

The low growing herbs may also be planted in a window box which may be fixed either outside or inside a sunny window or on a sunny wall of a courtyard. Here they are fixed by means of strong iron brackets, for they will be about 7 ft (2 m) above ground and must be made entirely secure. Window

Troughs made of cement on weathered stone and placed on a terrace or at the sides of a sunny courtyard will accommodate many low growing herbs. The trough should be filled with a porous loam after placing drainage materials in the base. Mountain (or wild) thyme is suitable to grow in troughs and one or two plants should be set at the sides. Other dwarf thymes can also be included and the small savory (Satureia rupestris), which makes a spreading mass of dark green mint-scented leaves. The stone crops can also be grown and a row of parsley and chives.

CHERVIL

HORSERADISH

SPEARMINT

BAY, PARSLEY, PEPPERMINT

Even a small flower pot placed on a windowsill can be used to grow herbs, either singly or in combinations. The photographs above suggest the range of possibilities.

Bay leaves are used in *bouquets garnis* and to flavor mild puddings, and just one or two are removed here and there as required. The plant is evergreen but in cooler climes is best grown in a small tub so that at the approach of winter it may be lifted indoors to protect it from frost damage. Plants may be grown on a single stem and trimmed into the shape of a ball or square, or they may be allowed to grow naturally. Keep them in trim by removing any long shoots as they form, and use them in the kitchen.

boxes are more easily tended when they can be reached from the ground, but a box made to the inner dimensions of a kitchen window which receives plenty of sunshine can just as easily be tended from the kitchen and can be equally successful. They may be planted with a wide variety of herbs which have many culinary uses, and those which would not do well outside can be grown indoors.

It will not be possible to grow enough plants for drying in window boxes, but if evergreens are planted, they can be used during most of the year, whatever the weather is like outside. There is nothing new in the idea. As long ago as 1574, Sir Hugh Platt, writing about the subject in Tudor England, said, "In every window you may make square frames either of lead or of boards, well pitched within. Fill them with some rich earth and plant such flowers or herbs therein as you like best."

Whether the box will be inside or outside the window, make it of wood, using timber 6 in. (15 cm) wide and ¾ in. (2 cm) thick. Make the box about 8 in. (20 cm) from back to front so that the end pieces fit inside the two longer pieces which will be the back and front. Use nails to secure the end pieces, since screws tend to part the wood. Oak is now difficult to obtain, but American red cedar is almost as durable and is equally impervious to water. Do not paint them, but treat the boxes inside and outside with wood preservative. Allow several days for the fumes to escape, then drill holes in the base and cover these with crocks or with a piece of wire netting to prevent loss of soil.

Make up a compost similar to that used for tubs, and after fixing the box securely with angle iron brackets, put in the compost and allow it to settle.

Sweet basil and knotted marjoram, which may be frost-tender in colder parts, may be grown in an inside window box, while outside you can plant low growing herbs which will not keep the sunlight from a room. You may include parsley (pot grown), chives, the various thymes, winter savory, germander, and nasturtiums to trail over the side.

Window box plants are kept tidy by the constant removal of the leaves or shoots and by pinching back those shoots which have made excessive growth. In dry weather, syringe the plants daily and they will respond by making plenty of new growth, but if you have to be away from home for several days at a time, or even weeks, herbs will come to no harm. Inside a window, pots of mustard and cress can be grown in winter and chicory forced in a cellar or shed in the dark.

Herbs may also be grown in terra-cotta earthenware pots, also in cement pots made to resemble stone and in vitrines and vases for which the rich colors of the herbs are in pleasing complement. The containers may be placed on a terrace or verandah or by the

PARSLEY

EET MARJORAM

A man's nature runs
either to herbs, or to weeds;
therefore let him
seasonably water the one,
and destroy the other.

Francis Bacon

heads with sacking in late autumn or, better still, lift the plants (in their pots) indoors, to a kitchen, sunny porch, or garden room where they will continue to grow and retain their leaves all winter. Bay laurel, if unprotected, will lose its leaves outdoors in severe weather and may be killed altogether. It can be grown in a garden room all year but will benefit from being placed outdoors at intervals during summer, whenever the weather is showery.

The scented-leaf geraniums are also grown in pots, for the plants require winter protection in northern Europe and North America and are lifted indoors before winter.

Hanging Baskets. With their informal habit, herbs are suitable plants for hanging baskets.

Several of the shrubby herbs such as rosemary and southernwood can be trained to cover a sunny wall. Here they will take up little garden space. A low retaining wall (as in the two photographs here) can be built close to the walls of a sunny courtyard. One can train scented roses and rosemary against the back walls, and plant all manner of herbs in the space between the low retaining wall and back walls. This will allow for many of the taller growing herbs to be planted, something which is not possible on a low wall built on a terrace or veranda. A complete herb garden can be planted in a space of 2 ft (60 cm) between back wall and retaining wall, which should be made about 16 in. (40 cm) high. Between the walls, drainage materials are provided, over which good-

side of a flight of steps, possibly leading from one part of the garden to another. This was where many herbs were grown in earlier times, when the plants would brush against the clothes of those who walked up and down the steps.

Many herbs can be grown in large pots, including rosemary and rue, sage and thyme, hyssop and balm, salad burnet and marjoram. Pots of parsley, sorrel, and the various mints will be appreciated if placed near the kitchen, and no plant is more suited to large pot culture than the bay laurel. If grown on a single stem, the heads can be clipped into squares or ball-shaped and they may be placed by the side of an entrance to the home or in various places on a terrace. If the winter climate is cold, either cover the

These may be suspended from the eaves of a bungalow or from the roof of a garden room. They may also be suspended from a strong wooden or an iron stake driven into the wall of a sunny courtyard. If a few seeds of trailing nasturtium are planted in the compost in spring, the plants will trail down to several feet (a meter or more) and will be a blaze of color all summer.

A hanging basket is made either of strong galvanized wire or plastic covered wire. A suitable size for herbs will be a basket of

quality loam is added to almost the top of the retaining wall.

Suitable plants to set behind a low retaining wall will be fennel and sweet cicely at the back, and bergamot and costmary in front. Set a plant of angelica in the corner of two high back walls. Other plants to use are chives and the sages; thyme and the savories; marjoram and hyssop; rue, tansy, and tarragon. Set a few plants of pinks at the front and nasturtium seeds for the plants to trail over the retaining wall to provide brilliant color in summer.

Where space is limited, a low wall *(below)* may be built at the front or side of a terrace or veranda, or to divide one part of the garden from another. It can be planted with low growing herbs. The wall is built with a core of soil and the herbs are planted at the top. When the wall, of brick or stone, is built up, the soil is added and the plants set out from pots at any time.

Herbs planted on a low wall: A plant or two of ground ivy, and a few nasturtium seeds pressed into the soil here and there, will trail over the sides and break up the hard lines of the stone. Suitable plants to use on a wall are marigold and thymes of all description; the marjorams and winter savory; a plant or two of chives; clove-scented pinks; the stonecrops and hyssop, each having many culinary uses and being colorful in leaf and in flower.

The scented-leaf geraniums (especially *Pelargonium felicifolium* or *P. capitatum*), while not the hardiest of herbs, make a most welcome addition to a hanging basket. They can be used outdoors in warm

climates; otherwise they should only be planted in baskets that will hang inside the house.

18–20 in. (45–50 cm) in diameter. Make up the basket in spring; to do so, place it on a table in a greenhouse or shed and place two bricks on opposite sides of the basket to prevent it from rolling about. Then line it with damp sphagnum moss to a depth of 2 in. (5 cm). The moss will retain moisture and prevent the compost from falling

through the wires, in addition to providing the baskets with a more pleasing appearance. Make the moss quite damp before using it: it is surprising how much water it will absorb. After lining the basket, fill it with compost. Use sterilized soil or fresh turf loam rather than soil from the garden, which will contain a large amount of weed seeds that will germinate and cause trouble later. To the loam, mix in 1 lb (½ kilo) of coarse sand to each basket of soil and a handful of lime rubble (mortar). A few pieces of charcoal placed in the compost will keep it sweet. Fill the basket to the top and allow it 2–3 days to settle down before planting. The soil should be in a damp but friable condition but not too wet.

Set out the plants from pots. If the basket is to be hung in a garden room or porch, or outdoors where there is a favorable climate, then at the center you can place one or two of the scented-leaf geraniums and plants of sweet basil. The latter is an annual but can be cut back to soil level at the end of each season and fresh plants put in next year. Several of the scented geraniums bear bright

pink or red flowers and all are attractive in leaf which they retain all year. Around the sides, plant two or three of the delightful ground ivy *(Nepeta glechoma)*, an herb used long ago to clarify ale. Its heart-shaped leaves with their indented edges are retained through winter and are dark green and often splashed with white. It is perennial and the stems will trail down to about 3 ft (1 m). It is a labiate, its small purple flowers appearing at the leaf joints. If, for instance, three plants are used, then set a few nasturtium seeds between them. These are annual and are removed at the end of summer. Other herbs to use are winter and summer savory, sweet marjoram and hyssop, each of which will appreciate being grown indoors or given the protection of the eaves of a house in all but the warmest gardens. Chives, parsley, and fragrant thymes will provide a suitable selection for kitchen use.

The baskets should go out during late spring. If the summer is dry, syringe the plants daily and keep the compost moist, but herbs in hanging baskets will survive several weeks without water if they have been correctly prepared.

The plants will soon begin to make bushy growth, but if used continually in the kitchen, removing a shoot here and there as required, they will not become too large. Any unduly long shoots are kept pinched back as they form.

Earthenware pots of 6 in. (15 cm) diameter, filled with compost, can also be suspended from the walls of a courtyard, by galvanized wire fixed beneath the rim of the pot. The pots are suspended about 16 in. (40 cm) from the stake fixed in the wall, which will allow the plants to make plenty of top growth unhindered.

PROPAGATION OF HERBS

Herbs are propagated in several ways, as discussed below.

From Seed. This is the method used for raising annual and biennial plants. In order to prevent root disturbance, which would cause the plants to take several weeks to re-establish themselves and so lose valuable time needed in ripening their seeds (and it is for their seed that annuals are mostly grown), the seed is almost always sown where the plants are to mature. A sowing is made early in spring, in small groups in the herb garden or in drills in the vegetable garden. Before sowing, take note of the height the plants will reach and sow accordingly.

Transplanting: Herbs from pots can be planted anytime except when the soil is frost-hard. Spring is the best time, for in the warmer days the plants will grow away quickly. Make the hole to take the soil ball or roots large enough so that the roots are not cramped, fill in with soil, and make firm. In dry weather, water the plants in. Do not plant too closely. Herbs need air and sunlight or they will die back.

needs biennial treatment if the seed is to ripen correctly, although in the Near East where the climate is more favorable, it is sown and harvested the same year. The herbs listed in the box at right are raised from seed and are given either annual or biennial treatment.

In northern parts of Europe and North America, anise, sweet basil, and summer sa-

PROPAGATED FROM SEED

Plant	Height
Alexanders	3–4 ft
Anise	18 in.
Black mustard	2 ft
Borage	2 ft
Caraway	2 ft
Celery	20 in
Chervil	16 in.
Coriander	10 in.
Dill	3 ft
Lamb's lettuce	10 in.
Nasturtium	trailing
Parsley	8 in.
Summer savory	8 in.
Sunflower	6–7 ft
Sweet basil	16 in.

Those which are tall-growing will be placed to the back; the most dwarf, to the front. Some will ripen their seed better if given biennial treatment, which means sowing the seed the year before that in which the plants mature. The slow-growing parsley is an herb that requires biennial treatment. The seed is also slow to germinate and if it has not been freshly saved, it may not germinate at all. There is an old country saying that "parsley goes nine times to the devil before it grows." Caraway also

vory are frost-tender and should not be sown or planted out until fear of frost has departed. In a cold climate, those herbs treated as biennials may be protected during winter by covering the plants with either glass or plastic cloches, which are removed in spring when the weather becomes warmer.

The seed is sown about 1 in. (2.5 cm) deep and thinly, for when the seedlings are about 4 in. (10 cm) high they will need thinning to about 10 in. (25 cm) apart to allow them

Propagation directly from seed: Annual herbs such as caraway and dill (those which are grown for their seed and mature in the year of saving) and biennials like borage and parsley (which are sown the previous year to that in which they mature) are usually sown directly into the open ground. There are perennial herbs (see list on next page) that may also be grown from seed. Shown above left are nasturtium and sweet basil, among the annuals propagated from seed.

One of the several ways of propagating herbal plants is from stem cuttings. In late summer, new wood is removed by hand from a main stem; an irregular tear is preferred to a neat cut with scissors or pruners. The shoots are treated with rooting powder and placed in soil in an earthenware pot. Thyme cuttings are being handled in the photograph at right.

Bottom: Parsley shoots which have been raised from seed, shown before transplanting. A slow-growing herb, parsley will require biennial treatment—that is, the seed is sown one year, and the plant matures the following year.

In addition to the annual herbs (listed on preceding page), many of the perennial herbs (list below) can be grown from seed just as easily. It is an expensive way of obtaining plants, but perennials such as sage and chives will take a year longer to produce usable plants than if purchased in pots. Annual herbs are sown where they are to mature; perennials are sown in pots or boxes, and when large enough to handle, are moved to individual pots or planted out.

PERENNIALS FROM SEED

Plant	Height
Angelica	5 – 6 ft
Balm	2 ft
Chamomile	prostrate
Chicory	10 in.
Chives	8 in.
Dandelion	6 in.
Fennel	4 – 5 ft
Good-King-Henry	2 ft
Hops	15 ft
Hyssop	2 ft
Lavender	3 – 4 ft
Lovage	3 ft
Rosemary	5 – 6 ft
Rue	2 ft
Sage	20 in.
Salad burnet	12 in.
Sorrel	10 in.
Sweet cicely	3 – 4 ft
Watercress	8 in.
Winter savory	12 in.
Wormwood	12 in.

room to develop. Thin coriander and summer savory to only 6 in. (15 cm); sunflower, to 2 ft (60 cm).

Most annual herbs (and some perennials, too) will seed themselves if several plants are allowed to shed their seeds before harvesting, though care must be taken to ensure that too much seed is not lost. In this way, the plants will perpetuate themselves. There are also those plants which are given annual treatment and which in Britain, northern Europe, and Canada are grown almost entirely under glass. These are the capsicums, the red peppers, which have so many culinary uses, and other tender plants such as the caper and okra. In the southern United States and in southern Europe, they are grown in the open; in colder parts, under glass. Seed is sown early in the year, in a temperature of 68 °F (20 °C), which may be provided by an electric propagating unit. Sow in sterilized loam, and when the seedlings are large enough to handle, transplant to individual pots and grow on in a temperature of 62 °F (17 °C). Keep the compost comfortably moist but not wet; otherwise the plants will damp off. As they grow larger, move to 8 in. (20 cm) pots or to deep boxes and grow on under glass, shielding them from the direct rays of the sun during the hottest days of summer.

There are many perennial herbs that may be raised from seed. They will take two years before they are large enough to set out in their permanent quarters but present little difficulty in their raising. Almost all perennials transplant well. If growing in gravel, lavender will usually seed itself and so will rosemary.

Perennials raised from seed are best sown in a frame or in a box or seed pan in a greenhouse. They may be sown in a sunny kitchen window or outside on a terrace or verandah, the seed box being covered with plastic or a sheet of glass to protect the seed from birds and mice and to warm the compost when the sun is shining and so speed germination. Always sow in sterilized loam from which weed seeds and disease spores have been eliminated. Add a handful of sand and one of moist peat to each kilo of loam and give a sprinkling of superphosphate of lime to encourage root activity and to keep the compost sweet. Distribute the seed evenly on the surface of the compost and give a light covering of compost. Spring is a suitable time to sow perennials, so that by the end of summer the young plants will be ready to move to small pots, containing a similar compost in which they will be sown. They will remain in the pots until the following spring when they are planted out. Perennial herbs which will grow readily from seed are listed in the adjacent box.

By Root Division. Many of the perennial herbs, but not the shrubby or woody ones, may be propagated in this way. It is the easiest of all methods and is done in autumn or spring when the plants die back. If they are lifted every four years and divided and replanted, this will keep them healthy and

Here we see a technique for planting seeds of perennials directly in a seed pan.
Below: Herbs such as shallots and onions are usually grown from small bulbs called sets, or in the case of garlic, from offsets or cloves.

Root division *(above)* is an easy way of increasing your stock of plants. This is done in autumn or spring, lifting the plants and gently pulling them apart.

vigorous, nor will they form any dead wood at the center. Lift the plants with a garden fork, shake away any surplus soil, and divide each plant into small pieces, each with a crown (from which new growth will begin) and some healthy roots. Gently tease the pieces apart and replant into clean, freshly prepared ground. They will begin to

make new growth almost at once.

By Stem Cutting. Most of the shrubby herbs grow from a single main stem and will not divide at the roots. The only way of propagation is either by sowing seed as described, or by taking and rooting stem cuttings and shoots. This is done toward the end of summer, removing the new season's wood which will be partially ripened by the sun. New wood will root more easily than older wood and can be made to root more quickly if the cuttings are treated with hormone powder. Remove the cuttings either just below a leaf joint or preferably with a "heel" attached. This is a wafer-thin piece of wood which comes away with the cutting when gently tugged from a main stem. The "heel" will give a greater rooting area than if the shoot is cut away with scissors or pruners. The lower leaves are carefully removed before treating the base of the shoot with the rooting powder. This is done by wiping the base with damp cotton wool so

that, when dipped in the rooting powder, it will adhere.

Hardwooded cuttings will root more quickly if inserted around the side of an earthenware pot, for they like to be in contact with the rough pot. Set the cuttings about 1 in. apart and in a compost containing sterilized loam (obtained from a nurseryman or garden shop) and sand in equal parts; here again, the cuttings like a gritty compost which encourages them to root. Most hardwooded herbs will root within about six months when they will be seen making new growth at the top. They should then be carefully lifted from the compost and replanted into small individual pots containing a similar "open" compost, perhaps fortified with a little decayed manure or bone meal. They are grown on for several months before being planted out where they will remain permanently.

From Root Cuttings. There are a number of herbs and spices that are propagated from their roots. Small pieces are removed when the plants are lifted for harvesting the roots. The pieces are then replanted. Licorice is propagated in this way, and horseradish in most of the temperate world; galingale in India, China, and Southeast Asia; ginger, too, which is mostly grown in Queensland, Jamaica, and Southeast Asia; and zedoary and turmeric which are cultivated in India, Malaysia, and Indonesia.

From Bulbs or Sets. Onions, shallots, and garlic are increased either from seed or by planting the small bulbs, also known as sets. With garlic, the bulbs are made up of cloves. Onion sets are specially prepared and kept in cold storage, while shallots and garlic sets are saved when the crop is harvested in autumn and kept over winter in a frost-free room to replant in spring. Small but firm tubers are used for planting and should be kept separately in boxes or bags from those stored for kitchen use.

PROPAGATION BY ROOT DIVISION

Plant	Height
Balm	2 ft
Bergamot	3 ft
Chives	8 in.
Cowslip	8 in.
Herb bennet	16 in.
Lady's smock	16 in.
Lovage	2 ft
Salad burnet	12 in.
Tansy	3 ft
Tarragon	2 ft

PROPAGATION FROM STEM CUTTINGS

Plant	Height
Balm	2 ft
Bay	15 ft
Juniper	20 ft
Lavender	3 – 4 ft
Oregano	12 in.
Rosemary	5 ft
Rue	2 ft
Sage	20 in.
Scented-leaf geranium	16 in.
Southernwood	3 ft
Spice bush	10 ft
Star anise	8 ft
Tansy	3 ft
Thyme	10 in.
Wintergreen	6 in.
Winter savory	12 in.
Wormwood	12 in.

Each of the different propagation techniques is suited only to particular types of plants. By consulting the four lists in this section, the reader can match a specific herb to its appropriate method.

A simple, inexpensive way of drying herbs such as sage, marjoram, and thyme is to string them up into small bunches and hang them on a cane or wooden bar fixed between the walls of a small shed or room or suspend the herbs from the rafters of an attic room.

Parsley can be cut fresh all the year if, in colder gardens, the plants are covered with a cloche in winter. Clip off the leaves with scissors. If the plant is to be dried, place the leaves in a warm oven for several days, turning them each day; or dry in the sun in an airy room. Parsley retains its freshness for several days.

Chives grow in dense clumps and when two to three years old produce numerous hollow pencil-like shoots which have a mild onion flavor. Remove them almost at soil level between spring and autumn and chop into small pieces to include in salads or with egg dishes. After four years, lift and divide the plants.

HARVESTING, DRYING, AND STORING HERBS

So important were herbs for cooking and for medicines in earlier times that it was essential to bring in the crop in as perfect a condition as possible—just as it is in harvesting grain today. Hence the saying "cut and dried," referring to a completed task or (as commonly used today) a foregone conclusion. In the monastic rolls of medieval times are numerous items of payment made for supplying those who tended the gardens with "knives for cutting herbs," which would be needed for cutting the hardwooded herbs such as rosemary, southernwood, the thymes, and sages. These plants need a sharp knife or pruners to cut off the woody stems, though the shrubby herbs must never be allowed to form an excess of old wood. If they do, the plants will fail to produce fresh new growth which is required to maintain the health and vigor of the plants and which will be more highly aromatic than old woody shoots. Any dead wood should be systematically removed each year.

Most herbs will be used fresh during summer, and those which are evergreen can be used all the year. The best-known example is rosemary: there is no necessity to dry it for winter use. The thymes, too, retain their green through winter, as does winter savory. Parsley, tarragon, tansy, and balm can be cut in summer when at their best and if blanched in boiling water for a few seconds, they may then be placed in plastic bags and in the deep freezer where they will keep fresh and retain their fragrance for a year or more. Tarragon leaves can be frozen in ice cubes in the refrigerator, to be used in summer drinks to which they impart their unique aromatic flavor.

Those herbs which lose their leaves in winter and will not freeze well are cut at the end of summer when most fragrant and are dried for winter use. Some herbs such as thyme will retain their scent and flavor better if dried, even though they do retain their leaves in winter.

Where herbs are growing under conditions they enjoy, it is usually possible to make two cuttings each year, the first about midsummer, the second early in autumn. This will also prevent the hardwooded herbs from making an excess of old wood. They are cut on a dry day, when dew has dried from the plants, using a sharp knife or secateurs (pruners) to remove the stems. The method is to hold the stems with one hand and to cut with the free hand. The stems are then placed the same way on a mat or on sacking to keep them from the soil or turf. If the day is sunny, they may be left out until late noon so that they will have become partially dry before taking them indoors.

Softwooded herbs such as balm and the mints are cut just above ground with sharp scissors. Those herbs which lose their leaves at the end of summer and die back—such as tarragon, balm, and bergamot—should have their leaves removed before they fall so that they can be frozen or dried for winter use.

The flowers of some herbs, such as borage and violet, can be candied when fresh, to use in confectionery and there are those herbs whose stems are used in the same way. Most

important is angelica which is cut at regular intervals during summer, for it is the young stems that are most wanted.

For information on the harvesting of specific garden herbs, the reader is referred to Reference Section II, which lists each plant singly, with details on planting and harvesting.

Herbs are dried by tying the stems into bunches and suspending them from the roof of a shed or attic—but do not use a shed with an asbestos cement or corrugated iron roof, for moisture will collect on the underside in winter and cause the herbs to become damp, when mildew will affect them. Dryness throughout is essential if herbs are to retain their quality. Should they become troubled by mildew, they take on a musty smell and lose flavor and scent. A drying rack will not only enable quite large quantities to be dried but will assist with their quicker drying.

A rack can be made by making a number of trays each about 4 ft (1 m) square, using ¾ in. (2 cm) timber, for the racks will not have to carry any great weight. About 1 in. (2.5 cm) should be allowed between each of the timbers to enable a free circulation of air to reach the herbs and fasten their drying. First make the frame of the rack, then nail to it the lengths of wood. Timber 4 in. (10 cm) wide should be fixed to the sides, and each rack is then fixed to four posts of 3 by 3 in. (7.5 cm square) timber. Fix the lower rack about 2 in. (5 cm) from the floor and others at intervals, allowing 10 in. (25 cm) between each rack. In this way, in a corner of an attic room, 6–8 racks can be constructed, depending on the height of the room, and will occupy very little space. Hessian is fixed to each rack to prevent the leaves falling through as the herbs dry out. An airing cupboard for clothes may be used as an alternative, covering the shelf timbers with clean hessian. The cupboard will be used for only a few weeks in their drying. If using a cupboard, leave the door slightly open to allow any moisture from the herbs to escape. In a warm dry room, whether strung up in bunches or dried on racks, herbs which were harvested in a dry condition will complete their drying in about 14 days. The leaves, which will now be brittle when touched, are then ready to rub from the stems. This is done by placing the herbs on a tray or in a box lined with clean white paper (shelf paper is the best) and the stems are rubbed with the palms of the hands until all the leaves are removed. The stems are then discarded or, in the case of

Dandelion roots can be covered in spring with an inverted pot to exclude light. This will blanch the leaves as they grow, so that they will be sweet and succulent.

Harvesting of marigold heads. The marigold is an annual, but if the weather is mild, continues to bloom all winter. The flower heads can be used fresh or dried. To dry, remove the heads in summer and spread them out on racks. Then pull the petals from the central boss and complete their drying. Store the petals in boxes.

A rack arranged in tiers, with space between each tier to allow for turning the herbs, is an ideal way to complete their drying. The racks are lined with hessian over which the herbs are spread, and are turned each day until quite dry. A dry, airy room or shed is necessary for quick drying. When quite dry, the herbs are rubbed down and placed in containers. Among those herbs grown for their leaves are marjoram, sage, and thyme, while lavender and marigold are grown for their flowers. They are dried in the same way.

In earliest times, the correct drying of herbs was considered of great importance, for they were indispensable in flavoring food and drinks. Herbs and spices today, whether as valuable commercial crops or when grown and harvested privately, must also be dried with particular care. To ensure evenness in drying, the plants or plant parts must be regularly examined on all sides and turned over at intervals (picture above).

lavender, are kept to burn like incense (after dipping in saltpeter solution and dried) in the home. The leaves are then rubbed through a fine-mesh strainer so that any small stems can be removed, and the herbs are then ready for the storage containers.

More difficult to dry is parsley, owing to its thick crinkled leaves. If the weather is warm and dry, cut the fronds when free from moisture and spread them out in a sunny attic or garden shed, turning the fronds reg-

ularly so that all parts receive some sunlight. If the weather is damp, parsley is best dried in an oven on low heat. Spread out the fronds and turn them every hour or so, keeping the oven door open to allow any moisture to escape. By this method, parsley will take two or three days to dry to the point where it will be crisp enough to rub down. But if not allowed to run to seed in summer, parsley will remain fresh for at least its first winter and possibly for another winter.

Parsley may be frozen and kept in the deep freezer for a year or more. Cut the fronds when at their best, blanch for a few seconds, and put into plastic bags before placing in the freezer.

Screw-top glass jars are suitable, or drums made of thin plywood; even cardboard boxes. Do not use tin boxes or plastic bags: both tend to sweat, and the herbs will also become damp and lose quality. Wood and cardboard will absorb moisture. Be certain to name each herb, for when the leaves are well broken down it is not always easy to remember which they are. They are then placed on a shelf in the kitchen or are kept in the attic, and small containers for kitchen use are kept filled from the storage containers. The herbs will be dried and ready to use by the late autumn and will, in most cases, take over from fresh herbs.

Seeds are the fruits of the plant. Great care must be taken with the harvesting of seeds of annual and biennial plants such as coriander, caraway, and dill. In cooler climes they will not ripen well except in a hot, dry summer; hence commercially they are grown in Spain and Portugal and around the Mediterranean, especially in North Africa where their harvesting presents no trouble.

The seed must be fully ripe before it is harvested; otherwise it will contain little essential oil nor will it have reached its fullness of flavor, and what little there is will soon be lost in storage. This is why annuals grown for their seed (and many of them have other culinary qualities as well) re-

Borage is one of the herbal plants that is best used fresh. Both its leaves and its attractive flowers can be harvested throughout the summer for immediate use. The same is true of dandelion, fennel, lovage, sorrel, and summer savory.

quire a long season to mature, in all but the hottest parts. If it is possible to treat the plants as biennial, so much the better for they will be well established by spring and will begin to grow as soon as the soil becomes warm.

As the seed becomes ripe, inspect the plants daily. The pods should be just on the point

brown and hard when placed on the palm of the hand, though with dill and cumin the elongated seeds are light brown. Smell also plays a part in determining a seed's maturity. Place a few seeds in the palm of one hand and press them with the palm of the other hand. The seeds should release their particular scents. Coriander seed when fully ripe will release an orange-like scent, which becomes more pronounced as the seed becomes drier. The principal constituent of the essential oil in the seed is the alcohol coriandrol which has the scent of bergamot orange, though the unripe seed smells of bedbugs; hence it is important that the seed be dry and fully mature before harvesting. Seeds vary in size and shape as well as in color. Dill is the smallest seed and an ounce (28 grams) will contain about 25,000. The seeds are paler than those of caraway and

Our seasoners utilize the most diverse parts of the herb and spice plants, as demonstrated in the six illustrations below. Among the plants cultivated for the sake of their *roots* are ginger, turmeric, and dandelion; the roots must be lifted out and dried in the sun. The *stem* is the plant part used in other cases, such as chives, whereas with balm, chamomile, marigold, lavender, cloves, and others, the *flower* or even the whole herb is used (the cloves sold in grocery stores are the dried unopened flower buds). Star anise (along with mustard, caraway, cumin, dill, peppers, and cardamon) is an example of a plant cultivated for its *seeds*, the ripe

ROOT (Dandelion) STEM (Chives) FLOWER (Balm) SEED (Star anise) LEAF (Myrtle) POD (Senna)

of opening (splitting) when harvested. If allowed to become fully open, they will shed the seed and it will be lost. It is also necessary to harvest the seed when the weather is dry. Thus, act as soon as the seed appears in the right condition and the weather is suitable; do not delay. When inspecting the capsules, press one or two with the fingers: if they appear dry and split open easily, they will be ready to harvest. In most instances, the seed will be black or dark

also flatter (caraway is curved). Cumin seed is similar but straighter.

Mostly, seeds are used whole but if required in the powdered form, they are broken (ground) down with pestle and mortar but only when completely dry. They will also lose their flavor if pounded too soon before use.

The fruits of cardamoms are much longer, measuring $\frac{1}{2}$ to $\frac{3}{4}$ in. (1–2 cm) long and are divided into three cells which contain

fruits being removed and dried in the sun so that the seeds can be extracted. *Leaves* are the flavorful parts of myrtle, bay, marjoram, sage, thyme, and so many other plants. With senna, vanilla, cocoa, and tamarind, it is the *pods* that are harvested. Other parts are also used; in saffron, it is the dried stigma of the flower that yields saffron powder. Cinnamon is the bark of a tree, taken from young branches. With garlic and shallots, it is the underground bulbs that are harvested.

101

After harvesting and drying, herbs must be stored in suitable containers and under dry conditions if they are to retain their quality. They may be stored in glass jars, plastic containers, or cardboard boxes, but not in tins, which sweat.

Mostly grown in India and Southeast Asia, cardamon seeds are wedge-shaped and dark brown, with an aromatic taste and smell. Those produced in Ceylon are larger and yellowish-red with a ginger-like odor.

Here we see herbs being packaged in a plastic bag in preparation for freezing. They can be kept as long as a full year.

the rich brown seeds. They are not separated from the pericarp until required to use. The aromatic flavor is only fully retained if the fruits are unbroken, and here too it is necessary to harvest them at exactly the right time. Even the seeds should not be powdered until ready to use in making up curry powders, for they lose their strength once broken. Cloves too, which are the unripe flower calyces of *Eugenia aromatica* and are imported from Zanzibar and the East and West Indies, will also better retain their fragrance of flavor if not pounded until required to be so used.

The moment the seeds are ripe for harvesting, cut away the seed pods with sharp scissors or secateurs and drop them into cloth or paper bags and take indoors to a dry room. There they are spread out on trays in an attic to complete their drying or they can be tied up in the bags and suspended from the ceiling (a beam is appropriate) for about two weeks. As the pods dry they will shed the seeds which are placed in muslin or paper bags or in small cardboard boxes and clearly named. Small quantities of seed are placed in wooden or pot containers for use in the kitchen. At this stage they can also be ground down to mix into curry powders. To retain their flavor and scent, seeds must be kept dry, like leaves, and they are best stored in the dark.

Roots are harvested in autumn after completing their growth from a sowing of seed made in spring. Celery can occupy the ground all winter; lift the plants and use the stems for flavoring when required.

The roots of herb bennet are clove-scented when dry, and a number of plants should be lifted in autumn and the roots cut off and stored in sand.

OUT-OF-SEASON HERBS

The roots of chicory are lifted in November for if seed was sown about the first of June, the roots should by then be as thick as a man's wrist. The foliage will have died down and the roots are lifted with a garden fork, to be forced in a cellar or shed. They are replanted in deep boxes containing 8 in. (20 cm) of old manure, and soil and light is excluded from them to blanch the shoots which in gentle warmth will be ready to use in three to four weeks.

The roots of some herbs such as licorice will remain in the ground for three to four years before they are economically long enough to use; similarly with elecampane. The plants are then lifted and the roots washed and dried and cut into small pieces before using. From the roots of licorice a juice is extracted which is used in confectionery and to flavor drinks.

To enjoy fresh mint during winter and early spring (and the plants will die back in autumn for their winter rest), the roots may be lifted in December and replanted in deep boxes filled with compost and placed in a greenhouse or garden frame. The compost should be of good-quality loam into which a small amount of sand and decayed manure are mixed. Only just cover the roots which are spread well out, and keep the compost nicely moist and in a temperature of about 50 °F (10 °C). The roots will soon begin to put out new shoots which may be cut and used when about 4 in. (10 cm) long. If the roots are lifted in February, artificial heat will not be necessary to force them into growth: the warmth from the spring sunshine will do so as high temperatures are not required.

If no glass is available, make up a mild hot-

Water mint *(Mentha aquatica)*. A stately perennial, growing 3 to 4 ft (1 m) tall, it is found by streams and in dark woodlands. The reddish-purple flowers are borne in whorls in summer, while the leaves, when pressed, release a scent of orange (bergamot) rather than mint.

bed outdoors. This is done in an out-of-the-way corner of the garden by enclosing an area of a square yard or square meter with deep boards held in place with wooden stakes driven into the ground. A hotbed is made by composting a quantity of straw with an activator.

As the mint stems may grow to 6 in. (15 cm) tall, if a hotbed is made in a frame, first remove several inches (cm) of soil, then put in the compost to a depth of 10 in. (25 cm) treading it well down to retain its warmth. Over the top, add 6 in. (15 cm) of riddled soil into which the roots are planted. Spread them out, but they can be almost touching. There should be about 2 in. (5 cm) of soil over the top of them. Water them and close up the frame; but if planting in a homemade frame or pit, place clear polyethylene sheeting over the boards to keep in the warmth generated by the hotbed, which will allow plenty of light to reach the growing mint. It must not be forced in the dark. The warmth of the early spring sunshine combined with that of the hotbed will soon cause the shoots to grow. The hotbed should be made up early in spring, to have forced mint with spring lamb.

Early mint can be enjoyed by covering the roots in early spring with cloches, over where they are growing, and they will soon begin to make new growth. Or roots can be lifted and planted in a deep box into which several inches of compost has been placed with a 4 in. (10 cm) covering with soil. Place the box in a garden room or outside on a verandah or terrace where it will receive some sunlight, and cover with clear plastic sheeting. There should be 6 in. (15 cm) from the top of the soil to the top of the box for the mint to grow. In this way, there will be fresh mint to use several weeks before that growing in the open ground and when it is most in demand.

After gently forcing the roots, they may be replanted in the open afterwards, in a well-nourished soil, but no stems should be cut for another two years. Top-dress in winter when the plants die down.

Growing and Processing

ROY GENDERS

Reference Section II

A tabulation of the 100 basic herb and spice plants, in which can be found classification data along with guidelines on propagation, planting or sowing, flowering, harvesting, and preservation. In specifying the parts of each plant that are used in seasoning, this section uses the following symbols:

 fruit / berry / cone

 leaf

 flower

 bud

 nut / bean

 bark

 seeds

 stem / shoots

 rootstock and tuber

roots

 bulb / clove

Growing herbs and spices might seem a purely utilitarian pursuit, which leaves no scope for artistry. But consider the herb garden. Its primary purpose may be to provide seasoners for the kitchen—that is, to cater to the aesthetic component of the sense of taste; but the herb gardener cultivates at the same time both the plant and the aesthetic elements proper to it. He arranges his plants in pleasing patterns, according to their respective heights, to the aspect of their foliage, to the colors of their flowers: he is appealing to the aesthetic component of the sense of sight. He does not neglect either one of the most subtle refinements of all: he is attentive to the fragrance of his plants, the aesthetic component of the sense of smell. The person who grows seasoners, like the cook, is practicing an art.

For the home gardener desiring to raise his own herbs or spices, the following pages offer a summary of our 100 selected plants. Roy Genders' chart offers a quick survey of the life cycle of each plant, from propagation and planting, to flowering, harvesting, and the preservation of the natural seasoners. These are of course norms and generalizations, rather than complete, exhaustive instructions. This section proposes an overview, for convenient classification of the plants. It is meant to be complemented by the Plant Lexicon and the chapter on gardening, the two sections immediately preceding, which contain advice on necessary climatic conditions for each plant and specific instructions for its cultivation, as well as a wealth of general background information. —*Ed.*

The marriage of beauty and utility *(left),* a kitchen herbal garden created for the Swiss Farm Show of 1939. Paths provide convenient access for cultivation, for picking fresh herbs, and for strolling by to enjoy their perfume.

Few gardeners will be constructing herbal plots on the regal scale illustrated in this eighteenth-century German scene. But whether one is planting herbs in an outdoor garden, or simply in a windowbox or hanging basket, there is no escaping the need for planning and timing. By consulting the reference chart on the following pages, read-

ers can quickly select plants of varying heights and complementary flowering season, to ensure a harmonious combination in a plot or pot.

REF. NO.	HERB OR SPICE	TYPE/HABIT	PROPAGATION FROM:	PLANT OR SOW	HEIGHT
72	ALLSPICE	Tree	Seed	Winter	35 ft (10 m)
81	ALMOND	Tree	Seed	Winter	20 ft (6 m)
11	ANGELICA	Perennial	Seed, division	Spring	6–7 ft (2 m)
73	ANISE	Half hardy annual	Seed	Early spring	20 in. (45 cm)
40	ASAFETIDA	Perennial	Seed	Spring	10 ft (3 m)
57	BALM	Perennial	Seed, root division, stem cuttings	Winter	2 ft (60 cm)
18	BAMBOO	Perennial	Stem cuttings	Autumn/winter	6–7 ft (2 m)
51	BAY	Tree	Stem cuttings, seed	Early summer	3–20 ft (1–6 m)
59	BERGAMOT	Perennial	Root division	Winter	2–3 ft (60–90 cm)
77	BLACK PEPPER	Perennial	Stem cuttings, seed	Spring	20 ft (6 m)
20	BORAGE	Biennial	Seed, root division, stem cuttings	Early summer	20 in. (50 cm)
74	BURNET	Perennial	Seed	Early spring	20 in. (50 cm)
93	CACAO	Tree	Seed	Winter	12–14 ft (4 m)
23	CAPER	Perennial	Stem cuttings, seed	Early summer	3–4 ft (1 m)
27	CARAWAY	Biennial	Seed	Midsummer	2 ft (60 cm)
37	CARDAMOM	Perennial	Root division, seed	Spring	6–7 ft (2 m)
13	CELERY	Annual	Seed	Spring	2 ft (60 cm)
12	CHERVIL	Annual	Seed	Spring	16 in. (40 cm)

FLOWERING TIME	PARTS TO USE	HARVEST	WHEN TO USE	HOW TO STORE
Summer		Late Summer	All year	Dry, in containers
February–April		Late Summer	All year	Dry, in containers
July–August		Summer	Summer	Candied
		September	All year	Store in containers
July–August		Summer	Summer	Use fresh
		September	All year	In seed containers
Summer		Summer	All year	In glass jars
July–September		Summer	Summer	Use fresh
			Winter (dried)	Dried and from freezer
August–October		Summer	Summer	Use fresh
		Autumn	All year	In containers
May–June		All year	All year (fresh and dry)	Dry in containers
July–September		Summer	Summer	Use fresh
			Winter	Dried and from freezer
Summer		Late summer	All year	Ground, in containers
June–August		Summer	Summer	Use fresh
July–August		Summer	Summer	Use fresh
All year		All year	All year	Ground, in containers
May–June		Summer	All year	Seeds in pickle
June–July		September–October	All year	In containers
Summer		Late summer	All year	Dry or powdered
July–August		Winter	Winter	Open ground
		September–October	All year	In containers
May–July		Summer	Summer	Use fresh
		August–September	All year	In containers

REF. NO.	HERB OR SPICE	TYPE/HABIT	PROPAGATION FROM:	PLANT OR SOW	HEIGHT
25	CHILI PEPPER	Annual	Seed	Early summer	3–4 ft (1 m)
6	CHIVES	Perennial	Seed, bulbils or bulblets	All year	16 in. (40 cm)
29	CINNAMON	Tree	Stem cuttings, seed	Winter	35 ft (10 m)
30	CITRON	Tree	Grafting, seed	Winter	15 ft (4 m)
39	CLOVE	Tree	Stem cuttings, seed	Winter	70 ft (20 m)
32	CORIANDER	Annual	Seed	Early spring	12 in. (30 cm)
53	CRESS	Annual	Seed	All year	3 in. (7.5 cm)
76	CUBEB	Perennial	Stem cuttings, seed	All year	15 ft (4 m)
35	CUMIN	Annual		Early spring	16 in. (40 cm)
92	DANDELION	Perennial	Seed	Spring	8 in. (20 cm)
10	DILL	Annual	Seed	Early spring	2 ft (60 cm)
86	ELDER	Tree	Seed, stem cuttings, suckers	Winter	12–15 ft (4 m)
41	FENNEL	Perennial	Seed	Spring	5–6 ft (1.5 m)
95	FENUGREEK	Annual	Seed	Spring	6 in. (15 cm)
8	GALINGALE	Perennial	Root division	All year	3–4 ft (1 m)
5	GARLIC	Bulb	Seed, bulblets or bulbils	Spring/autumn	16 in. (40 cm)
100	GINGER	Perennial	Rhizomous division	March	4–5 ft (1.5 m)
28	GOOD-KING-HENRY	Perennial	Seed	Early spring	2 ft (60 cm)

FLOWERING TIME	PARTS TO USE	HARVEST	WHEN TO USE	HOW TO STORE
June–August	🍅	Summer	All year	Fruits in pickle
	▒	Summer	All year	Seed in containers
July–August	●	All year	All year	Use fresh and from freezer
May–September	▯	All year	All year	Dried
	🍅	Summer	All year	Dried
March–September	🍅	Summer	All year	Use fresh and from freezer
All year	◖	August–November	All year	Dry, in containers
July–August	●	Summer	Summer	Use fresh
	▒	September–October	All year	In containers
—	●	All year	All year	Use fresh
May–September	🍅	Late summer	All year	Store dry
July–August	▒	September–October	All year	In containers
March–November	● ◖	Summer	Summer (fresh)	Use fresh
June–July	●	Summer	Summer	Use fresh
	▒	Autumn	All year	In containers
July–August	🍅	August–October	Winter	As preserve
July–September	⚶	Summer	Summer	In freezer
	●	Summer	Summer	In freezer
	▒	September	All year	In containers
June–July	▒	Summer	All year	Dry, in jars
March–July	⚘	Autumn	All year	Dry, in containers
July–August	⚜	August–October	All year	In frost-free room
Summer	⚘	March	All year	In boxes or jars
July–August	⚶	Summer	Summer/winter	Use fresh and from freezer

REF. NO.	HERB OR SPICE	TYPE/HABIT	PROPAGATION FROM:	PLANT OR SOW	HEIGHT
33	HAZEL	Tree		Winter	16 ft (5 m)
42	HERB BENNET	Perennial	Root division	Autumn/spring	16 in. (40 cm)
46	HOP	Perennial	Cuttings from underground stems	Spring	16 ft (5 m)
15	HORSERADISH	Perennial	Root cuttings	Autumn/winter	2 ft (60 cm)
47	HYSSOP	Perennial	Seed, stem cuttings, division	Spring	16 in. (40 cm)
50	JUNIPER	Tree	Stem cuttings	Winter	40 ft (10 m)
52	LAVENDER	Perennial	Stem cuttings, seed, root divisions	Spring	1–4 ft (30–120 cm)
4	LEEK	Annual	Seed, bulblets or bulbils	Spring/autumn	2 ft (60 cm)
94	LEMON THYME	Perennial	Stem cuttings	Spring/early spring	4 in. (10 cm)
55	LEMON VERBENA	Perennial		Spring	6–7 ft (2 m)
44	LICORICE	Perennial	Seed, root division	Autumn	3–4 ft (1 m)
54	LOVAGE	Perennial	Seed, root division	Midsummer	3–4 ft (1 m)
22	MARIGOLD	Annual	Seed, special color types from cuttings	Spring	12 in. (30 cm)
9	MELEGUETA PEPPER	Perennial	Root division	Spring	6–7 ft (2 m)
56	MELILOT	Biennial	Seed	Late summer	3 ft (90 cm)
17	MUGWORT	Perennial	Root division, seed	Spring	3–4 ft (1 m)
21	MUSTARD, BLACK	Annual	Seed	Early spring	3–4 ft (1 m)
21	MUSTARD, WHITE	Annual	Seed	All year	4 in. (10 cm)

FLOWERING TIME	PARTS TO USE	HARVEST	WHEN TO USE	HOW TO STORE
March–April	◉	October–November	All year	Store dry
June–August	⚘	All year	All year	Use fresh
July–August	⚘	Early summer	Early summer	Use fresh
	✿	September	Autumn	Store dry
June–August	⚘	All year	All year	Use fresh
July–September	✿ ◆	All summer	Summer (fresh)	Store dry
Early summer	◉	Summer (2nd year)	Fresh	Use fresh
June–August	✿	September	Summer	Use fresh
			Winter	Store dry in containers
July–August	⚘	All winter from open ground	Winter	Use fresh and in freezer
July–August	◆	Summer	All year	Dry, in containers
July–August	◆	Summer	Summer	Use fresh
June–July	⚘	October	All year	After drying
June–July	◆	Summer	Summer	Use fresh
	▦	September	All year	In containers
All year	◆ ✿	Summer	All year	Use fresh; flowers dry from containers
March–July	▦	Late summer	All year	In containers when ground
June–September	▦	Late summer	All year	In glass jars
July–August	◆	Summer	Summer	Use fresh
			Winter (dried)	In dry room
June–August	▦	August–September	All year	In containers
—	◆	All year	All year	Use fresh

111

REF. NO.	HERB OR SPICE	TYPE/HABIT	PROPAGATION FROM:	PLANT OR SOW	HEIGHT
62	MYRTLE	Tree	Seed, stem cuttings	Winter	6–8 ft (2 m)
96	NASTURTIUM	Annual	Seed	Spring	Trailing
60	NUTMEG	Tree	Seed and grafting	Winter	30 ft (9 m)
65	OLIVE	Tree	Stem cuttings, seed, suckers, seedlings	Winter	20 ft (6 m)
2	ONION	Bulb	Seed, bulblets or bulbils	Spring	18 in. (45 cm)
67	OREGANO	Perennial	Seed, stem cuttings	Autumn/spring	16 in. (40 cm)
24	PAPRIKA	Annual	Seed	Early summer	3–4 ft (1 m)
70	PARSLEY	Biennial	Seed	Early spring	12 in. (30 cm)
14	PEANUT	Annual	Seed	Spring	12 in. (30 cm)
58	PEPPERMINT	Perennial	Root division, stolons, runners	Winter	16 in. (40 cm)
75	PINE	Tree		Winter	100 ft (30 m)
78	PISTACHIO	Tree	Seed, budding, grafting	Spring	20 ft (6 m)
71	POKE	Perennial	Seed	Autumn	10 ft (3 m)
68	POPPY	Annual	Seed	Spring	20 in. (50 cm)
66	POT MARJORAM	Perennial	Seeds, stem cuttings	Autumn/spring	12 in. (30 cm)
79	PURSLANE	Half hardy annual	Seed	Early summer	6 in. (15 cm)
7	ROCAMBOLE	Bulb	Seeds, bulblets or bulbils	All year	2 ft (60 cm)
38	ROCKET	Perennial	Seed	Autumn	2–3 ft (1.5 m)

FLOWERING TIME	PARTS TO USE	HARVEST	WHEN TO USE	HOW TO STORE
July–August		Autumn	All year	Dry, in jars
June–October		Summer	Summer	Fresh
		Summer	Summer	Seeds in pickle
All year		All year	All year	Dry, in jars
May–July		Late summer	All year	Oil or fruit, in glass jars
July–August		September–October	All year	In dry room
July–September		Summer	Summer	Use fresh
			Winter (dried)	Dry, in container and in freezer
June–August		Summer	Summer	Use fresh
			Winter	From freezer
July–September		All year	All year	Fresh; dried or in freezer
		Autumn (2nd year)	All year	
Summer		Late summer	All year	In containers
July–September		Summer	Summer	Use fresh
			Winter (dried)	Dry and rub down or chop for freezer
Summer		Autumn	All year	Dry, in jars
Early summer		Summer	All year	In glass jars
June–August		Fresh	Summer	Use fresh
July–September		Summer; autumn	All year	In seed containers
July–September		Summer	Winter (dry)	Dry in containers; and in freezer
July–September		Summer	Summer	Use fresh
May–August		Autumn	All year	In frost-free room
Summer		Summer	Use fresh	Use fresh

REF. NO.	HERB OR SPICE	TYPE/HABIT	PROPAGATION FROM:	PLANT OR SOW	HEIGHT
82	ROSEMARY	Perennial	Seeds, stem cuttings	Spring	5 ft (1.5 m)
84	RUE	Perennial	Root division, seeds	Spring	2 ft (60 cm)
26	SAFFLOWER	Annual	Seed	Early summer	30 in. (75 cm)
34	SAFFRON	Bulb	Root division	May	4 in. (10 cm)
85	SAGE	Perennial	Seeds, stem cuttings	Spring	20 in. (50 cm)
80	SALAD BURNET	Perennial	Seed, root division	Autumn/spring	16 in. (40 cm)
87	SAVORY, SUMMER	Half hardy annual	Seed	Early summer	8 in. (20 cm)
87	SAVORY, WINTER	Perennial	Stem cuttings, root division	Spring	12 in. (30 cm)
3	SCALLION, WELSH ONION	Perennial	Seed, bulblets or bulbils	Spring	6 in. (15 cm)
69	SCENTED-LEAF GERANIUM	Perennial	Stem cuttings	Early summer	20 in. (45 cm)
31	SCURVY GRASS	Annual	Seed	Early spring	12 in. (30 cm)
89	SESAME	Annual	Seed	Early spring	3–4 ft (1 m)
1	SHALLOT	Bulb	Seed, bulbils	Early spring	16 in. (40 cm)
83	SORREL	Perennial	Seed	Winter	12 in. (30 cm)
43	SOYBEAN	Annual	Seed	Spring	16 in. (40 cm)
58	SPEARMINT	Perennial	Root division, stolons, or runners	Winter	12 in. (30 cm)
48	STAR ANISE	Tree	Stem cuttings, seed	Winter	30 ft (9 m)
88	STONECROP	Perennial		Winter	10 in. (25 cm)

FLOWERING TIME	PARTS TO USE	HARVEST	WHEN TO USE	HOW TO STORE
March–June	[leaf]	All year	All year	Dry, in containers
	[flower]	March–June	Spring	Use fresh
	[seed]	September–October (in warm climate)	All year	In seed containers
July–September	[leaf]	All year	All year	Use fresh
Early summer	[flower]	Summer	Summer	Dry, in containers
	[seed]	Late summer	All year	Dry, in containers
August–September	[flower]	Autumn	All year	In containers
July–September	[leaf]	Summer	All year	Dried and from freezer
	[seed]	October	All year	In containers
June–August	[leaf]	Summer	Summer	Use fresh
July–August	[leaf]	Summer	Summer	Use fresh
July–September	[leaf]	Summer	Winter	In freezer
July–August	[leaf]	All year	All year	Use fresh
All year	[leaf]	All year	All year	Use fresh; and from freezer
May–June	[leaf]	Summer	Summer	Use fresh; and from freezer
May–July	[seed]	Late summer	All year	Dry, in jars
July–August	[bulb]	September–October	All year	In dry room
June–August	[leaf]	Summer	Summer	Use fresh
			Winter	From freezer
Summer	[seed]	Late summer	All year	Ground, in jars
August–September	[leaf]	Summer	Summer	Use fresh
			Winter (dried)	Dry and rub down, or chop for freezer
Spring	[seed]	Autumn	All year	Dry, in jars
July–August	[root] [leaf]	Summer	Summer	Use fresh

REF. NO.	HERB OR SPICE	TYPE/HABIT	PROPAGATION FROM:	PLANT OR SOW	HEIGHT
45	SUNFLOWER	Annual	Seed	Early spring	10 ft (3 m)
64	SWEET BASIL	Half hardy annual	Seed	Early summer	16 in. (40 cm)
61	SWEET CICELY	Perennial	Seed, root division	Spring	4–6 ft (1.5 m)
66	SWEET MARJORAM	Perennial	Seed, stem cuttings	Autumn/spring	16 in. (40 cm)
24	SWEET PEPPER (PAPRIKA)	Annual	Seed	Early summer	3–4 ft (1 m)
90	TAMARIND	Tree	Seed	Winter	35 ft (10 m)
91	TANSY	Perennial	Seed, root division	Winter	3–4 ft (1 m)
16	TARRAGON	Perennial	Seed, root division	Autumn/spring	2 ft (60 cm)
94	THYME	Perennial	Stem cuttings, root division	Spring	10 in. (25 cm)
97	TRUFFLE	Fungus		Spring	Underground
36	TURMERIC	Perennial	Root division	Spring	20 in. (50 cm)
98	VANILLA	Perennial	Stem cuttings	Spring	Climbing
99	VIOLET	Perennial	Seed	Spring/autumn	3 in. (7.5 cm)
49	WALNUT	Tree		Winter	100 ft (30 m)
63	WATERCRESS	Perennial	Seed, root division	Spring	8 in. (20 cm)
19	WINTER CRESS	Perennial	Seed	Spring	8 in. (20 cm)
36	ZEDOARY	Perennial	Root division	Spring	16 in. (40 cm)

FLOWERING TIME	PARTS TO USE	HARVEST	WHEN TO USE	HOW TO STORE
Late summer	(symbol)	Autumn	All year	As cooking oil
July–September	(symbol)	Summer	Summer	Use fresh
			Winter (dry)	Dry in containers; and in freezer
May–June	(symbol)	Summer	Summer	Use fresh
	(symbol)	September	All year	In freezer; in containers
July–September	(symbol) (symbol)	Summer	Summer	Use fresh
			Winter (dry)	Dry, in containers; and in freezer
June–August	(symbol)	Summer	Summer	Use fresh
			Winter	From freezer
January–June	(symbol)	Late summer	All year	Dry, in jars
July–September	(symbol)	Summer	Summer	Use fresh
			Winter	Dry in containers; and in freezer
June–July	(symbol)	Summer	Summer	Use fresh
			Winter (freezer)	In dry room; and from freezer
July–September	(symbol)	Summer	Summer	Use fresh
			Winter (dry)	In dry room; in freezer
—	(symbol)	All year	All year	Use fresh
Summer	(symbol)	Late summer	All year	Dry or powdered
April–June	(symbol)	Autumn	All year	As essence
March–May	(symbol)	Spring	Spring (fresh)	Candied
Early summer	(symbol)	Autumn	All year	Dry, in containers
June–August	(symbol)	Summer	Summer	Use fresh
			Winter	From freezer
June–August	(symbol)	Autumn; winter	Autumn; winter	Use fresh and from freezer
Summer	(symbol)	Late summer	All year	Dry or powdered

Zam weiß senff

Coriander.

Borragen.

The Art of Seasoning

NIKA HAZELTON

This chapter and the Reference Section immediately following are devoted to cooking. A general orientation to the uses of herbs and spices is provided in the present chapter. It includes several multi-purpose recipes, such as for marinades, herbal bouquets, and vinegars. More elaborate recipes for complete dishes will be found in the Reference Section, on pages 137–151.

Happiness is a row of fragrant herbs on a sunny windowsill and a rack of pungent, aromatic dried herbs and spices. For here we have the elements of good cooking, the elements which transform the primitive gratification of hunger into a pleasurable, aesthetic experience.

All of us are familiar with at least a few fresh or dried herbs and with some whole or ground spices. I am thinking of parsley and chives that are used fresh, of thyme and sage that come to us most frequently dried, of stick cinnamon and ground mace, to mention just a very, very few of the flavorings that gladden our cooking. This book introduces a full hundred herbs and spices, which offer a wide range of choice.

The present chapter is intended as a general guide to the art of seasoning. Beginners and advanced cooks alike would do well to heed this basic advice before plunging into individual recipes. We are sometimes apt to forget how to make the most of these flavorings and how to keep them fresh and good for further use. Leaving fresh herbs aside for the moment, let me begin by reminding you of some general rules that apply to dried herbs and spices.

Opposite page: This photographic still-life suggests some of the aromatic riches of natural herbs and spices. More than thirty different seasoners are combined here for scenic effect. What pleases the eye, however, could be disastrous to the taste: cooks are advised to limit the number of herbs and spices they combine in any one dish. The appropriate combination of different seasoners is a subtle art.

Right: A jovial cook in a Venetian trattoria, where seasoners are applied with a graceful light touch. Amateur cooks who heed basic guidelines can capture at home some of the distinctive, rich flavor that many of us associate with ''ethnic'' or ''exotic'' restaurants.

The preceding pages show three woodcuts from the *New Kreüterbuch* of Leonard Fuchs, printed in Basel, 1543: white mustard, coriander, and borage.

The basics: Shown here are three fresh herbs, essential to almost any kitchen, which make up the basic herb bouquet: thyme and parsley *(below)*, and bay leaf *(right)*.

DRIED HERBS AND SPICES: SOME BASIC REMINDERS

Buy in small quantities and do not keep longer than one year at most. Especially dried herbs have a shelf life rarely longer than 4 to 6 months.

Store in tightly capped, airtight jars away from the light and heat and in a cool, dry place. A shelf near or above the kitchen stove will not do. If there is no cool place in your kitchen, store tightly covered in the refrigerator.

Open your herb and spice jars once a month and sniff for freshness. If stale, replace or your cooking will suffer.

Use dried herbs and spices with discretion and discrimination in any single recipe, particularly if you are not familiar with them. Remember that it is easy to add seasonings or flavorings to a dish, and very difficult if not impossible to remove them.

Avoid too many herbs and spices in the same dish unless a recipe calls for them. Use only one strong-flavored seasoning in a food which may be combined with several mild-flavored ones.

Do not flavor more than two dishes in a meal with herbs or spices. And do not forget that their purpose is to enhance the flavor of food and not to disguise it. If the taste of your cooking is overpowered by the seasoning, that dish is a failure.

Experiment with unfamiliar herbs and spices. Add a pinch or so to a little of the dish they are meant for and let stand at room temperature for 5–10 minutes so that the flavors are able to develop fully. Then taste and decide if you want less or more or none at all.

When you double or triple a recipe, do *not* double or triple the amounts of dried herbs and spices. These are the proper amounts: For double the recipe, use $1\frac{1}{2}$ times the amounts called for. For triple the recipe, use twice the amounts called for.

ABOUT FRESH HERBS

Cooks newly beginning to flavor their foods with herbs may be mystified by the names of groups of herbs called for in many recipes. Here are the terms most frequently used and their explanations:

Sweet herbs are plants whose leaves, seeds, or roots make them suitable as seasonings, thanks to their aroma. Thyme, sage, chives, and mint are such sweet herbs.

Pot herbs are plants whose leaves and stems are used for food rather than seasoning. Cabbage, spinach, dandelion greens, and beet tops are pot herbs.

Salad herbs are any herbs used to flavor salads.

Herb bouquets are combinations of herbs used together to flavor soups, stews, braised meats, vegetables, and sauces; the combination depends on the dishes in which herb bouquets will be used. When fresh, the herbs are tied together with string; when dried, they are wrapped in a piece of washed cheesecloth and tied. The reason for tying the herbs is to prevent them from dispersing in the food and from being skimmed off, and also to make it easy to remove them. The most basic and common herb bouquet is the *bouquet garni*, essential in French cooking. A simple *bouquet garni* consists of 2 sprigs of parsley, ½ bay leaf, and 1 sprig or ⅓ teaspoon dried thyme. Other herbs to be added to a *bouquet garni* are always specifically mentioned, such as a medium bouquet with fennel or celery or marjoram.

Fine herbs (better known in the French form *fines herbes*) is also a combination of fresh herbs. However, these are minced and remain in the finished dish. A blend of parsley, chives, tarragon, and chervil are the standard *fines herbes* of French cookery, most often used in egg and cheese dishes.

Herbs and spices need not be restricted to *haute cuisine;* a cold picnic offers many opportunities to use them, in everything from the sesame seed crackers at far left, to truffles and olives with cream cheese, various herb butters and spreads, and watercress with tomato.

SIMPLE BOUQUET GARNI

2 sprigs parsley
½ bay leaf
1 sprig fresh thyme or ⅛ teaspoon dried thyme

HERB BOUQUETS FOR SEVERAL MEATS

Lamb stew: rosemary, parsley, celery.

Veal stew: parsley, thyme, and a piece of lemon rind.

Beef stew with tomatoes: basil, parsley, bay leaf, clove.

Although some dishes call for the use of a whole branch or sprig, fresh herbs are usually trimmed and chopped up before being added to food. A chopper like that shown in this close-up *(left)* proves especially effective in cutting or mincing your herbs to allow their full flavor to emerge. Dried, chopped herbs should be crushed between the fingers to release their aroma as they are added to a dish. For those fortunate enough to have an herb garden like that shown below, the seasoners will be available in their freshest state for months on end.

HOW TO USE FRESH HERBS

To prepare for cooking: Snip potted herbs frequently, for this promotes growth. But do not snip off more at one time than needed. Snip each stalk separately with scissors and never sheer off the top of potted herbs in a crew cut. Wash cut herbs gently in a bowl of cool water by swishing them up and down. Drain, shake dry gently, and pat dry with paper toweling. Crush, chop, or mince fresh herbs before cooking; this releases their flavor. Strip leaves off larger and coarser herbs before mincing, as their stems are tough. Wispy herbs like dill, fennel, and even parsley should be gathered in six to a dozen strands or heads and snipped straight across with a pair of sharp scissors.

Storing fresh herbs. Wrap loosely in damp paper toweling. Or wash, shake dry thoroughly, and pack into tightly closed jars, then refrigerate. Store whole herbs since minced herbs keep poorly.

Use leftover minced herbs to make herb butter (see pp. 131, 132).

Use whole herbs to make herb vinegar (see pp. 132–133).

If you are left with parsley stems having used the parsley heads elsewhere, tie the stems together and add them to slow-cooking dishes for flavoring. Discard the stems before serving.

Add fresh herbs to a dish during the last 15 minutes cooking time unless the recipe specifies otherwise.

To cold dishes in which fresh herbs are an essential ingredient (such as vegetable cocktails, salads, and cheeses) add herbs several hours or overnight before serving.

To salad dressings add fresh herbs about 15 minutes before serving.

Fresh herbs used as a garnish, such as parsley and chives, are sprinkled only at serving time over the dish they are to enhance.

Equivalents: One tablespoon minced fresh herbs corresponds to about $\frac{1}{3}$ teaspoon ground and to about $\frac{1}{2}$ tablespoon crushed dried herbs. However, this proportion depends on the kind and on the freshness of the dried herbs. Be sure to taste as you add either fresh or dried herbs to your cooking.

Cooking with fresh garlic. Unpeeled garlic cloves will give a mild, subtle flavor to your cooking. Add whole and unpeeled to your

dish. When cooked, each clove may be squeezed firmly and the ensuing puree may be spread on bread or mixed into hors d'œuvres or into a salad dressing.

For a whiff of garlic, peel a clove or more and spear each clove with a toothpick for easy removal. Add to your food and cook for 10 to 20 minutes, remove and discard.

Warning! A crushed or mashed garlic clove has two to three times the strength of a minced one.

Dried herbs such as oregano *(above)* are more effective if reconstituted by soaking or simmering in a liquid that can then be added to the dish.

Right: Pepper, black and white, whole and ground. The white variety is used in pale-colored dishes for good visual effect. A pepper mill is a must: your fresh ground pepper has incomparably more flavor than storebought ground.

ABOUT DRIED HERBS

Dried herbs will release more flavor to your food if you crush or crumble them well between the palms of your hands before adding them to your cooking; your body heat will release the herbs' flavorful essential oils.

Always reconstitute dried herbs for full flavor. Before using, soak dried herbs from 10 minutes to 1 hour in a liquid that you can add to your recipe, such as water, milk, bouillon, lemon juice, salad oil, wine, or vinegar. If possible, warm the liquid first. Or you may simmer dried herbs over low heat in a little butter for a few minutes. If you cannot add both liquid and herbs to your food, strain out herbs and use them alone.

When in a hurry and you want to add dried herbs to sauces, salad dressing, and mayonnaise, pour boiling water over dried herbs and let stand 1 minute. Drain and pat dry between kitchen paper before use. Or place measured herbs in a small tea strainer, dip in boiling water for 1 minute, then dip quickly in cold water, drain, and pat dry.

For long-cooking foods such as soups, stews, and casseroles, add herbs at the beginning of cooking time. This way they will blend in with the other ingredients. However, another school of cooks advocates adding dried herbs only during the last 30 to 45 minutes of cooking time or else their flavor will be lost. I subscribe to the first but you may prefer the second solution.

For quickly cooked foods, such as hamburgers, be sure to reconstitute your dried herbs as described above before blending them into your cooking.

In salad dressings, let dried herbs stand in the unchilled oil dressing for 15 to 30 minutes.

Both garlic and onion are available dried in varied forms. Garlic is found as instant minced, powdered, granulated, and garlic salt. Onion is available as flakes, instant minced, diced, chopped, sliced, powdered, granulated, and as onion salt. Instant minced garlic and onion, and onion flakes, diced, chopped, and sliced onions should be rehydrated for about 5 to 10 minutes with an equal amount of water. Drain before using. Fresh garlic and onions are infinitely preferable to dried ones. However, if for convenience's sake you must use the dried garlic and onions, treat them with great discretion for they are assertive and not always desirably so.

ABOUT SPICES

Sniff spices for freshness. Ground spices lose strength more rapidly than whole spices. If a spice smells stale, discard it for it will not flavor your cooking.

Keep spices dry, since moisture will cause deterioration. Never dip a moist spoon or knife tip into a spice jar. Discard spices that have begun to cake.

In cooking, put whole spices into a little cloth bag (such as a cheesecloth bag) or into a stainless steel metal tea ball; do *not* use tea balls made of any other metal. This way, spices are easier to remove from the finished dish. If no bag or tea ball is used, it will be necessary to strain the liquid.

FIRST AID FOR OVERSEASONED COOKING

Strain out bits of herbs and spices.

A raw, peeled, and quartered large potato simmered for 15 minutes in your cooking

Whenever possible use freshly ground rather than ready-ground or powdered spices. Freshly ground pepper or nutmeg make all the difference in flavor.

Grind whole spices just before using. A mortar and pestle, a pepper mill, a coffee grinder, a blender, or a food processor will do the job. For small amounts, use mortar and pestle or a pepper mill.

The flavor of whole spices, such as peppercorns, cardamom, coriander and cumin seeds, cinnamon sticks, whole cloves, and vanilla beans, is more pronounced than that of ground or powdered spices.

will absorb some of the excess seasoning. Remove potato pieces and discard.

If food is overly salty, first use potato as described and then stir a little sugar or brown sugar into your food. Start with ¼ teaspoon and taste before adding more, up to 1–2 teaspoons depending on the food and the quantity.

If food is overly sweet, add about ½ to 1 teaspoon lemon juice, cider or white vinegar, tasting as you add.

If food is overly seasoned, prepare an *unseasoned* second batch and combine the two.

This engraving of an eighteenth-century manorial kitchen presents cookery as a somewhat diabolical, or at least a frenetic, art. The picture is from a guide to housekeeping published in Nuremberg in 1722, at a time when the French already wielded a strong influence on European cooking. The scene suggests a more adventurous, rather than "classical," cuisine, however, and one that was no doubt richly flavored. The woman seated at left appears to be working with a mortar and pestle.

Having examined the ingredients themselves, the basic seasoning elements and tools, we now proceed to some guidelines on the various foods with which they can be combined, in a series of subsections extending from soups to desserts. Each type of dish requires a specific approach.

SOUPS

Clear soups may be sprinkled at serving time with finely minced chives, watercress, mint, basil, or chervil. For a nice touch, add a dab of whipped cream to each helping of soup and concentrate your minced herbs on the whipped cream.

A chiffonade of fresh herbs improves both fresh and canned soups. Use any herbs at hand that harmonize with the soup's flavor. Allow 1 to 2 tablespoons fresh herbs to 1 pint of soup. Add a few tablespoons of the soup to the herbs and puree in a blender or food processor. Return the blended herbs to the soup and mix well. If you have no

Each different type of food will, because of varying texture and flavor, require separate consideration for purposes of seasoning. Even the simplest fare, such as this grilled T-bone steak, profits from the judicious application of herbs and spices, provided that the specific qualities of the food are kept in mind. Reference Section I ("Choosing Your Herbs and Spices") will prove useful in matching the 100 seasoners to various foods.

blender, simply mince the herbs very, very fine. Chives do not combine well with other herbs; they should be added separately.

Experiment with different spices in your soups. Add a dash of ground allspice to green or yellow pea soup, or a dash of ground mace or cardamom to cream soups and seafood chowders, and two to three cloves to vegetable soups. Add spices at the beginning of cooking; use discretion.

Almost all, if not all, soups profit from a sprinkling of minced parsley at serving time. It will improve both the appearance and the flavor of the soup. Parsley is the one herb whose flavor is compatible with the flavor of the soup, whatever other herbs may have already been used in its preparation.

FINES HERBES

A classic fresh herb mixture for soups, sauces, cheese, and nonsweet egg dishes. Add at the last minute to the dish that is being cooked. The cooking will release their essential oils but since it is for a short time only, the herbs will keep their freshness.

Equal parts of:
parsley
tarragon
chervil
chives

Mix herbs and mince with a sharp knife. Do not grind or blend.

SAUCES

Sauces fulfill two functions: either to enhance a food gently or to be sufficiently assertive to add interest to foods with personalities that are not strong enough to stand on their own. However, a few basic principles apply to all sauces. Be careful about salting a sauce. Reducing a sauce concentrates the salt and if you are using stock or bouillon, this also will add salt. Add pepper near the end of cooking time because in a delicate sauce, the long cooking of pepper may develop a bitter taste. If sprigs of parsley or other herbs or whole spices are cooked in a sauce, lift them out before straining or pureeing the sauce or you will

boiling point. Drain into a bowl thoroughly and dry between paper towels. Use the mushroom liquid for the sauce or save it for use in other sauces, stews, or wherever a savory liquid is called for.

To flavor the milk for a white sauce or a béchamel add a small onion to the milk and bring to boiling point. Lower heat and keep the onion in the milk until you think the milk sufficiently flavored. Remove onion before using the milk. For a more pronounced flavor, stick the onion with 1 or 2 cloves and cook. A peeled garlic clove may be used instead or with the onion and treated as described above.

When a recipe calls for a dash of nutmeg, cloves, or other spice, add it to the sauce during the last 2 to 3 minutes of cooking time. Longer cooking may cause flavor to be lost or exaggerated, depending on the spice.

Tartar sauce, consisting of mayonnaise and herbs, can be made quickly using fresh ingredients. An egg yolk is beaten with a dash of dry mustard. Add droplets of salad oil one at a time, beating continually until a good consistency is obtained (³/₄ to 1 cup oil will be needed). Combine with fresh chopped herbs (1 to 2 tablespoons), plus 1 tablespoon each of capers and chopped pickle if desired.

have a sauce flecked with unattractive dark spots. By the same token, use white pepper in a white or light sauce.

When preparing mushrooms to add to a sauce, cook the mushrooms in water to cover and add to the water a little salt and a little lemon juice to avoid darkening. Drop the mushrooms, whole, quartered, or thickly sliced into boiling water and cook for 2 minutes after water has returned to

Uncooked sauces containing fresh herbs keep for about a week in the refrigerator; some, like pesto, can be frozen successfully. Use on vegetable salads, pasta, cold fish, or meats.

When making a sauce dominated by spices, such as curry, fry the spices in a little butter or oil for 2 to 3 minutes, stirring constantly. This will allow their full flavor to be released and captured in the sauce.

FISH

When steaming fish, add a bundle of fresh herbs to the liquid. Parsley, fennel, thyme, mint, and balm, single or in combination, are suited to the purpose.

Add fresh or dried herbs to fish cooked in foil.

Sprinkle sauteed fish with *fines herbes* during the last 3 minutes of cooking time providing no other herbs have been used. Vary the flavor of court bouillons with different herbs.

Add a dash of ginger, mace, or allspice to shellfish dishes.

Spread fish with herb mayonnaise before broiling.

EGGS AND CHEESE

When making an omelet, a frittata, or scrambled eggs, add half of the *fines herbes* or any other herbs or herb mixtures to the beaten eggs before cooking. When eggs are almost set, sprinkle with the remaining herbs.

Give interest to bland cheeses such as cottage cheese or cream cheese by mixing with minced garlic, minced fresh herbs, reconstituted dried herbs, fennel, or aniseed. For a sweet cheese, use a pinch of sugar, grated nutmeg, ground cloves, and ground cinnamon or ground cardamom or mace.

A flavorful spread can be made from leftover cheeses.

Mash remaining bits of the same kind (that is, soft or hard cheeses), thin them a little with dry white wine, sherry, or brandy, and flavor with herbs or spices.

Add a dash of nutmeg or allspice to a cheese soufflé batter.

MEATS AND POULTRY

Whether you are grilling, broiling, roasting, or pan-frying meats, or cooking them by moist heat (that is in a liquid), add salt at the end or just before the end of the cooking because salting before browning draws out the juices. Pepper may be added earlier. Marinated meats require less salt, pepper, or flavorings. Taste as you add them to your cooking.

To distribute garlic evenly on roasts, mash a garlic clove into 2 tablespoons olive oil or melted butter. Spread over the meat's surface. If you wish to insert whole or halved garlic cloves, cut pockets into the meat and insert garlic making sure none shows on the surface. Any garlic bits on the surface of the meat will scorch and produce an unpleasant flavor. The same applies to any herb stuffing.

To add flavor to roasting meats, baste them with an herb baste made by simmering together for a few minutes white or red wine,

---

LEMON HERB BUTTER

About ½ cup

For boiled or grilled fish

½ cup butter, at room temperature
1 tablespoon grated lemon rind
½ teaspoon minced fresh chives
½ teaspoon minced chervil or basil
1 teaspoon minced parsley

Cream the butter with the lemon rind and the herbs until thoroughly mixed. Spread on fish while the fish is very hot. Or spread butter on raw fish and grill.

MUSTARD SAUCE

About 1 cup

For fish, seafood, and cold meats Make at least 2 hours before serving.

9 tablespoons salad or olive oil
3 tablespoons white vinegar
2 tablespoons Dijon mustard
¾ teaspoon salt
¼ teaspoon freshly ground white pepper
2 tablespoons sugar
⅛ teaspoon ground cardamom

Combine ingredients and blend thoroughly. Beat with wire whisk or fork before serving.

HERB BASTE

About 1½ cups

Use dry red wine for beef; dry white wine for lamb, veal, or pork. Vary herbs according to food and taste. Chicken bouillon makes for a lighter base than beef bouillon. Start basting after about 30 minutes of cooking.

1 cup chicken or beef bouillon
½ cup dry red or white wine
1 garlic clove, mashed
1 teaspoon dried thyme or savory
½ teaspoon crumbled rosemary
½ crumbled bay leaf
½ teaspoon allspice (optional)

Combine all ingredients. Simmer covered over low heat for 5–10 minutes. Keep liquid hot while basting but do not boil. To make gravy, strain all pan juices, scraping up the brown bits at the pan bottom. Use as is or thicken with flour or cornstarch and butter.

MAITRE D'HOTEL BUTTER

About ¾ cup

For steaks and grilled meats

½ cup butter, at room temperature
2 tablespoons minced parsley
2 tablespoons minced chives
2 tablespoons fresh lemon juice

Cream the butter with the parsley and the chives, adding the lemon juice a little at a time. Mix thoroughly. Turn onto a piece of waxed paper and shape into a roll. Refrigerate and cut into slices. Place one slice on each portion of steak or other grilled meat.

SEASONED BREADCRUMBS FOR FRIED FOODS

Use for fish, chicken, and any food that is to be breaded before frying. Vary the seasonings to your own taste.

1 cup finely sifted dry breadcrumbs or cracker crumbs
½ teaspoon salt
¼ teaspoon paprika
3 tablespoons grated Parmesan cheese
½ teaspoon any dried herb such as crumbled rosemary, sage, tarragon, or majoram

Combine ingredients and mix thoroughly.

---

or broth or a mixture of both, with garlic, onion, herbs, and spices. Keep the herb baste hot while basting, and when basting liquor is used up, use liquids in bottom of pan. Or rub seasoned salts into meat.

If you have a rosemary bush, use branches of this herb for brushing oil over roasting lamb. Use branches of any preferred herbs dipped into a basting sauce for basting roasting, broiling, or grilling meats. This also applies to barbecues and out-of-doors over-the-coals cookery.

Crush and press green or black peppercorns into steak before broiling.

When preparing kebabs, add a few bay leaves to the skewer, alternating them with the meats or vegetables. For pot roast, add either a few cloves or a few mustard seeds to the cooking liquid.

Use marinades (pages 133–134) to tenderize and flavor meats and poultry.

Use seasoned breadcrumbs for fried foods (see recipe above).

When cooking out of doors on an open fire, throw all the prunings and trimmings of the herb garden on the fire during the last few cooking moments. Their smoke will flavor the food deliciously.

Spread any food to be broiled or grilled with herb oil. This is made by soaking 1 or 2 preferably fresh herbs in a jar of olive oil. Let stand at room temperature for several days before straining and rebottling.

HERB AND SPICE VINEGARS

GENERAL RULES

Use only the best quality vinegars, such as cider or wine or white vinegars. (As a rule, white vinegars are sharper.)

It is preferable but not necessary (as shown in many recipes) to heat the vinegar before adding it to the herbs and spices. If you do, *heat only just below boiling point; do not boil.* Herb or spice vinegars mellow with time, losing their sharpness.

Do not use metal caps when bottling your vinegars; their chemicals do not agree and the vinegar may turn black.

The type of vinegar used will determine the flavor of the finished product.

Remove garlic from any herb or spice vinegar after 24 hours steeping or it will wreck the flavor of the vinegar.

FRESH HERB VINEGARS

Select herb leaves just before the plants are in full bloom. Gently bruise the leaves before placing in a jar. Start making herb vinegars with just one or two herbs. Combinations of more herbs require a good knowledge of the strength and flavors of each fresh or dried herb. Strongly flavored herbs will kill the flavor of milder ones.

Proportions for fresh herb vinegars

1 cup freshly minced herbs to 1 pint (2 cups) or 16 fluid ounces (U.S.).

DRIED HERB VINEGARS

It is preferable to heat the vinegar before adding to the dried herbs.

Proportions for dried herb vinegars

Infuse 10 days to 2 weeks. 2–3 teaspoons dried herbs (depending on strength) to 1 pint vinegar.

To make the dried herb vinegar, proceed as in *fresh herb vinegar.*

SPICE VINEGARS

The vinegar must be heated to just below boiling point.

Herb vinegars can be made with virtually any herb that is desired. The picture at left shows fresh dill. Other popular choices are shallot and tarragon.

The seeds or spices must be crushed coarsely or bruised to release their essential oils. Do this with a mortar and pestle, or place the seeds or spices between waxed paper and pound with a rolling pin or a bottle. Combine seeds and spices carefully for congeniality.

Proportions for spice vinegars
Infuse 2 weeks. ½ ounce preferred seeds or spices to 1 pint vinegar.
To make spice vinegar, proceed as in *fresh herb vinegar*.

MARINADES

Marinades are liquids in which foods, especially meats, are soaked to tenderize them when tough, and to impart flavor. All marinades contain an acid such as vinegar, wine, or lemon juice which soften the tough fibers of the food. Marinades can be cooked or uncooked. Cooked marinades are preferable for foods that must marinate for 12 hours or more, as in the case of venison or in some beef dishes such as sauerbraten.

UNCOOKED MARINADE

About ¾ cup

Use for fish or chicken to be broiled

¼ cup salad or olive oil
½ cup dry white wine
1 tablespoon lemon juice
1 minced garlic clove
½ teaspoon grated lemon rind
½ teaspoon dried tarragon, thyme,
  or crumbled rosemary
½ teaspoon salt
½ teaspoon white pepper

Mix all ingredients thoroughly. Refrigerate for 2 hours or overnight in a covered jar. Marinate for about 3 hours, turning pieces at least once. During broiling, baste with marinade.

Below: Illustration from the title page of a sixteenth-century German cookbook.

COOKED MARINADE FOR BEEF AND VENISON

About 8 cups

½ cup olive or salad oil
1 cup thinly sliced onions
1 cup thinly sliced carrots
½ cup thinly sliced celery
2 chopped garlic cloves
6 cups full-bodied dry red wine
1 cup red wine vinegar
1 cup water or
2 cups red wine vinegar
½ cup parsley heads, no stems
2 bay leaves
1 tablespoon allspice berries
1 teaspoon whole cloves
1 tablespoon crushed juniper berries
1 teaspoon peppercorns
1 tablespoon salt

Heat oil in a large saucepan. Add onions, carrots, celery, and garlic. Sauté vegetables over low heat for about 5 minutes until the onions are golden, but do not let anything brown. (This flavors the vegetables and prevents them from getting sour.) Add remaining ingredients and simmer covered over low heat for 1 to 1½ hours. Strain and cool. Refrigerate marinade; refrigerated, it will keep for weeks.

dried herbs are equally suited to marinades. When draining the food, wipe it clean of bits of herbs and spices before further cooking. Strain marinade and use for basting or in sauces.

When dry white wine for marinades is not available, use half the quantity called for of French vermouth and add water to bring up quantity. Since French vermouth contains herbs, go easy on the flavorings.

SALADS

Add minced or chopped fresh herbs to a salad just before tossing with the dressing, provided the dressing is plain. If you are using an herb dressing, omit salad herbs.

When using herb oils or herb vinegars, use salad herbs with discretion and only use herbs harmonious with the herbs flavoring the oil or vinegar.

The following herbs are suited for salads: parsley, chervil, tarragon, chives, dill, basil, mint, thyme, marjoram, and fresh dill and fennel sprigs.

Do not use too many different herbs; combine their flavor carefully, or they will cancel each other out.

Any marinade container must be made of glass, china or ceramic, or stainless steel, and *never* of aluminum, iron, or any other metal.

Do not over-marinate any foods or their flavor will be lost. Marinate cubed meat as for kebabs for 2 to 3 hours; larger pieces of meat (5 to 10 pounds and more) overnight, for 24 to 48 hours and more, depending on the age of the meat. Make sure the food is totally immersed in the marinade and turn it occasionally. Allow about ⅔ cup marinade for every pound of food. Place marinating foods in the refrigerator if marination is for more than 1 to 2 hours.

Marinades often depend on the cook's tastes in flavoring herbs and spices. Go easy as you are trying out new combinations. Fresh or

UNCOOKED LAMB MARINADE

About 1½ cups

1 small onion, chopped
1 garlic clove, minced
1 tablespoon minced fresh rosemary
  or crumbled dried rosemary
10 peppercorns
1 teaspoon salt
4 tablespoons olive oil
1 cup dry sherry or French vermouth

A table virtually groaning beneath the weight of a profusion of fruit and pastries, from a late sixteenth-century painting by Lodovico Pozzoserrato. Renaissance cooks delighted in waffles and cakes, often spiced with cinnamon, nutmeg, and cloves. Today we often bake with allspice, which resembles these three flavors combined.

DESSERTS

Sweet herbs and spices can add new interest to desserts of many kinds. Sweet herbs suited for the purpose are rosemary, balm, rose geranium, bergamot, angelica, and sweet cicely. Sweet spices include nutmeg, vanilla, mace, cinnamon, ginger, cardamom, and aniseed.

The use of both sweet herbs and spices, when not specified in a recipe, is largely a matter of personal preference. Sweet herbs may be added to a fruit salad, to a sweet soufflé batter, to pies and cakes. When making a dessert that requires cooking, such as fritters, waffles, crepes, soufflés, and custards, herbs are added to the batter. They may be removed before cooking, as when flavoring a custard with bay leaf or rosemary, or they may be cooked into the finished dish. Whether to mince or not to mince fresh herbs used for this purpose depends on their size and on the cook's discretion. However, whole or minced herbs may be floated on a fruit salad, baked fruits, or fruit tarts. When using dried herbs, reconstitute them in a little water or fruit juice before adding to the food.

A sprinkling of spices adds new interest to familiar desserts. Sprinkle ground or freshly grated nutmeg on vanilla ice cream, yogurt, and other creamy desserts. Sprinkle ground ginger, mace, or cardamom on melon. Use crushed aniseed in cooked and uncooked fruit desserts such as rice pudding and fruit compotes. Add the crushed aniseed to cooked desserts before cooking them, and add to uncooked desserts half an hour or more before serving to develop flavors. Ground black pepper, a pinch or two of it, adds to the spices in a pudding or spice cake. Surprisingly, black pepper sprinkled on ripe strawberries accents their flavor. For fruit salads, make a sugar syrup with a preferred spice like whole cloves, cardamom, or aniseed. Cook for 10 minutes and strain onto fruit salad. Chill before serving.

To flavor sugar for desserts and cakes, bury a vanilla bean in a container filled with granulated or confectioners' sugar. Close tightly and let stand for a week before using.

Cooking with Herbs

PAULA WOLFERT

It is a characteristic of man that he tends to add an aesthetic element to any activity he undertakes, even the most primitive and the most elementary. None of his preoccupations is more basic than the providing of food, a necessity for the preservation of life. It hardly requires adornment; but it receives it, through the art of gastronomy. There are many means by which the preparation of food has been elevated to a fine art: the most direct is by the use of seasoners. This is not even a development of civilization, with its sophisticated refinements. It antedates civilization, if, indeed, it is not one of the factors which developed it. We may be inclined today to think of prehistoric man as a brutish creature, devoid of subtle sentiments, whom we envisage as gulping down his food greedily, almost without tasting it; but

OPERA DI BARTOLOMEO SCAPPI

MASTRO DELL'ARTE DEL CVCINARE, con laquale si può ammaestrare qual si voglia Cuoco, Scalco, Trinciante, o Mastro di Casa.

DIVISA IN SEI LIBRI.

IN VENETIA, Per Alessandro de' Vecchi. M DC XXII.

Left: A good stock of culinary herbs and spices, both fresh (in season) and dried, are essential to any kitchen. Stored in tightly capped, airtight jars in a cool, dry place, dried herbs can be used for four to six months.

Our uses of herbs and spices today, as demonstrated in the recipes on the following pages, draw on the great cooking traditions of both East and West. The spirited group seen wielding chopsticks in this open-air restaurant in Singapore *(right)* are probably enjoying a highly spiced dish. Western cuisine is tamer, though the great masters such as the sixteenth-century Italian Bartolomeo Scappi *(top)* often combined six or seven herbs and spices in a dish.

Stone Age man was already seasoning his food. The recipes by Paula Wolfert collected here encompass a great variety of dishes, from soup to dessert, ranging from very simple to elaborate productions, and derive from a whole spectrum of national cuisines. Not all meant for timid eaters, none of them will cause the lips to blister. –*Ed.*

DISH	INGREDIENTS	DIRECTIONS

MEDITERRANEAN FISH SOUP

Serves 6

3 small white fleshed fish heads and spines, washed and with all traces of blood and organs removed
1 leek cut up
$\frac{1}{2}$ medium onion cut up
$\frac{1}{2}$ large carrot cut up
1 fennel stalk cut up
6 parsley sprigs
1 teaspoon fennel seeds
1 bay leaf and 1 pinch dried thyme
1 pound ripe tomatoes
3-inch dried orange peel
2 cloves garlic, halved
2 teaspoons salt
$\frac{3}{8}$ teaspoon pulverized saffron
1 tablespoon Pernod, flamed
2 medium-sized fillets of red snapper, or flounder, or sole boned
Garnish:
Julienned carrots
Julienned zucchini
Julienned turnips
Blanched orange zest—very little

Put fish heads and spines, cut-up vegetables, herbs, tomato, orange peel, garlic, and salt in 5-quart casserole. Add 3 quarts water and bring to a boil. Lower the heat to a simmer and cook uncovered for 30 minutes or until reduced to half. Skim off scum as it rises to the top.
Strain through a fine-meshed strainer. Add saffron and the Pernod. Bring to a boil and simmer for 2 minutes.
Meanwhile slice the fish, leaving the skin on, crosswise on a slight bias, into strips about 3 inches long and 1 to $1\frac{1}{2}$ inches wide. Arrange 4 pieces of fish in each flat soup bowl.
Blanch the julienned vegetables in the simmering soup and refresh. Place in the center of each bowl.
Just before serving, pour very hot fish soup over the raw fish, just to cover. The hot soup will cook the fish.

MEXICAN FISH SOUP

Serves 4 to 5

$\frac{1}{4}$ cup olive oil
$\frac{1}{2}$ cup finely diced onions
$\frac{1}{2}$ cup finely chopped celery
1 large clove garlic, finely sliced
$\frac{1}{4}$ teaspoon red pepper flakes
$\frac{1}{4}$ teaspoon ground cumin seeds
$\frac{1}{3}$ cup diced red bell pepper (pimiento)
$\frac{1}{2}$ cup diced green bell pepper
$\frac{3}{4}$ pound mixed cubed fresh fillets of fish (red snapper, halibut, tilefish, etc.)
$\frac{1}{4}$ pound fresh shrimp, peeled and deveined
3 tablespoons chopped fresh green coriander leaves
$\frac{1}{2}$ cup peeled, cubed, and seeded tomatoes
12 littleneck clams, shelled
$\frac{1}{2}$ cup dry white wine
3 cups fish stock or $1\frac{1}{2}$ cup fish stock and $1\frac{1}{2}$ cups clam juice
Lemon juice
Salt and pepper to taste

In a large skillet, heat the olive oil; add the onion, celery, garlic, pepper flakes, cumin, red and green bell peppers, and cook over medium heat for 2 minutes, swirling to blend flavors. Add the shrimp, fish, green coriander leaves, tomatoes, clams and their liquor, and wine. Bring the pan juices to the boil. Add the fish stock and simmer 5 to 7 minutes, stirring often. Skim off the foam that rises to the surface. Add a dash of lemon juice, salt, and pepper. Serve at once.

ORIENTAL MEATBALL SOUP

Serves 4

4 ounces ground pork
1 tablespoon soy sauce
1 tablespoon sherry
1 slice boiled ham
2 scallions
1 quart chicken stock, well degreased
Salt

Mix ground pork with soy sauce and sherry. Form into 12 smooth equal-sized balls.
Dice the ham. Chop the green shoots and the white bulbs of the scallions to make 3 tablespoons.
Bring 1 quart water to a boil in a wide saucepan. One by one, gently drop in the meatballs. Reduce heat and poach for 5 minutes.
Use a slotted spoon to lift the meatballs out of the simmering water and let them drain on a flat dish. Discard the poaching water.
Heat chicken stock. Drop in the meatballs and cook 5 minutes. Season the stock with salt if necessary.
Add the diced ham and chopped scallions. Let them heat through. Serve at once.

DISH	INGREDIENTS	DIRECTIONS

ALMOND SOUP

Serves 4 to 5

2 tablespoons butter
½ cup chopped onions
2 tablespoons flour
1 quart boiling chicken stock
½ cup ground blanched almonds
½ cup heavy cream
Salt and freshly ground white pepper

Melt the butter in a saucepan, add the onions, and cook until soft but not browned. Stir in the flour. When blended add the boiling stock, stirring briskly. Allow to simmer a few minutes. Stir in the ground almonds. Cook at the simmer 20 minutes. Stir in cream and allow to heat through. Season with salt and pepper to taste. Serve hot.

RUSSIAN FISH SOUP

Serves 4

2 pounds fish trimmings: heads, tails, and bones of a sole, bass, red snapper, or any other white-fleshed fish
2 tablespoons butter
2 medium-sized onions, sliced
2 ribs of celery with leaves, sliced
½ cup sliced carrots
½ tablespoon salt
½ teaspoon cracked peppercorns
2 sprigs parsley
5 sprigs fresh dill
1½ quart water
1½ tablespoons tomato paste
½ teaspoon sugar
Juice of 1 lemon
1 cup sauerkraut juice
½ pound fresh salmon or sturgeon, boned, skinned, and cut into 2-ounce portions
12 capers, rinsed and drained
4 black olives, halved
¼ cup diced dill pickle
4 thin slices of lemon
2 tablespoons chopped fresh dill

Wash fish trimmings under cool running water; cut away any traces of blood, liver, intestines, or eggs; set aside.
In a heavy 4-quart saucepan melt the butter and sauté the onions, celery, and carrots for a few minutes, stirring. Add the fish trimmings, salt, peppercorns, parsley, and dill sprigs. Moisten with water and stir over high heat until it comes to a boil. Skim. Stir in tomato paste and sugar. Simmer, covered, for 30 minutes, skimming when needed; strain. Add lemon and sauerkraut juices. Return strained soup to a clean saucepan and reheat to a simmer. Poach fish pieces in the soup very gently for 5 minutes (7 minutes if the pieces are very thick.) Arrange 1 piece of fish in each soup bowl; add to each bowl 3 capers, 2 olive halves, 1 tablespoon diced pickle, 1 lemon slice, ½ tablespoon chopped dill. If the soup is too sour for your taste, add pinches of sugar.

VIETNAMESE SOUR SOUP

Serves 4

1 ounce tamarind pulp
⅔ cup hot water
1-inch thick ring of fresh pineapple, cored and peeled
1 quart water
2 tablespoons Nuoc Mam (oriental fish sauce)
1 tablespoon lemon juice
1½ tablespoons peanut oil
¼ cup finely sliced shallots
2 cloves garlic, thinly sliced
6 ounces fresh or frozen shrimp, peeled and deveined
Sugar (optional)
Salt and freshly ground pepper
1¼ cups fresh bean sprouts
3 tablespoons roughly chopped fresh coriander leaves

Soak the tamarind pulp in hot water for 2 to 3 hours. Press through a sieve set over a small bowl. Using your fingers, separate the fruit and squeeze to release as much liquid pulp as possible. Discard the contents of the sieve, reserving only the strained liquid.
Finely dice the pineapple. In an enameled 3-quart saucepan combine 1 quart water, fish sauce, tamarind, and lemon juice, and bring to boil. Add the pineapple and simmer gently, uncovered, for 10 minutes.
Heat the oil in a small skillet, fry the shallots and garlic in it, stirring, until golden brown and crisp; drain. Set aside. Add the shrimp to the soup and continue to cook 3 to 5 minutes longer. If the soup is too sour for your taste, stir in a small amount of sugar. Taste for salt and pepper. Bring soup to boil; stir in the bean sprouts; then immediately remove from the heat.
Ladle into individual bowls, scatter crisp shallots and garlic over each serving, and top with coriander leaves. Serve hot.

BASIL SAUCE FOR ROAST LAMB OR CHICKEN

Serves 6

2 cups extra rich chicken stock
1 tablespoon finely chopped shallots
½ clove garlic, finely chopped
½ cup dry white wine
½ cup white port
1¼ cups heavy cream
Salt and freshly ground white pepper
2 dozen medium-large basil leaves (2 tablespoons finely chopped leaves)

In a saucepan combine chicken stock, shallots, garlic, white wine, and port. Reduce almost to a glaze. Add the cream and reduce again to a napping consistency. Strain; return to the saucepan, season with salt and pepper, and fold in the basil.

DISH	INGREDIENTS	DIRECTIONS
CHIVE BUTTER FOR GRILLED FISH Makes 1 cup	1 bunch fresh chives 16 tablespoons sweet butter, softened to room temperature Salt and pepper Lemon juice to taste	Puree fresh chives in workbowl of food processor. Add butter, tablespoon by tablespoon, and process to combine. Rub through a sieve. Chill. In a small saucepan bring 2 tablespoons water to the boil. Quickly beat in the chive butter piece by piece over medium-high heat. The butter must foam and start to boil. Boil 5 seconds, whisking. Pour into a small bowl. Season with salt, pepper, and if desired, a drop of lemon juice.
CLASSIC WHITE BUTTER SAUCE Makes about 1 cup serving 5 to 6	¼ cup dry white wine 2 tablespoons white wine vinegar 2 tablespoons finely chopped shallots 12 tablespoons unsalted butter; firm but not cold and cut into tablespoons ¼ teaspoon coarse salt Scant ¼ teaspoon ground white pepper	In a 1½ or 2 quart non-aluminum saucepan combine the wine, wine vinegar, and chopped shallots. Bring to a boil, lower the heat and cook, uncovered, until reduced to a glaze, in about 5 minutes. Remove the saucepan from the heat. Touch the bottom of the inside of the pan with your index finger. It should be just hot enough to withstand the heat for 2 seconds. Quickly whisk in 2 chunks of butter. When soft and creamy return the saucepan to very low heat. Whisking constantly, continue adding chunks of butter, a few at a time. Add more butter only when the previous addition has been absorbed. The consistency of the mixture must be creamy and thick. Remove pan from heat whenever butter appears to be melting rather than thickening and foaming. Strain the sauce into a bowl. Season with salt and pepper. Set in a warm, but not hot, place until ready to serve.
GREMOLATA (Recipe by Nika S. Hazelton)	2 tablespoons minced parsley, preferably Italian parsley 1 medium garlic clove, minced ½ teaspoon grated lemon rind	Mix ingredients and sprinkle on food during the last 5 minutes of cooking. Simmer covered over very low heat to let flavors be absorbed by the food. An Italian mixture of seasonings for sauces and pan gravies. The classic use is in Osso Buco, a dish of braised veal shanks. Do not use gremolata in white sauces or creamed dishes.
PESTO Fresh Basil Sauce Makes 1 cup (Recipe by Nika S. Hazelton)	2 cups loosely packed fresh basil leaves, no stems 2 garlic cloves, or to taste, chopped ¼ cup pine nuts or walnuts (optional) 2 tablespoons grated Romano cheese and 2 tablespoons grated Parmesan cheese (or 4 tablespoons either Romano or Parmesan) 4–6 tablespoons olive oil Salt, freshly ground pepper	Put the basil, garlic, and nuts into the container of a blender or food processor. Blend at low speed for a few moments or until ingredients are coarsely chopped. Add cheese and half of the olive oil and blend again. Scrape the mixture down from the sides of the container. Turn speed to low and trickle in remaining olive oil while blending. By hand, stir in salt and pepper to taste. To refrigerate pesto, turn into a jar and add a thin film of olive oil to cover the top.
OLIVE AND CAPER RELISH Makes approximately 1 cup	1 two-ounce tin anchovy fillets, rinsed and drained 1 cup black Mediterranean-type olives, pitted, and roughly chopped 2 tablespoons capers, rinsed, drained 1 tablespoon lemon juice ½ teaspoon Dijon mustard Freshly ground black pepper 2 tablespoons cognac ¼–½ cup fruity olive oil	Blend anchovy fillets, olives, capers, lemon juice, mustard, freshly ground pepper to taste. Add cognac until pasty. Still blending, pour in just enough olive oil in a steady stream to obtain a smooth, thick sauce. Scoop into a pretty pottery bowl and chill well before serving.
SAUCE BÉARNAISE **(FOOD PROCESSOR METHOD)** Serves 4 to 6	3 tablespoons dry white wine ¼ cup tarragon vinegar 2 tablespoons minced shallots 3 tablespoons finely chopped fresh tarragon or tarragon leaves packed in vinegar, divided 2 egg yolks ½ teaspoon salt ¼ teaspoon white pepper Cayenne pepper 12 tablespoons unsalted butter, melted and kept hot	In a small non-aluminum saucepan, combine the white wine, vinegar, shallots, and 1 tablespoon tarragon. By boiling, reduce to 1½ tablespoons. Scrape into the workbowl of a food processor; add the egg yolks, salt, and pepper, and process 1 minute. With the machine on, spoon the hot butter through the feed tube. Taste and readjust the seasoning. Add a pinch of cayenne for a sharper taste if desired. Fold in remaining 2 tablespoons tarragon.

DISH	INGREDIENTS	DIRECTIONS

SPAGHETTI WITH OLIVE SAUCE

Serves 10 to 12

½ pound juicy black Greek olives, rinsed, pitted, and finely chopped
½ pound green olives, rinsed, pitted, and finely chopped
2-ounce tin anchovy fillets, rinsed and mashed
1 tablespoon capers, rinsed and drained
2–3 tablespoons chopped pickled or raw mushrooms (optional)
2 tablespoons chopped parsley
2–3 fresh basil leaves, chopped (optional)
2–3 cloves garlic, finely chopped
Freshly ground black pepper
Olive oil
2 pounds spaghetti
Salt

Combine olives, anchovies, capers, mushrooms, herbs, garlic, and pepper in the mixing bowl. Pour over enough olive oil to cover. Allow to stand and marinate 2 hours, turning the ingredients often and adding more oil if necessary to keep the olive mixture completely covered.
Cook the spaghetti in boiling salted water until tender. Meanwhile in a saucepan heat the olive and oil mixture but do not allow it to boil. Drain the spaghetti, pour over the sauce and serve at once. Serve without grated cheese.

SPICE MIXTURE FOR COFFEE

Makes ⅓ cup mixture

2 whole nutmegs (about 4 teaspoons ground nutmeg)
4 blades cinnamon (about 1 teaspoon ground cinnamon)
6–8 dried rosebuds
½ teaspoon ground cloves
1 tablespoon ground ginger
½ teaspoon ground galingale or 2 small pieces
2 allspice berries (about ⅛ teaspoon ground)
¾ teaspoon ground white pepper
3 blades mace (about ½ teaspoon ground mace)
15 white cardamom seeds or pods
1 teaspoon fennel seeds
1 teaspoon aniseed
1 tablespoon sesame seeds

Combine spices in an electric spice grinder or blender. Sieve and bottle carefully to preserve the freshness and aroma. When making coffee, add ¼ teaspoon to every ½ cup ground coffee grinds before making coffee in your usual fashion. (It makes no difference whether you are making black Turkish-style coffee or American roast.)

CARROT SALAD

Serves 4

1 pound carrots
1 clove garlic
⅛ teaspoon ground cinnamon
¼ teaspoon ground cumin
½ teaspoon sweet paprika
Pinch of cayenne pepper
Juice of 1 lemon
⅛ teaspoon granulated sugar
Salt, olive oil, chopped parsley

Wash and peel carrots. Boil whole in water with the garlic until barely tender. Drain. Discard the garlic and dice or slice the carrots.
Combine the spices with the lemon juice, sugar, and salt to taste, and pour over the carrots. Chill. Sprinkle with oil and chopped parsley just before serving.

COOKED TOMATOES AND SWEET GREEN PEPPER SALAD

Serves 6

16 red, ripe tomatoes (about 4 pounds), peeled, seeded, and chopped
Olive oil for frying
9 sweet green peppers, grilled, cored, seeded, and chopped
2 cloves garlic, peeled and chopped
1 teaspoon paprika (optional)
Salt and cayenne to taste

Fry the tomatoes in a small amount of oil, mashing and turning them with the spoon as they cook down. When they are very thick add the chopped green peppers, garlic, optional paprika, and some salt and cayenne to taste. Continue to reduce the mixture until all the liquid has evaporated and it starts to fry in the released oil. (At this moment you must give the dish your full attention, turning the tomatoes and peppers over and over in the skillet to avoid scorching.) When everything is very thick and has reduced to about 1½ cups, remove from the heat and drain. Serve cool.

CUCUMBER SALAD

Serves 4

2 cucumbers, peeled, seeded, and grated
1 tablespoon granulated sugar
1 teaspoon vinegar
1 tablespoon olive, salad, or peanut oil
¼ teaspoon salt
⅛ teaspoon thyme or oregano; or a mixture of two
Handful of cured black olives

Drain off excess liquid from the cucumbers, then combine with the sugar, vinegar, oil, and salt. Crush the herbs between your fingertips and sprinkle over the cucumbers. Mix well with two forks, then chill. Decorate with the olives just before serving.

DISH	INGREDIENTS	DIRECTIONS

GREEK MIXED SALAD

Serves 6

Assorted salad greens (Boston, bibb, romaine, escarole, and watercress)
½ clove garlic
1 crisp cucumber, sliced, salted
1 diced green pepper
1 jar pitted black olives
4 tablespoons imported olive oil (virgin is best)
1 tablespoon red wine vinegar
Freshly ground black pepper
1 can anchovy fillets, drained and cubed
Dried oregano, crumbled between fingertips to release oils
¼ cup feta cheese, crumbled

Wash greens and dry well. Tear into bite-size pieces. Rub wooden salad bowl with garlic. Salt cucumber ½ hour. Drain and pat dry. Toss greens with cucumber slices, green pepper, and olives. Mix oil and vinegar, pepper, anchovies, and a good pinch of oregano in a small mixing bowl; blending well. Toss dressing with the salad and garnish with feta cheese and more oregano.

ORANGE AND GRATED CARROT SALAD

Serves 4 to 6

1 pound carrots
1 navel orange
1 teaspoon ground cinnamon
2–3 tablespoons lemon juice
1½ tablespoons granulated sugar
1 teaspoon orange flower water
Pinch of salt

Clean and grate the carrots. Peel and section the oranges, reserving the juice. Mix orange juice with the remaining ingredients. Stir in the orange sections. Toss with the grated carrots. Chill before serving. Partially drain if necessary.

PURSLANE SALAD

Makes 6 cups

2 quarts purslane
1 or 2 small dried red chili peppers
1 teaspoon salt
10–12 cloves garlic
1 cup chopped parsley
1 cup chopped green coriander
Salad oil
¼ pound cured black olives
2 teaspoons paprika
2 teaspoons ground cumin
Juice of 2 lemons
Lemon wedges

Wash the greens under running water. Drain and cut small. Fill the bottom of a steamer with water and bring to a boil. Fasten on the perforated top, add the greens, and steam, covered, for 30 minutes. Remove from the heat and allow to cool, uncovered. When cool enough to handle, squeeze out as much moisture as possible.
Pound the chili pepper in a mortar with 1 teaspoon salt and the garlic. Gradually add the chopped parsley and coriander and continue pounding until it becomes a paste.
Heat 3 tablespoons oil in the casserole and slowly cook the olives with the paprika and cumin 2 to 3 minutes. Add the herb paste and the lemon juice, cover, and cook 5 minutes. Pour in ½ cup oil, add the greens and cook together, stirring frequently, for 20 minutes, or until all the moisture has evaporated and the mixture is very thick. Salt to taste. Serve with lemon wedges.

TUNISIAN MIXED SALAD

Serves 4 to 6

1 cup peeled, seeded, and diced ripe red tomatoes
1 cup chopped onions
1 cup seeded, de-ribbed and diced sweet green peppers
1 tablespoon seeded and finely chopped hot green chili pepper
1 cup peeled, cored, and diced raw green apple
1½ tablespoons vinegar
4½ tablespoons olive oil
1 tablespoon pulverized dried mint leaves
Salt to taste
Freshly ground black pepper to taste

Combine the tomatoes, onions, peppers, and apple in a serving bowl. Add the vinegar and oil and toss well.
Sprinkle with the pulverized mint, salt, and pepper. Mix thoroughly. Serve at room temperature.

ZUCCHINI AND CARAWAY SALAD

Serves 4 to 6

1½ pounds small firm zucchini, trimmed
1½ teaspoons chopped garlic
1½ teaspoons ground caraway seed
4 tablespoons olive oil
1 tablespoon wine vinegar
Salt and freshly ground pepper to taste
Cayenne pepper to taste

Boil the zucchini until just tender. Place in workbowl of food processor or jar of electric blender and puree. Combine with garlic, caraway seed, oil, vinegar, and seasonings, mixing well. Chill before serving.

DISH	INGREDIENTS	DIRECTIONS

**SEAFOOD SAUSAGE
LE PLAISIR**

Makes 6 sausages

¾ pound fresh or frozen sea scallops
⅓ pound fresh or frozen shrimps
1 tablespoon finely minced shallots
1½ tablespoons unsalted butter
1 heaping tablespoon finely minced carrots
1 tablespoon finely minced celery rib
½ teaspoon crumbled thyme leaves
Salt and freshly ground pepper
18 fresh well-dried and shredded sorrel leaves
2 yards sausage casings, soaked 1 hour in water
2 cucumbers
Sugar and 1 teaspoon butter for glazing
1 recipe White Butter Sauce (see p. 140)
2 tablespoons finely chopped fresh peeled tomato
Chopped parsley

Rinse and dry scallops. Cut into small cubes. Puree in food processor. Peel and devein shrimp. Cut into small pieces. Soften shallots in butter. Add carrots and celery and sauté gently 1 minute. Sprinkle with thyme, salt, and pepper. Cool. Mix seafood, vegetable mixture, and sorrel and force into sausage casings. Knot sausages.
Peel, seed, and cut cucumbers into small olive shapes. Cook in salted boiling water 1 minute; drain and pat dry. Glaze in a skillet with ½ teaspoon sugar and 1 teaspoon butter.
Steam sausages 10 minutes or poach 15 minutes. Spoon white butter sauce onto serving plates. Place one sausage on each. Decorate with glazed cucumber, "dots" of tomato, and parsley. Serve hot.

**SEAFOOD, HAM,
AND OKRA GUMBO**

Serves 6 to 8

1 ham hock
⅓ cup bacon fat, lard, or vegetable oil
⅓ cup flour
1¾ cups chopped onion
1 green bell pepper, chopped
⅓ cup thinly sliced green scallion shoots
2 tablespoons finely chopped parsley
2 cloves garlic, peeled and chopped
1 pound small tomatoes, sliced
1 pound fresh okra, chopped or one 10-ounce package frozen okra, defrosted and chopped
¼ teaspoon cayenne pepper
Salt, preferably rock salt
1 teaspoon dried thyme leaves
Crab Boil (see below)
Juice of 1 lemon
12 live, medium-sized, hard-shelled blue crabs (optional) or substitute 2 cups cooked lump crabmeat
2 pounds raw shrimp

"CRAB BOIL" For Louisiana Gumbos

6 allspice berries
2 crumbled bay leaves
Pinch of grated nutmeg
5 dried hot peppers, crumbled
2 teaspoons coriander seeds
1 tablespoon black mustard seeds
2 cloves
Mix and wrap in a cheesecloth bag. Enough for the gumbo.

The day before you plan to serve the gumbo, simmer the ham hock in 3 quarts water for 2 hours. Then make the gumbo soup base. Heat the bacon fat in a 4-quart saucepan and blend in the flour, stirring. Cook over low heat, stirring constantly, until the mixture turns a nice chocolate brown. Do not allow the flour to burn.
Add the onion, green pepper, scallion, parsley, and garlic and cook, stirring, for 10 minutes. Add tomatoes, okra, cayenne, 2 teaspoons salt, and the thyme. Add the ham hock and 1½ quarts of its cooking broth. Bring to a boil, cover, and simmer for 1 hour. Cool and allow to ripen in the refrigerator overnight.
The following day, bring 4 quarts water to a boil in a large pan; add the Crab Boil mixture, the lemon juice, 1 tablespoon salt and boil for 10 minutes, covered. Add the crabs, bring back to the boil, and boil crabs for 12 minutes or more, depending upon their size. Remove the crabs and allow to cool. Add the shrimp and bring to the boil again. Remove from the heat and let stand 10 minutes, covered. Remove the shrimp and let cool. Boil down the cooking liquid to half. Add 2 cups of this liquid to the gumbo. Remove the ham hock from the gumbo: discard the fat and the bone and cut the meat into bite-size pieces. Add to the gumbo. When the crabs and shrimp are cool, they can be shelled and added to the gumbo. Reheat to boiling and serve hot.

**FRIED HALIBUT OR POLLOCK
WITH PARSLEY SAUCE**

Serves 4

¾ cup roughly chopped parsley
½ teaspoon chopped garlic
Juice of ½ lemon
Salt and freshly ground black pepper
4 one-inch-thick halibut or pollock steaks
Flour seasoned with salt and pepper for dredging
½ cup olive or vegetable oil
2 tablespoons chopped onion
1 tablespoon flour

Place the parsley and the garlic in the blender jar. Add ¼ cup water. Whirl until smooth. Thin with another ¼ cup water. Add lemon juice, salt, and pepper. Set aside.
Dip the fish steaks into seasoned flour and shake off any excess. Fry in hot oil until nicely browned on both sides. When cooked remove to a warmed serving dish. Pour off half the oil. Cook the onion in the remaining oil and pan drippings until soft and golden. Add the flour and cook until light brown, stirring. Add the parsley mixture. Cook, stirring, 2 minutes. Pour over the fish and serve at once.

DISH	INGREDIENTS	DIRECTIONS

CHINESE STEAMED FISH

Serves 6

2 pounds sea bass
2 Chinese black mushrooms (cloud ears)
1 scallion, bulb and green shoot
1 slice boiled ham
2 slices ginger
2 tablespoons soy sauce
1 tablespoon sherry
1 tablespoon vegetable oil
$\frac{1}{4}$ teaspoon each: salt, pepper
$\frac{1}{2}$ teaspoon sugar

Wash whole fish under cold running water. Wipe dry. Score with a sharp knife; make 1-inch diagonal slits at 1-inch intervals on both sides.
Soak cloud ears in warm water 30 minutes. Slit the scallion in half and cut on diagonal, into strips 1 inch long and $\frac{1}{4}$ inch wide. Shred the ham and ginger into matchsticks. Wash cloud ears thoroughly to remove sand. Pat dry, then cut into match-sticks.
Place the fish on an oven-proof platter which must be a bit smaller in diameter than the steamer so it can be easily removed. Leave the head and tail on the fish if it will fit. Spoon soy sauce, sherry, and vegetable oil over fish.
Sprinkle with salt, pepper, and sugar. Scatter ginger, cloud ears, scallion, and ham on top.
Steam over 2 inches of boiling water 15 minutes with tightly covered lid. Serve fish whole as soon as possible.

POTTED SALMON

Makes about 1 to $1\frac{1}{3}$ cups

Court-bouillon: $\frac{1}{2}$ cup dry white wine; 1 small carrot, scraped and cut into rounds; 1 small celery rib, sliced; 1 small onion, sliced; 6 black pepper-corns; herb bouquet: parsley, bay leaf, and thyme
5 ounces fresh raw salmon
1 shallot, peeled and halved
9 tablespoons unsalted butter, cut into chunks
5 ounces smoked salmon, picked over for small bones
2 teaspoons Armagnac or Cognac
1 teaspoon fines herbes
Salt and freshly ground white pepper
Thin slices of buttered toast

Make a court-bouillon in a small saucepan with the ingredients listed here. Bring to a boil, reduce the heat, and cook at the simmer 10 minutes. Slip in the sliced salmon and poach it until the flesh flakes easily when prodded with a fork. Remove; drain, discard any skin and bones. Cool and break the flesh into large pieces.
Finely chop the shallots. In bowl of food processor blend butter, shallot, smoked and cooked salmon until well mixed but gritty in texture. Add Armagnac, herbs, salt, and pepper. Let ripen 2 hours in refrigerator before serving. Serve with hot buttered toast.

SEA SCALLOPS IN PAPILLOTE WITH WATERCRESS AND TOMATOES

Serves 4

1 pound red ripe tomatoes
2 tablespoons olive oil
Salt and freshly ground pepper
1 bunch watercress with thick stems removed
1 cup heavy cream reduced to half
16 sea scallops
2 ounces unsalted butter

Peel, core, halve, and seed the tomatoes. Cut into small cubes. Soften in hot olive oil, stirring, for 4 minutes. Drain in a colander to remove excess moisture. Season cooked toma-toes with salt and pepper.
Wash and dry watercress leaves and pat dry on paper towels. Mix the tomato and reduced heavy cream.
Have ready four 12 by 16 inch pieces of foil. On half of each sheet, place a few of the watercress leaves. Spread about 2 tablespoons of the tomato mixture over the leaves and top with 4 sea scallops. Cover with two more tablespoons of tomato and a few more leaves. Dot each package with butter. Fold securely around the edges, leaving some room for steam to expand during baking.
Bake on a cookie sheet in a preheated 500 degree oven for about 5 minutes, or until the foil package puffs up. Serve at once.

ARTICHOKE FLAN

Serves 6

1 package frozen artichoke hearts (9 or 10 ounces)
1 lemon
Flour
$\frac{1}{4}$ cup olive oil
6 eggs
1 teaspoon salt
$\frac{1}{4}$ teaspoon pepper
$\frac{1}{4}$ cup milk
$\frac{1}{2}$ teaspoon summer savory

Thaw the artichokes and drain dry on paper towels. Sprinkle with juice of 1 lemon for flavor. Preheat the oven to 400 de-grees. Dust the artichokes with flour. Heat the olive oil in a skillet and fry the artichokes until golden brown on all sides. Arrange, cut side up, on the bottom of an ovenproof skillet. In a mixing bowl, beat the eggs with salt, pepper, milk, and savory until frothy. Pour over the hot artichokes and cook over moderate heat for 30 seconds to set eggs on the bottom. Then transfer skillet to preheated oven and bake for 8 to 10 minutes, or until eggs are firm.
Remove from the oven and let the flan rest a few minutes. Use a spatula to loosen the sides and bottom and turn out onto a round serving dish. Cut into wedges and serve at room temperature.

DISH	INGREDIENTS	DIRECTIONS

 EGGS IN BRIOCHE WITH MUSTARD TARRAGON SAUCE

Serves 4

4 stale brioches
¾ cup dry white wine
3 tablespoons finely chopped shallots
1 tablespoon finely chopped parsley
1 tablespoon finely chopped fresh tarragon or 1½ teaspoons dried tarragon
Dried mustard
⅓ cup heavy cream
8 tablespoons unsalted butter, cut into 8 pieces
Salt and freshly ground pepper
4 fresh eggs

Remove the tops of each brioche about ⅕ of the way down and reserve. Scoop out the centers without piercing the outside. Be sure each hollow is large enough to hold one egg.
In a small, heavy non-aluminum saucepan, combine the wine, shallots, parsley, and tarragon. Bring to the boil, lower heat, and cook slowly until the liquid is totally evaporated and the shallots are very moist and soft but not browned. Add 1 teaspoon mustard and the cream and reduce quickly to 2 tablespoons. While the pan is still hot, beat in the butter, tablespoon by tablespoon, off the heat. The butter should be foamy and thick, not oily. Readjust seasoning, adding more mustard if necessary. Set aside.
Break an egg into each brioche, season lightly with salt and pepper. Bake in a preheated 400 degree oven for 7 to 10 minutes, or until the whites are set.
Spoon a little sauce over each egg; set the top of the brioche in place and serve at once.

 SCRAMBLED EGGS WITH CHERVIL

Serves 4

8 very fresh eggs
5 tablespoons butter, plus enough to coat bowl
Salt and freshly ground pepper
2 tablespoons heavy cream
2 tablespoons finely minced chervil

About 1 hour before serving, break the eggs into a fine wire strainer set over a bowl. Gently crush the yolks with the back of a wooden spoon. Let them drip; do not press or beat the eggs, though you can stir them from time to time if desired. Butter the sides and bottom of a glass or ceramic mixing bowl. Set over a saucepan filled with simmering water. Add the eggs, salt, pepper, and 1 tablespoon butter. Cook slowly over simmering water, stirring constantly with a rubber spatula. Be sure to move the spatula along the sides and bottom of the bowl to avoid curds forming. When the eggs begin to thicken add remaining butter tablespoon by tablespoon. When the eggs begin to hold together with as few curds as possible, but still very creamy and saucelike, remove the pan from the heat, still stirring. Fold in the cream and half the herbs.
Spoon equal amounts of scrambled eggs into small ramekins and garnish each with a pinch of the remaining chervil.

 CHILI CON CARNE

Serves 4 to 5

1¾ cups finely chopped onion
4 tablespoons vegetable oil
1 pound ground lean beef
½ pound ground lean pork
1¼ teaspoons finely chopped garlic
¼ cup chili pepper powder
2 tablespoons oregano
1 tablespoon cumin seeds
1 quart fresh tomatoes: peeled, seeded, and chopped
Salt and pepper
1 whole clove
1 tablespoon red wine vinegar
½ tablespoon sugar
2 tablespoons grated chocolate

Soften the onion in the oil in a deep pan. Add the meat and stir to break up. Add garlic, chili pepper powder, oregano, cumin, and tomatoes. Bring to the boil, stirring. Simmer uncovered 1½ hours. Skim off fat before seasoning with salt, pepper, and clove. Stir in vinegar and sugar and cook 15 minutes longer. Add the chocolate and bring back to the boil. Serve hot with garnishes of chopped onion, sour cream, and cooked kidney beans.

 LAMB STEW WITH MARJORAM

Serves 4 to 5

3 pounds lamb shoulder, cut into 1½-inch chunks
3 tablespoons salad oil
1 cup grated onion
¼ teaspoon pulverized saffron
1 teaspoon ground black pepper
Salt to taste
1 teaspoon chopped garlic
5 tablespoons chopped parsley
2½ pounds zucchini, preferably small ones
2 teaspoons marjoram

Trim and discard excess fat from the lamb. In a casserole brown the meat on all sides in oil. Add grated onion, spices, salt, garlic, and parsley. Toss to coat the meat. Add 2 cups water and cook at the simmer, covered, 2 hours or until the meat is almost falling off the bones. Add small amounts of water whenever necessary.
Top and tail the zucchini and cut into ¾-inch slices. Salt lightly and let drain 20 minutes, then rinse and drain again. Sprinkle with 1 teaspoon marjoram and set aside.
Remove meat from the casserole and arrange in a shallow baking dish. Degrease the sauce. Add the zucchini and cook 10 minutes. Spread zucchini over the meat. Boil down the sauce to thicken. Pour over the meat and reheat in a hot oven. Serve at once, with a small sprinkling of remaining marjoram.

DISH	INGREDIENTS	DIRECTIONS

LAMB STEAKS WITH OLIVE SAUCE

Serves 6

Two 1¼ pound lamb steaks
  (each 1½ inches thick)
Salt
Grapeseed or vegetable oil
1 cup chicken or lamb stock
¾ cup juicy black Mediterranean style
  olives, rinsed, pitted, and chopped
1 ounce anchovy fillets, rinsed
  and mashed
1 tablespoon finely chopped parsley
½ teaspoon finely chopped garlic
Lemon juice to taste
⅛ teaspoon cayenne pepper

Lightly season the lamb with salt. Brush both sides of lamb steaks with oil. Set aside until 35 minutes before serving.
In a saucepan combine stock, olives, anchovy fillets, parsley, garlic, 1 tablespoon lemon juice, and cayenne pepper. Heat, stirring, until flavors blend. Correct the seasoning. Keep hot. Broil lamb steak 4 inches from heat, 3 minutes each side. Let rest in warm place 20 minutes. Meanwhile preheat oven to 475 degrees. Place lamb in baking dish and set in oven to roast 8 minutes for rare, 9 or 10 minutes for medium-rare, and 11 minutes for well done.
Cut immediately, slightly on the diagonal, into thin slices. Surround with the sauce and serve immediately.

LIVER BROCHETTES WITH BAY LEAVES

Serves 3 to 4

10 imported bay leaves
1 pound calf's liver, cut into 1-inch cubes
Salt and freshly ground black pepper
Pinch of grated nutmeg
Vegetable oil
1 lemon, quartered

In a mortar pound 3 of the bay leaves until almost a powder. In a mixing bowl toss the liver cubes with the ground bay leaves, salt and pepper, grated nutmeg, and 3 tablespoons oil. Allow to stand 1 hour.
Cut the remaining 7 bay leaves into 1-inch pieces. Thread seasoned liver cubes alternately with bay leaves. Brush with oil. Broil quickly on all sides, 2 or 3 inches from a broiler flame until the first drops of light pink liquid ooze up. Serve at once with lemon quarters.

MME CHU'S STAR ANISE BEEF

Serves 6

2 pounds boneless stewing beef cut in
  1-inch cubes
2 scallions
2 tablespoons vegetable oil
½ cup dry sherry
¼ cup soy sauce
2 thin slices ginger
1 whole star anise or eight sections
1 teaspoon salt
1 tablespoon sugar

Wash the beef and pat dry with paper towels. Slice scallions in half and cut into 2-inch lengths on the diagonal, using both green shoots and white bulbs.
Heat the oil in a saucepan over high heat. Using a wooden spoon to turn the meat, sear well on all sides, a few pieces at a time. Add sherry, let boil 1 minute, then add soy sauce and 1 cup water.
Mix in the ginger, scallions, star anise, salt, and sugar. Cook for 3 minutes. Bring again to boil. Reduce heat to simmer and cover pan. Cook for 30 minutes. Stir to baste the meat and continue cooking for 30 minutes longer. Remove ginger slices and whole star anise. Serve hot.

MIDDLE EASTERN LAMB TARTLETS

Makes 16

Tartlet crust:
⅔ cup cream cheese
8 tablespoons sweet butter
2 cups all-purpose flour
½ teaspoon salt
Filling:
2 tablespoons butter
½ cup finely chopped onions
1 pound ground lamb
Salt and freshly ground black pepper
⅓ teaspoon ground allspice
2 tablespoons chopped parsley
½ cup pine nuts
⅓ cup unflavored yogurt

To make the crust: Blend the cream cheese and butter together. Work in the flour and the salt. Press to knead the dough in order to incorporate the flour evenly. Wrap in plastic wrap and chill at least 2 hours. Roll out between sheets of plastic wrap and cut out sixteen 2½-inch rounds. Make small rims to hold in the following filling. Fill the tartlets and bake in a preheated 350 degree oven 30 minutes. Serve hot.
To make the filling: melt the butter in a skillet and in it cook the onions, without browning, until soft. Add the meat and continue cooking 3 to 4 minutes breaking up any lumps of meat with a fork. Add salt, pepper, and allspice. Mix in the parsley and the pine nuts. Allow to cool, then stir in the yogurt. Fill, bake, and serve hot.

RIB STEAKS IN THE STYLE OF ROME

Serves 4 to 5

2 boned rib steaks, 1 inch thick
1 tablespoon finely chopped fresh
  rosemary, or ½ tablespoon dried
2 cloves garlic, peeled and chopped
½ cup olive oil
¼ teaspoon freshly ground black pepper
Salt
Lemon quarters

The day before serving pound the slices of meat between sheets of wax paper until somewhat thinner. In a mortar pound the rosemary and the garlic to a paste. Stir in the olive oil and season with pepper and a little salt. Marinate the meat overnight in the oil mixture, turning the meat once or twice. Remove the meat and pat dry with paper towels. Broil 4 minutes on each side or until done to taste. Place on a warmed serving dish, sprinkle with lemon juice, and serve at once.

DISH	INGREDIENTS	DIRECTIONS

ROAST LAMB, ARAB STYLE

Serves 10

1 forequarter lamb (10 pounds)
1½ tablespoons ground coriander seed
4 to 5 cloves garlic, peeled and mashed
2 teaspoons ground cumin
1 teaspoon sweet paprika
6 tablespoons sweet butter, softened
Salt to taste

Carefully remove extraneous fat from the lamb, then make deep incisions under the foreleg bone along the breastplate. Blend all the other ingredients into a paste and rub into the meat. Let stand 10 minutes.
Preheat the oven to 475 degrees.
Place the lamb, fatty side up, in a large roasting pan. Place on the middle shelf of the oven and roast 15 minutes. Reduce the heat to 350 degrees and continue to roast for about 3 hours, or until the meat can easily be removed from the bones with your fingers. Baste every 15 minutes with the juices in the pan. Serve at once, while still burning hot. Eat with your fingers and have a bowl of ground cumin and salt ready for those who like to dip their meat.

CHICKEN LIVERS ON CROUTONS

Makes 12

8 ounces chicken livers, picked over to remove green bile
1 small onion, finely chopped
¼ cup butter
1 California bay leaf or 2 European bay leaves
½ teaspoon crumbled sage leaves
¼ teaspoon freshly ground black pepper
½ cup dry white wine
3 tablespoons cognac
3 fillets of anchovies, rinsed, drained, dried, and chopped
2 teaspoons capers, drained and chopped
12 slices of French or Italian bread

Roughly chop the livers. Soften the onions in half the butter for 1 to 2 minutes. Add the bay leaves and the sage. When the onions turn golden, add the roughly chopped livers. Stir with a wooden spoon over moderate heat for 2 to 4 minutes. Add pepper. Pour in the wine and cognac and raise the heat. Let bubble for 5 minutes. Remove bay leaves when livers and sauce are almost dry.
Blend the chopped anchovies and capers with the remaining 2 tablespoons butter. Reheat chicken livers and when hot beat in the anchovy butter mixture. Blend well. Pile on toasted bread rounds and serve at room temperature. Serve with drinks.

CHICKEN WITH FORTY CLOVES OF GARLIC

Serves 4 to 5

3½-pound ready-to-cook chicken
Salt and freshly ground black pepper
2 bouquets garnis of Provençal herbs: bay leaf, parsley, thyme, celery leaves, savory, and a little rosemary
¼ cup olive oil
40 cloves of garlic, unpeeled
2 tablespoons anisette, pastis, or anisina
Flour and water paste

Preheat the oven to 350 degrees.
Rub the chicken with salt and pepper. Stuff with one of the herb bouquets, then truss the chicken. Place in the casserole. Combine oil, garlic cloves in their skins, anisette, salt and pepper, and remaining herb bouquet and dump over the bird. Cover and seal the casserole with a ribbon of flour and water paste. Set in the oven to bake 1 hour 15 minutes.

CHICKEN WITH MOROCCAN SPICE MIXTURE

Serves 4

2½ to 3 pound chicken, quartered
¼ cup vegetable oil
1½ cups finely chopped onions
Salt and freshly ground black pepper
2 teaspoons of Moroccan spice mixture (below)
2 ripe tomatoes, peeled, seeded, and chopped
4 sprigs each: fresh green coriander and parsley
2 tablespoons lemon juice
1 cup Greek green-cracked olives

MOROCCAN SPICE MIXTURE FOR LAMB AND CHICKEN STEWS
1 tablespoon each: ground ginger
ground black pepper
ground turmeric
½ tablespoon ground cinnamon
1 teaspoon grated nutmeg

Brown the chicken quarters in hot oil. Add the onions and stir-cook 3 to 4 minutes. Add salt, pepper, and spice mixture. Cook over medium heat 5 minutes, tossing and turning the chicken quarters often. Add the tomatoes. Cook over high heat until the pan juices are well reduced. Add ½ cup water and cook over moderate heat, stirring, until evaporated. Add another 1½ cups water, a little at a time, stirring constantly. When the pan juices are thick, add the herbs. Cover tightly and cook over low heat until the chicken is tender.
Add lemon juice and olives and cook 5 minutes longer to blend flavors.

DISH	INGREIDENTS	DIRECTIONS

FRIED CHICKEN WITH SESAME SEEDS

Serves 4

4 leg and thigh pieces of chicken, halved
Salt and freshly ground black pepper
1 egg, lightly beaten
2/3 cup all-purpose flour
1 cup sesame seeds
2 teaspoons paprika
Oil for frying

Preheat the oven to 350 degrees.
Rub the chicken pieces with salt and pepper. Beat the egg with 1/2 cup water in a shallow bowl. Combine flour, sesame seeds, paprika, and salt to taste in a plastic bag, mixing well. Place the chicken pieces, 2 or 3 at a time, in the egg mixture then in the plastic bag. Close and shake until the chicken is nicely coated with the sesame seed mixture. Remove to a dish. Repeat with the remaining pieces of chicken.
In hot but not smoking oil brown the chicken pieces on both sides. Transfer to a baking sheet, set on the middle shelf of the preheated oven to finish the cooking in about 20 minutes.

GINGERED CHICKEN STEW WITH CHICK PEAS

Serves 6 to 8

1 pound dried chick peas
2 chickens, quartered
1 teaspoon ground Jamaican ginger
1 rounded teaspoon freshly and finely ground black pepper
1 teaspoon salt
1/4 teaspoon pulverized saffron
3 tablespoons finely chopped parsley
Pinch of ground cinnamon
1 leek, thinly sliced
1/4 cup butter
1 cup thinly sliced onion
Salt

Soak chick peas overnight in water to cover.
Rub chickens with a mixture of ginger, black pepper, and salt. Drain chick peas, place in saucepan, cover with fresh water and cook, covered, 1 hour. Drain and submerge in a bowl of cold water. Rub chick peas to remove their skins. Place spiced chicken in deep casserole. Add saffron, parsley, cinnamon, leek, and butter. Cover with 1 1/2 quarts water and bring to a boil. Reduce heat, cover, and simmer 1 hour, turning the chickens frequently in the resulting sauce.
Remove chickens when tender and keep warm.
Add finely sliced onions, peeled chick peas, and cook until the onions are soft and the sauce has reduced to a thick gravy. Reheat the chickens in the sauce. Taste for salt and serve hot.

ITALIAN ROAST SQUAB WITH JUNIPER BERRIES

Serves 6

1/2 cup long grain rice
6 squabs and their livers
4 slices prosciutto or Canadian bacon
12 juniper berries, toasted in a dry skillet until shiny
Salt and freshly ground black pepper
6 slices bacon
4 ounces unsalted butter
1/3 cup dry white wine
1/3 cup chicken stock

Boil rice for five minutes; drain.
Puree livers with prosciutto in workbowl of food processor. Crush juniper berries in a mortar and rub through a sieve. Mix drained rice, pureed livers, and juniper berries. Season with salt and pepper. Stuff the squabs with this mixture. Place 1 strip of bacon across each breast and truss each bird. Rub roasting pan with 2 tablespoons butter. Rub each bird with 1 tablespoon butter. Roast at 350 degrees for about 1 hour. Degrease pan. Deglaze pan with white wine. Add stock and boil down to intensify flavors. Strain juices over the squabs.

GRATED POTATO CAKE STUFFED WITH LEEKS

Serves 6

1 pound leeks, whites plus 1-inch shoots, roots trimmed, well-washed, and dried
5 tablespoons unsalted butter
1/2 cup heavy cream
Salt and pepper
2 pounds potatoes, peeled
1/4 cup clarified butter

Thinly slice the leeks. Melt 2 tablespoons butter in a heavy casserole. Add leeks, cover, and cook gently for 6 minutes. Uncover. Add remaining butter and stew the sliced leeks 5 minutes longer. Add the cream and boil down to thicken. The leeks must not be runny. Season with salt and pepper. Cool.
Grate the potatoes or cut into very thin matchsticks. Rinse in several changes of water. Drain; spread them out on a kitchen towel to dry. Roll the towel and potatoes up like a rug and squeeze tightly to extrude all excess water. Potatoes will keep in this state for at least an hour.
Heat clarified butter in a large skillet. Spread out half the potatoes to cover bottom. Top with braised leeks, leaving an inch margin around the edge. Cover with remaining potatoes and pat into a cake-like form, about 10 inches in diameter. Cover and cook 5 minutes, shaking the pan often to keep the potatoes from sticking. The bottom should be golden and crusty. Invert and continue cooking, uncovered, over low heat 10 to 15 minutes, or until the potatoes are tender. Sprinkle with salt. Serve hot, cut into wedges.

PUREED GREEN CELERY WITH CORIANDER SEED

Serves 8

2 bunches celery with green leaves attached
3/4 pound peeled potatoes
3 tablespoons sweet butter
1/8 cup heavy cream
1/4 teaspoon ground coriander seed
Salt and freshly ground pepper

Wash each celery rib and cut into 2-inch pieces. Do not remove green tops or scrape away strings. Cook the ribs with the potatoes in boiling salted water. Drain, and let cool slightly. Rice potatoes or rub through a food mill. Puree celery stalks and leaves in workbowl of food processor. Combine in a gratin pan. Add butter, cream, and seasoning to taste. Reheat in a 350 degree oven. Serve with grilled lamb.

DISH	INGREDIENTS	DIRECTIONS

ARTICHOKE HEARTS IN RED WINE

Serves 6

1 cup cubed, blanched lean salt pork
6 raw artichoke bottoms, quartered
1 cup cubed prosciutto
1½ cups chopped onions
½ cup chopped mushrooms
⅔ cup minced scallions
1 cup sliced carrots
2 teaspoons sliced garlic
2 teaspoons tomato paste
1 bottle coarse full-bodied red wine
2 bay leaves
1 sprig of thyme
3 parsley sprigs
6 black peppercorns
Salt
¾ cup brown sauce (or gravy)
Pinch of sugar
2 tablespoons olive oil
1½ tablespoons brandy
2 tablespoons sweet butter
½ tablespoon minced parsley

In a skillet, lightly brown the salt pork. Add the trimmings of the raw artichokes, the prosciutto, onions, mushrooms, scallions, carrots, and garlic. Sauté 1 minute, stirring. Blend in tomato paste. Add red wine, herbs, peppercorns, and salt to taste. Reduce heat and cook gently 1½ hours. Stir in the brown sauce. Simmer 5 minutes longer. Strain, pressing down on the vegetables to extract all their juices. You should have about 2 cups sauce. Reduce if necessary. Adjust seasoning adding a pinch of sugar if necessary to balance flavors.
In a clean skillet, sauté artichoke pieces in hot olive oil until lightly browned around the edges. Add brandy and reduce to a glaze. Add red wine sauce and simmer 15 minutes. Swirl in butter to thicken. Sprinkle with parsley.
Serve with grilled meat or poultry or alone as a first course.

PAELLA

Serves 8

¾ cup olive oil
1 cup grated onion
½ pound boneless pork shoulder cut into 1-inch cubes
3-pound chicken, cut into 8 pieces
1 teaspoon finely chopped garlic
2 cups peeled, seeded, and chopped tomatoes
2 bay leaves
4 sprigs fresh parsley
Salt and freshly ground black pepper
½ teaspoon pulverized saffron
12 mussels, well scrubbed
½ pound small clams, scrubbed and soaked in cold water 30 minutes to eliminate sand
¼ pound sweet green peppers, seeded, deribbed, and cut lengthwise into thin strips
¼ pound green beans, trimmed and cut into 1-inch lengths, or 9 ounces frozen artichoke hearts, thawed
3 cups raw imported Spanish or Italian rice
7-ounce jar roasted red peppers, drained and cut into thin strips
½ pound shelled and deveined shrimp
¼ pound fully cooked chorizo sausage, skinned and thinly sliced
2 lemons, quartered

In a large casserole heat ⅓ cup olive oil and in it cook ½ cup grated onion for 2 minutes, stirring. Add the pork and chicken and sauté for 5 minutes, stirring. Then add the garlic, tomatoes, herbs, salt, pepper, and saffron. Cover and cook over medium heat about 25 minutes, stirring from time to time.
Meanwhile steam the mussels and clams in 1 cup water until they open, about 5 minutes. Discard any that do not open. Reserve the mussels, clams, and cooking liquor and discard the shells. Strain the liquor.
Add the green peppers and green beans or artichokes to the casserole. Cook, covered, 5 to 10 minutes longer.
Meanwhile heat the remaining olive oil in the paella pan and cook the remaining ½ cup grated onion 1 minute. Add the rice and cook, stirring until all the grains are coated, 8 to 10 minutes.
Add the mussel and clam liquor plus 7 cups water to the casserole. Bring to the boil. Slowly pour the bubbling sauce over the rice. Then slide the remaining contents of the casserole evenly over the sizzling rice. Add the red peppers, shrimp, chorizo slices, mussels, and clams. Stir once. Cook, uncovered, over brisk heat until the liquid is absorbed and the rice is tender, about 20 minutes. Rotate and shake the pan from time to time to cook the rice evenly. Allow the contents to rest 5 minutes before serving. Serve directly from the pan with the lemon wedges.

STUFFED TOMATOES

Serves 4

8 firm red tomatoes
Salt
¼ loaf French or Italian bread
2 cloves garlic, peeled and crushed
Olive oil
2-ounce tin anchovy fillets
¼ cup pine nuts
¼ cup yellow raisins plumped in water, then drained
2 tablespoons chopped fresh parsley
Freshly ground pepper

Cut a slice off the top of each tomato, scoop out the pulp and seeds, and discard or reserve for some other use. Salt the shells and set them upside down to drain.
Thinly slice the bread, rub with garlic, and cut into ¼-inch cubes. Brown lightly in olive oil and set aside to drain on paper towels.
Drain, rinse, drain, and mash the anchovies. Mix with remaining ingredients. Stuff tomatoes, cover with tops, and fit into baking dish. Bake 20 minutes in a hot oven. Serve hot.

149

DISH	INGREDIENTS	DIRECTIONS

ANDRÉ DAGUIN'S PEPPER COOKIES

Makes 7 dozen

1½ cups all-purpose flour
¼ cup sugar
4 tablespoons (½ stick) unsalted butter
¼ cup olive oil
⅞ teaspoon freshly ground white pepper
1 small egg, lightly beaten

In the workbowl of a food processor fitted with the metal blade, combine the flour, sugar, butter, and olive oil and process for 10 seconds. Add the pepper and egg; blend again until just combined. Form the dough into a ball; wrap in waxed paper or plastic wrap; and chill overnight.
Line a baking sheet with parchment paper and preheat the oven to 350 degrees.
Roll the dough out between floured sheets of waxed paper or plastic wrap to a 9 by 12 inch rectangle. Beginning at the wide end, fold the dough up ¾ inch and over itself using the paper or wrap as an aid. Cut along the width of the fold and then cut the resulting strip into ¾-inch pieces.
Repeat the process with the remaining dough.
Transfer the cookies to the prepared baking sheet, and bake in the preheated oven for 10 minutes, or until the cookies are just golden, not brown. Cool on racks. They will keep a long time in an airtight jar or metal container.

CLOVE ORANGE ICE

Makes 1½ quarts

2¾ cups granulated sugar
2 cups water
2 whole cloves
1 quart orange juice, strained
½ cup strained lemon juice
½ tablespoon grated orange rind

Combine sugar, water, and cloves in a large saucepan. Cook, stirring, over medium heat until the sugar is dissolved. Boil the syrup for 5 minutes. Strain into a mixing bowl and let cool. Combine orange juice, lemon juice, and grated rind. Stir into sugar syrup. Set in the freezer compartment until the mixture is mushy but set around the edges of the bowl. Use an electric beater and beat until smooth. Return to the freezer for 4 to 5 hours. Beat again, pour into mold, and freeze it until almost firm.

FILBERT CRISPS

Makes 45 crisps

5 tablespoons unsalted butter, softened
1 cup sugar
½ cup egg whites (about 4 egg whites)
¾ cup ground hazelnuts
2 teaspoons grated orange rind
⅔ cup cake flour

Preheat the oven to 425 degrees.
Place the butter and the sugar in the mixing bowl; beat until creamy. Beat in the egg whites. Fold in the ground nuts and the grated orange rind. Using a rubber spatula gently stir in the flour 2 tablespoons at a time. Pack into a pastry bag. Drop small rounds of batter onto the greased baking sheets, leaving 3 inches between each round. Using a knife dipped in cold water, flatten each into a thin oval shape. Bake until the edges are golden brown—about 10 minutes.
Use a spatula to detach the crisps and allow to cool on wire racks. Store in an airtight tin.

SAUTÉED APPLES WITH LEMON OR ORANGE MARMALADE

Serves 4

2 large tart green apples
3 tablespoons unsalted butter
4 tablespoons imported lemon marmalade
Grated nutmeg
Confectioners sugar

Peel, core, and slice the apples into 12 pieces each.
In a small skillet, melt 1½ tablespoons butter.
Add the apple slices and sauté them, turning them often, for 1 minute or until they are barely soft. Push the apples to one side of the skillet, add the marmalade and remaining 1½ tablespoons butter, and mix with the pan juices.
Fold in the apple slices and cook over high heat, turning the apple slices constantly until caramelized around the edges. Sprinkle with grated nutmeg and confectioners sugar. Serve hot.

SWEET AND SOUR CHERRIES WITH MACE

¾ pound firm, not too sweet cherries
1 cup red wine vinegar
⅔ cup sugar
Ground mace

Wash and prick each cherry once or twice with a needle. Trim each stem, leaving about 1 inch attached. Heat the vinegar in an enameled or stainless steel pan, add the sugar and cook, stirring, over low heat until the sugar is dissolved. Raise the heat and boil for 3 to 4 minutes. Stir in a good pinch of ground mace. Cool slightly.
Place the cherries in a ¾-quart preserving jar and pour the liquid over them. Seal closely and leave at least 6 weeks before using.

DISH	INGREDIENTS	DIRECTIONS

MOROCCAN BREAD

Makes 2 six-inch round loaves

1 package active dry yeast
1 teaspoon granulated sugar
3½ cups unbleached flour
1 cup whole-wheat flour
2 teaspoons salt
½ cup lukewarm milk
1 teaspoon sesame seeds
1 tablespoon aniseed
Cornmeal

Soften the yeast in ¼ cup sugared lukewarm water. Let stand 2 minutes, then stir and set in a warm place until the yeast is bubbly and doubles in volume. Meanwhile, mix the flours with the salt in a large mixing bowl.

Stir the bubbling yeast into the flour, then add the milk and enough lukewarm water to form a stiff dough. (Since flours differ in their ability to absorb moisture, no precise amount can be given.) Turn the dough out onto a lightly floured board and knead hard with closed fists, adding water if necessary. To knead, push the dough outward. (It will take anywhere from 10 to 15 minutes to knead this dough thoroughly and achieve a smooth, elastic consistency. If using an electric beater with a dough hook, knead 7 to 8 minutes at slow speed.) During the final part of the kneading, add the spices. After the dough has been thoroughly kneaded, form into two balls and let stand 5 minutes on the board.

Lightly grease a mixing bowl. Transfer the first ball of dough to the greased bowl and form into a cone shape by grasping the dough with one hand and rotating it against the sides of the bowl, held by the other hand. Turn out onto a baking sheet that has been sprinkled with cornmeal. Flatten the cone with the palm of the hand to form a flattened disk about 5 inches in diameter with a slightly raised center. Repeat with the second ball of dough. Cover loosely with a damp towel and let rise about 2 hours in a warm place. (To see if the bread has fully risen, poke your finger gently into the dough—the bread is ready for baking if the dough does not spring back.)

Preheat the oven to 400 degrees.

Using a fork, prick the bread around the sides 3 or 4 times and place on the center shelf of the oven. Bake 12 minutes, then lower the heat to 300 degrees and bake 30 to 40 minutes more. When done, the bread will sound hollow when tapped on the bottom. Remove and let cool. Cut in wedges just before serving.

HONEY CINNAMON CAKE WITH WALNUTS

1¼ cups sugar
¾ cup honey
1¼ teaspoons ground cinnamon
Juice of ½ lemon
1¾ cups chopped walnuts
1½ cups all-purpose flour, sifted
1 teaspoon double-acting baking powder
4 tablespoons sweet butter, softened to room temperature
4 eggs, separated

To make the syrup: Cook ¾ cup sugar and ¾ cup water in a small saucepan, stirring. Bring to the boil. Simmer 5 minutes. Stir in the honey, ¼ teaspoon ground cinnamon, and the lemon juice. Cook at the simmer 5 minutes longer. Allow to cool completely.

Preheat the oven to 350 degrees.

Combine 1¼ cups nuts, remaining cinnamon, flour, and baking powder. Set aside. Cream remaining ½ cup sugar with butter until light and fluffy. Add egg yolks, one at a time, beating well after each addition. Beat in the walnut mixture. Separately beat the egg whites until stiff. Gently fold the egg whites into the walnut mixture. Put the mixture into the prepared cake pan. Sprinkle the top with the remaining ½ cup chopped walnuts. Set in the oven to bake until the cake tests done.

Remove the cake from the oven. Cut into diamond shapes in the cakepan. Pour cool syrup over the hot cake. Cover and allow to stand overnight before serving.

Seasoners of the World

WAVERLEY ROOT

Flavor is the gift of Asia. Of the two most important categories of plants which add tastiness to food, spices and herbs, the first are almost solely Asiatic; the second, though also Asiatic, come from a part of Asia which shares its largesse with Europe.

The great majority of the principal spices of the world (cinnamon, cloves, ginger, mace, nutmeg, pepper) are natives of an area which extends from India to the Molucca

A meditative merchant waits for customers in the marketplace of Fez, the spectacularly picturesque Moroccan city reputed to know alone the secret recipe for *Ras el Hanout,* the national seasoning blend. Moroccan consciousness of spices is implicit in a folk saying used to blast ignorance: "What does an ass understand about ginger?"

Opposite page: The heat of the tropical sun created the heat and color of these spices displayed in the open-air market of Guatemala city.

Islands. The great majority of the principal herbs of the world (anise, basil, bay leaf, chervil, coriander, cress, fennel, fenugreek, marjoram, mint, oregano, rosemary, sage, tarragon, thyme) come from an area which starts in Iran but spreads through Asia Minor along the northern shore of the Mediterranean into southern Europe. The onion-garlic family, whose members are important seasoners, is believed to have originated in Central Asia. Citrus fruits serve as flavorers too: they probably started in China.

Seasoners are not the most decisive factors in shaping the character of a cuisine, but they are the most spectacular. They force themselves first upon our attention. When we enter a strange country, we learn at once what sort of cooking we may expect from the nature of the condiments we find waiting for us on restaurant tables.

In France there used to be, on each table, a four-place cruet containing olive oil, vinegar, salt, and pepper, to permit the diner to make his own salad dressing in accord with his own taste, a habit now, unhappily, in decline. In Italy there is grated Parmesan cheese, in Germany, probably, grated horse-radish. Scandinavia offers chopped dill or dill-mustard sauce; England, mustard or Worcestershire sauce; and the United States, of course, ketchup (which is of Asiatic origin, as is Worcestershire sauce).

Everywhere in Latin America you will find tiny hot chilies chopped into vinegar or vegetable oil or both, to which Brazil will add a shaker of manioc meal. Everywhere in southeastern Asia you will find a salty liquid derived from fermented fish which is identical with the all-purpose seasoner of ancient Rome, *garum;* in the Far East, soybean sauce. (In India, there is nothing; Indians do not eat in the restaurants. They are for foreigners.)

Ethiopia offers its fiery red *berberé* sauce, perhaps the hottest all-purpose seasoner in the world, with the possible exception of the Latin American chili condiment. But you have only to move on to North Africa to meet its complete antithesis. In the luxury restaurants of the Maghreb (Tunisia, Algeria, Morocco) your eyes will delight in the graceful shape of a tall slender vase, often of silver, which looks as though it were meant to hold a single orchid; but even an orchid stem could not pass through the narrow opening at its top. It is designed to release its precious contents only drop by drop. It holds rose water.

SEASONERS AND STAPLES

If Asia is the principal source of the world's seasoners, why doesn't food everywhere taste Asiatic? Twice during the world's history it did. When the Roman Asiatic Army returned to Italy in 185 B.C. bringing strange flavorers with it, Roman food foundered in Asiatic excess. When the Crusaders returned from Asia Minor in the Middle Ages, Europe wallowed briefly in Oriental spicing. "Modern Indian cookery probably comes closest to medieval," Anne Willan wrote. But Eastern spices were soon tamed by incompatibility with Western staples: wheat married less easily with vivid seasoning than rice, meat less easily than fish.

EUROPE
The basic grain of Europe is wheat and its basic meat beef, both of which accord best with what we might call reasonable unsensational seasoning. Italy, which uses much rice and prefers veal to beef, is accordingly a country which spices its food with bravura. In Central and Slavic Europe, rye bread and pork encourage flavors sometimes strong and sour, while the pungent spicing of Scandinavia developed in function of its fish, especially the herring.

FISH
Dill

MEAT
WHEAT
Basil

Garlic

Olive oil

Couscous

Okra
Baobab

MILLET
Berberé sauce

MAIZE

WHEAT

Dried lemons

Asafetida
Pepper
Ginger
Cardamom

Cinnamon

RICE

Ginseng

Soybean sauce

RICE
FISH
Seaweed

FISH

Nuoc Mam

Nutmeg
Cloves

ROSEMARY, "dew of the sea" (because it grows well on coasts), is an herb much used in European cooking.

SWEET PEPPERS, common vegetables in Europe, are natives of America, brothers to the more pungent chilies.

GINGER, widely us[ed] Asia, probably origin[ated] in India, for its r[oot] comes from the Sa[nskrit] sringavera, "horn-r[oot]"

NUTMEG, originally confined to a few small islands in the Moluccas, was the last Asiatic spice to reach Europe, in 1190.

AFRICA
South of the Sahara, Africa originally knew few cereals, but ate much game; consequently seasoning was bland before the sixteenth century.

INDIA
When the Aryans invaded India from the north, where dairy cattle were important, they brought with them a cuisine which cooked with butter, in the form of ghee (but the poor used sesame or mustard-seed oil, the very poor, safflower oil); the south continued to use vegetable oils or coconut milk. The north ate wheat, the south rice. These differences made the south even more receptive than the north to imaginative seasoning.

SOUTHEAST ASIA
The diet of Southeast Asia is dominated by rice and fish——two foods which cry out for vivid or subtle seasoning and here receive it. The "salt" of this region is a liquid made from fermented fish, almost identical, curiously, with the all-purpose seasoner of ancient Rome, *garum*, made from fermented fish too.

Indian food is colorful. Ingredients for a holiday meal assembled at Jangri, southern India——wheat flour, sugar syrup, saffron——are a joyful yellow.

The water buffalo shown tilling a flooded Asiatic rice in this eighteenth-century woodcut is not quite outdated yet.

ANGLO-SAXON cooking is anything but reticent in its seasoning, partly because of the forthright nature of its staples——wheat (oats in Scotland, potatoes in Ireland), beef (with Worcestershire sauce), and mutton (with mint sauce), but even more, perhaps, because of climate. Cold, damp winters help make the Briton one of the world's greatest overeaters of sugar, a warming energy-building food.

Mustard

THE FAR EAST

Except in the distant north, rice is the basic cereal in the Far East (and in Southeast Asia too, for that matter); and the area harbors the world's greatest fish eaters, the Japanese. Both rice and fish demand assertive spicing, and get it in the form of that universal all-purpose seasoner, the salty soybean sauce.

Maple sugar

MAIZE

WHEAT

MEAT   Peanuts

Chili

NORTH AMERICA

Hearty foods——wheat and beef——and for much of the United States rigorous winters, encourage the use of strong seasoners rather than subtle ones: for instance, the white mustard, whose plant is shown above. A unique North American seasoner is maple sugar.

LATIN AMERICA

Maize (bland), cassava flour (insipid), and the potato (modest) are the staples of Latin America; the sharp bite of the native chilies lifts their low taste thresholds. Subtropical and tropical climates are consistent with chilies too, and also with the luscious, aromatic velvety vanilla and allspice.

MAIZE

POTATO

Vanilla
Allspice
Cassava

MEAT

The eating habits of a large part of the world were changed when sugar cane was transplanted from its native Asia (India?) to the West Indies, with such success that sugar, previously a luxury food, decreased in price and became available to everybody.

A familiar scene in every Latin American market is the chili seller, his brightly colored wares spread out on the ground before him. It is familiar too in other warm countries, for the New World chili has conquered the Old World.

Peppers soak up the heat of the Indian sun twice: on the shrub, and then, spread out to dry, on the ground. Thus deprived of their water content, they deliver a concentrated incandescence to the mouth.

INDIA

For Westerners, the taste of India is the taste of curry; but curries are only one manifestation of what really characterizes Indian cooking—the skillful use of spices. India probably uses more different seasoners than any other area in the world; and it uses them more subtlely.

"The variety, the combination, and the use of spices are the major factors that distinguish Indian cooking from any other cuisine in the world," Santha Rama Rau has written. "Through the choice of spices, through their proportion and blending, a good Indian cook expresses imagination, ingenuity, individuality, subtlety, adventurousness"; and she reminds us that in some parts of India a bride stands barefooted on the stone used for grinding spices, while in others she brings her own private mortar and pestle with her to her husband's home. "Indian cooks," wrote Caroline Bates, "combine spices as painters mix colors, striving for the proper proportion, balance, and nuances of tone and grinding different mixtures... for every dish.... Indian cooking owes its distinctive character to the refined use of spices."

Most Westerners know by now that curry powder does not come from a single plant, like cinnamon or nutmeg, but is a mixture of seasoners; many persons, however, still think that it is an invariable mixture, compounded always of the same spices in the same proportions. Actually no standardized curry powder exists in India except what is called, disdainfully, "railway curry." Dining cars are ill equipped for subtlety; the

conditions under which they operate oblige them to stock a single mixture which, being designed to go with everything, does not go well with anything. No Indian housewife would use the same powder for every curry she cooks, any more than a Western housewife would flavor everything from soup to desserts with the same seasoners. The difference between the Indian cook and the Western cook is that the latter puts the different herbs and spices called for by her recipe into the dish separately, one by one; the Indian cook assembles all the seasoners first, works them into a common blend, and puts the resulting mixture into the dish. The ideal is that the flavor of the curry should be the flavor of the *blend*; the

NATIVE SEASONERS USED COMMONLY IN INDIA

Cardamom, Cinnamon, Ginger, Lemon, Mung bean sprouts, Pepper, Poke, Sesame, Tamarind, Turmeric, Zedoary root

Zedoary root

AFGHANISTAN
Asafetida
Pistachio

NORTHERN CUISINE (WHEAT)
Dry masalas
No garlic
Cooking in ghee
Curries—chutneys

INDIA

SOUTHERN CUISINE (RICE)
Wet masalas
Garlic
Cooking in vegetable oils
and coconut milk

CEYLON
Cinnamon

IMPORTED SEASONERS USED COMMONLY IN INDIA

Anise, Asafetida, Chili, pepper, Coriander, Cress, Cumin, Dill, Fennel, Fenugreek, Garlic (in south only), Mustard, Onion, Peanut, Pistachio, Saffron

Right: These enormous sacks of natural unadulterated spices on sale in bulk at New Delhi pay eloquent testimony to the importance of seasoners in Indian cooking.

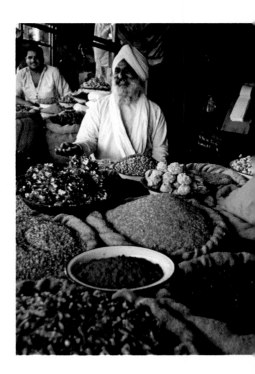

different ingredients which have gone into it should not be individually identifiable. What the Westerner calls a curry powder, the Indian calls a dry masala; there are wet masalas too, semiliquid pastes compounded also of a variety of flavorers. Curries are not all hot, as Westerners are inclined to think: they run from the fiery to mixtures so bland that foreigners with taste buds less finely attuned than those of Indians find it difficult to perceive their savor at all. This is true also of chutneys—relishes—which range from sweet jam-like kinds made chiefly with fruit through sweet-and-sour varieties to hot spicy sour concoctions never found outside India. A wide variety of spices accounts also for the soul of achars, Indian oil pickles. There is a marked difference in India between the cuisines of the north and the south. The basic cereal of the north is wheat: the south and the east eat rice. The common cooking fat of the north is ghee, clarified butter; that of the south is vegetable oil (but never olive oil, which would falsify the subtle seasonings of Indian cooking by adding another flavor of its own) or sometimes coconut milk. As a result, the south uses many more herbs and spices than the north, and prefers them, if possible, fresh. The north, where many dishes call for slight seasoning or none at all, is often content with dried seasoners. Garlic is popular in the south, but is rarely eaten in the north, where orthodox Hindus frequently refuse to use it at all.

The spice which goes oftenest into curries is turmeric, whose aromatic, slightly bitter, and somewhat musty flavor represents for many Westerners the typical taste of curry; when it is not turmeric it is probably coriander, second only to turmeric in frequency of use, though it is not native to India, or even fenugreek, which may not be native either, though in this case there is room for doubt. The widely used chilies, which make hot curries hottest, are also foreign.

After these, the seasoners most used are black pepper, cumin, cardamom, aniseed, dill, mustard, sesame, fennel, saffron, ginger, and mung bean sprouts. India also employs a number of flavorers not much found elsewhere: the seeds of the jackfruit, which might be described as the poor man's breadfruit; powdered pumpkin rind; *tamarind*, sharp but refreshing; *anvla*, a fruit which looks like a gooseberry but is sharp in taste;

asafetida, whose gum is the part used; *camphor*, combined in a dessert with bananas; *tamarish manna*, an excretion provoked when insects damage the twigs of this tree; a small dark-brown flower called *badiani khatai*; a South Indian fruit, *kokum*, described in Sanskrit literature as resembling in color

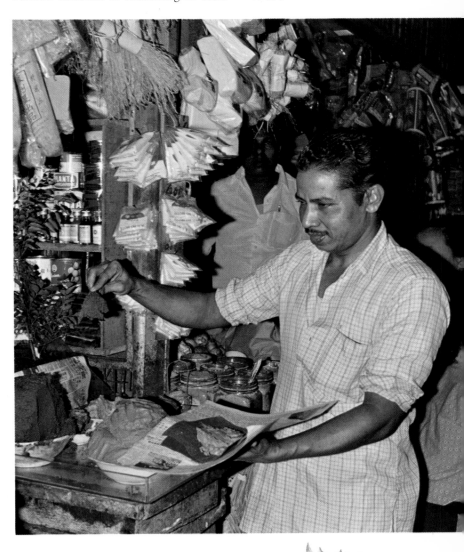

Pounding its ingredients together with a pestle, an Indian spice seller prepares a dry masala (curry powder) for his customers. What Westerners recognize as the taste of curry is usually that of turmeric, pictured below.

and texture the mouth of a beautiful woman (but not, one hopes, in taste, for it is extremely acid); and we might add also the flavoring of the Bengal *undhya* ("upside-down"), a vegetable dish flavored with salt, red pepper, cumin, coriander, fenugreek, fennel, ginger, and garlic, turned out of its cooking pot onto moistened hay, which gives it, unexpectedly, a smoky flavor. The hay is not eaten, but as its function is to contribute taste, it is entitled to be called a condiment.

157

SOUTHEAST ASIA

SEASONERS
OF SOUTHEAST ASIA

Burma
Coconut milk, Curries,
Fermented fish sauce, Peanut oil,
Sesame oil, Shrimp paste,
Soybean sauce (in north)

Malaysia
Candlenut, Coconut milk,
Chilies, Lemon grass

Thailand
Chilies, Coriander (leaves),
Curries, Fermented fish sauce,
Lemon grass, Lotus (root, seeds),
Mung bean sprouts, Peppermint,
Pessicary, Saffron, Soybean sauce

Indochina
Bamboo shoots, Cassia, Curries,
Fermented fish sauce, Ginger,
Jellyfish, Lemon grass,

The chief unifying elements in the cooking of Southeast Asia are a cereal (rice) and a seasoner (*nuoc mam* in Vietnam, *tuk trey* in Cambodia, *nam pla* in Thailand, *ngapi-yet* in Burma, *patis* in the Philippines, *bagoong* in Hawaii) which has been described as "a smelly liquid redolent of rancid fish, unpleasing to Western palates." Actually the fish is not rancid, but salted and fermented; the liquid pressed from it, which Indochinese gourmets enrich with ground *karung*, a water bug which looks like a cockroach, is the salt of Southeast Asia, used to bring out the taste of many kinds of foods, just as salt is used in the Occident. Northern Burma bows to Chinese influence by using soybean sauce as its universal

BURMA
LAOS
Nuoc Mam
THAILAND
VIETNAM
Limes
CAMBODIA
Cassia
PHILIPPINES
Coolest spicing
MALAYSIA
SUMATRA
White pepper
BORNEO
Camphor
MOLUCCAS
Nutmeg
Mace
CELEBES
NEW GUINEA
JAVA
Black pepper
BALI
Hottest spicing

Lily petals, Soybean sauce,
Star anise, Water chestnut,
Water convolvulus

Indonesia
Bay leaf, Black pepper (Java),
Chilies, Cloves (Moluccas),
Coconut milk, Coffee (Java),
Garlic, Ginger, Keluak nut,
Mace (Moluccas), Mung bean
sprouts, Nutmeg (Moluccas),
Onions, Peanut oil, Sesame
seeds, Soybean sauce, Turmeric,
White pepper (Sumatra)

Philippine Islands
Chilies, Fermented fish sauce,
Garlic, Lime, Onions,
Shrimp paste, Tamarind

gional preferences by employing the characteristic fermented fish sauce. Its original native seasoning was probably mild, which has survived in its bland soups, flavored with musky coriander leaves or with a herb popular in many parts of Southeast Asia—citronella or lemon grass.

"The delicate perfume of an herb or a leaf constitutes perhaps the greatest contribution of Vietnam to the universal cuisine," according to *The Song of Pounded Rice*, a Vietnamese cookbook. Some are indeed delicate, like a number of borrowings from China (water chestnuts, star anise, bamboo shoots, mung bean sprouts); the ever-present basil; *nghe*, described as a sort of saffron, though it seems closer to safflower; the water convolvulus, which tastes like a cross between cabbage and kale; and its own specialty, dried lily petals. Others are more authoritative, for Vietnamese cooking is distinguished by the wide range of its seasoners. *Rau ram*, or persicary, also known in English as lady's-thumb, is peppery. Among mints, Vietnam prefers the sharp purple-stemmed varieties derived from peppermint and goes them one better with a local type called *tia to*, whose lacy purple leaves are sharp in odor and flavor. What appears to be a variety of chives is stronger than European chives, and the ginger-like root called *rieng* outdoes ginger. The strangest seasoner in the Vietnamese pantry is *sua*—jellyfish.

Laotian seasoners are much like those of Vietnam, used with greater finesse. Each

seasoner, but in the south this gives way to the ubiquitous fermented fish condiment, along with another almost as common, a salty shrimp paste. Indian influence causes Burmese meals to be built around curries, sometimes cooled by cooking in coconut milk, though the normal cooking fats are sesame or peanut oil. Many Burmese dishes are too acid to please Westerners.

Thailand bows to Chinese influence by using water chestnuts, lotus roots or seeds, and soybean sauce (on salads); to Indian by using much curry *(khaeng phed)*; and to re-

The Philippine Islands enjoy the coolest cuisine of Southeast Asia. The fermented fish sauce and spicy shrimp paste are still found here, but both are blander than anywhere else. A favorite seasoner is lime juice or peel, from a local variety, the *calamansi*. Philippine food strikes Westerners as being basically sour.

The chief links between the cooking of Southeast Asia and the Pacific Islands are coconuts and rice, the latter a comparatively recent arrival. Before its advent, the basic food of the Islands was *poi*, the sour purplish paste pounded from the taro root, a discourager of seasoning; the Pacific Islands were in any case poor in native spices or herbs, though Hawaii, like the Philippines, has developed its own citrus fruit, the Kaffir lime; its favorite nut is the macadamia, which is anything but pungent. What faint

Everywhere in Southeast Asia the basic cereal is rice, a bland food which calls for spicing, one of the reasons why the peoples of this area have developed a genius for seasoning. Despite the introduction of new strains of "miracle rice" (whose flavor and texture most Asiatics dislike) and of modern machinery, many rice paddies are still worked by hand *(center, left)*. Recent studies have shown that there is no significant difference in yield between rice farms which use tractors and those which stick to bullocks and hand labor.

spice or herb is cooked separately for its optimum time until the moment arrives when they all go into the pot together. Laos sometimes strews over its dishes an aromatic herb not thought of as a seasoner in the West—marijuana. Cambodia sprinkles flowers on its rice.

The cuisine of Malaysia is modeled on that of India, but uses mild sweet spices where India might prefer stronger ones. One of its favorite seasoners is the mild-flavored candlenut, and the cooling coconut milk is often used for cooking.

It is Indonesia which eats the hottest, spiciest food of Southeast Asia. Bali, where Indian influence is strong, likes the most fiery food of all. Its standard seasoning mixture is *tabia bun*, made from turmeric, sesame seeds, bay leaves, onion, garlic, ginger, and two pungent roots which seem to have no names in European languages, *kentjur* and *laos*. Borneo produces a flavorer of minimum use—camphor.

Yet the favorite seasoners of Indonesia are, inconsistently, mild: soybeans, peanuts, and mung bean shoots, in that order. A local condiment which is less restrained is the black bitter *keluak* nut; the Moluccas, contrarily, grow a milder nut, the *kenari*, which has been compared to the almond. These are the original Spice Islands, once the only habitat in the world of mace, nutmeg, and cloves. They still produce 70 percent of the first two, but export more than they use, while the clove trade has been lost to Zanzibar.

flavoring Pacific foods have is often applied from the outside—by the leaves in which meat, fish, vegetables, or fruit are wrapped for cooking. The broad leaves of the native *ti* plant are the most popular for this purpose, but the slightly musty savor they exude, while appreciated in fish, is inappropriate for fruits, which are therefore wrapped in banana leaves. Peculiar to Tahiti are the leaves of the wild *fafa* plant, employed especially to envelop chicken, because, it is explained, "they don't scratch the throat."

Southeast Asia is all islands and peninsulas; no spot is very far from the sea. The area therefore eats more fish than meat; besides, fish is cheaper. Like rice, fish calls for seasoning, and demands even more imperiously that it should be ingenious and subtle. Thus the basic foods of the region conspire to encourage the development of the art of using herbs and spices skillfully, which is characteristic of this part of the world.

159

"There are dishes of all flavors," explained the Chinese poem *The Summons of the Soul* (third century B.C.), "bitter, salt, sour, hot, and sweet." Among the examples of fine foods cited in the same poem was "seethed tortoises highly seasoned, but not so much as to spoil the taste." This is the basic principle of Chinese cooking—plenty of condiments, but used always to accent the natural flavors of food, not to call attention to their own tastes.

The universal seasoner of the Far East is the salty, pungent soybean sauce; but the Chinese use it with commendable moderation. Soybeans appear as condiments in many other forms also—as bean sprouts; as soybean cake; as soybean "milk," often given to children instead of cow's milk, scarce in

Soybean sauce, made from beans fermented with the aid of bacteria and yeast, does not have to be as pungent as the liquid we are accustomed to encountering on the tables of Chinese restaurants. There are many kinds, some of them flavored by other substances—aromatic leaves, ginger, citronella, onions, fermented fish, or even fermented chicken. In China as in India, olive oil is not used as a cooking fat, though peanut oil, sesame seed oil, and even the not quite neutral soybean oil are common.

China is unlike India in using standardized seasoning mixtures. Five-Spice Powder, in its commonest form, is compounded of finely ground star anise, Szechwan pepper, fennel, cloves, and licorice root. Master Sauce starts with a small amount of Five-Spice Powder in soybean sauce, and adds more star anise, ginger, tangerine peel, salt, and sugar; it is kept for repeated cookings, growing richer with time from the flavors of the foods which have been cooked in it, and kept "alive" by regular replenishing of its seasoners. Hoisin Sauce is a sweet-and-spicy combination of seasonal vegetables with soybean sauce, chili pepper, garlic, sugar, and salt. The chutney-like *duk* sauce is

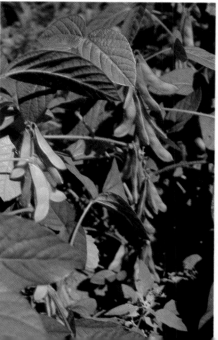

cattle-poor China, which is why the soybean is called "the cow of the East"; but soybean curd, which looks like custard, is "meat without bones" for those who think it tastes like beef extract. Other Chinese liken it to strong cheese, little liked in China, and call one type *chou tofu*, stinking curds. Soybean grains, bitter if mature, are eaten only unripe, when their flavor is agreeable.

made from red plums. Oyster sauce has no fishy taste, and indeed not much flavor of its own, but it brings out other flavors. Northern Chinese cooking (Peking, Honan), versatile and vinegary, also likes the scorched meat of Mongolia, where meat is cooked very simply, but is served accompanied by a host of relishes, sauces, and seasoners, echoed in Peking when coriander leaves, vinegar, shrimp sauce, sesame jam, chili oil, mashed bean curd, and soybean sauce are placed on the table, with a bowl for each diner in which he can mix for himself the seasoning of his heart's desire.

FENNEL

SZECHWAN PEPPER

LICORICE ROOT

STAR ANISE

CLOVE PLANT

The ingredients of Chinese Five-Spice Powder, a basic blend used either on its own or as a foundation for complicated sauces.

Coastal food (Shanghai) is only lightly spiced. It is characterized by much use of the technique called "red cooking," the color produced by braising foods in the standard combination of soybean sauce, wine, star anise, ginger, and sugar. This cuisine is relatively sweet and, in the opinion of Chinese from other regions, greasy, for lard is the usual cooking fat.

Southern cooking (Canton) is in many opinions China's best; but when this assessment comes from Americans it is partly a tribute to familiarity, for American Chinese cooking is a branch of Cantonese—the first Chinese to settle in the United States. The flavoring, though a trifle salty, is on the cool side. Garlic sauce is used, but black bean, oyster, and lobster sauces are more characteristic.

The cooking of the interior (Szechwan) has a worldwide reputation for hot spicing which is not entirely deserved; its chief characteristic is the wide variety of seasoners used rather than their strength; it also tends to be oily. One reason for this reputation may be the success of Szechwan pepper (*fagara*, not the same as Indian pepper) in forcing itself upon your attention. Ordinary pepper registers its effect immediately and then fades away; Szechwan pepper, barely tasted when swallowed, develops a rapid crescendo which can leave you gasping. Szechwan cooking is hot only in comparison with other Chinese cuisines; it has resisted the more violent influences of its neighbors, India and Vietnam. One of its superficial characteristics is much use of crunchy bamboo shoots, which are certainly mild enough.

Bamboo shoots are much liked elsewhere in China too, and so are dried mushrooms (the meaty Japanese *shi-i-take* or the southern Chinese cloud ear or tree ear); dried tiger-lily buds, alias "golden needles"; black and white sesame seeds; dried jujubes; lotus leaves, roots, fruits, and seeds; "dragon's eyes," the lichee-like fruit which looks like russet-yellow grapes and tastes sweet or sub-acid; orange peel; dried shrimps; baby fish, squid, and scallops, used curiously as condiments; minced smoked ham; the licorice-flavored star anise; ginger; icicle radish; water chestnuts; scallions and green onion sprouts; soybean and mung bean sprouts; black vinegar; Chinese cabbage, Chinese celery cabbage, and Chinese parsley (which is coriander, used more for its leaves than for its seeds); but, strangely, little Chinese cinnamon, no doubt because this is the sharp coarse cassia, and China prefers the subtler spice of Ceylon.

Japan, once tributary to China in many domains, was once its gastronomic satellite also, and its seasoning, consequently, was dominated by soybean sauce. But when, in the ninth century A.D., Japan withdrew into self-imposed isolation, it became bad form to put soybean sauce on the table. The ascetic military tradition stamped it as an effete luxury, and besides it was Chinese, an unwelcome reminder of the abandoned servitude. The soybean survived all the same, but the sauce (*shoyu*) made from it, less sharp in Japan than in China, has been relegated to a secondary role as one ingredient among many in marinating mixtures, in cooking liquids, or in dips.

Instead of the Chinese Five-Spice Powder the Japanese have Seven-Pepper Powder, of quite different ingredients—mustard seeds, sesame seeds, poppy seeds, rape seeds, hemp seeds, dried tangerine peel, and pepper leaf (*sansho*), which comes from the prickly ash, whose leaves and bark also serve as a substitute for ordinary black pepper.

At breakfast the Japanese begins his day with an extremely bitter pickle, usually in the form of the tiny very sour red plum called *umeboshi*, guaranteed to wake one up as effectively as a cold shower; and he is accustomed to cleansing his mouth at the end of each meal with another pickle, plum, ginger, cucumber, or, likeliest of all, the giant white radish called *daikon,* which tastes like turnip.

In the typically Japanese tempura cooking (more prosaically, deep frying), flavor is imparted to foods by the liquids in which they are cooked. Since the role of the cooking oils is now precisely that of contributing taste, the Japanese do not rule out olive oil as the Chinese and Indians do, but they use it in discreet quantities. Each tempura cook has his own favorite blend: one may use 85 percent cottonseed oil, 10 percent olive oil, and 5 percent sesame seed oil, another 75 percent peanut oil, 20 of sesame seed oil, and 5 of olive oil. Tempura-cooked food is usually placed before the diner accompanied by several little bowls containing such condiments as lemon juice, chopped horseradish, or a sharp sauce made from dried bonito. *Sashimi,* the Japanese specialty of fillets of raw fish, are served with *wasahi,* a soybean sauce rendered uncharacteristically pungent by the addition of a hot variety of fresh ripe horseradish, especially in summer, when the fish served is likely to be red-fleshed and oily, like tuna; in winter white-fleshed fish are eaten with *ponzu,* a dip of soybean sauce and the lime-like *yuzu* juice.

A favorite dry seasoner for sprinkling over cooked vegetables is *katsuobushi,* the tuna-like bonito dried until it is as hard as wood; it has to be shaved into flakes with a special kitchen tool. Combined with *kombu* (kelp), this becomes *dashi,* which not only flavors vegetables, but is used as the basis for fish stock. A similar concoction is *tsukudani,*

tiny fish and kelp boiled down until all the liquid has been eliminated, when it is powdered for sprinkling over rice dishes. Japan uses half a dozen different kinds of seaweed to flavor salads and soups.

Other condiments much used in Japan are dried *shi-i-take* mushrooms; chestnuts, cashew nuts, and gingko nuts (which taste like dried almonds that have somehow acquired a vaguely fishy flavor); Chinese cabbage; the mild rice vinegar; *kanpyo,* dried gourd, sold in strips; *gobo,* burdock root; *shirataki* and *konnyaku,* both made from a sort of yam; mustard, chives, scallions, and onions; fresh ginger and *shoga,* pickled red ginger; *takano tjume,* small whole red peppers, probably the hottest condiment in the Japanese repertory; pickled sea urchin; bamboo shoots and lotus roots; *junsai,* "the slippery vegetable," because it is difficult to hold onto the viscous coating of its spindle-shaped edible part; *goma,* black or white sesame seed; and *goma-abura,* sesame seed oil; the icicle radish, which tastes about as *daikon* does; and even, but rarely, the leaves of Japan's national flower, the chrysanthemum.

Korea lies between China and Japan gastronomically as well as geographically, but unlike them has taken chilies to its bosom, producing dishes much hotter than either of its neighbors. Like them also, it makes heavy use of the soybean; its fermented *hamanatto* is exported to Japan, where it is more popular than that country's own *nat-to.* Its seasoners are much like those of its neighbors—bean sprouts, sesame seeds, nuts—and in addition one peculiar to itself: *insam,* which resembles ginseng.

This Mongolian family *(above),* seated on the hut floor to dine, has reached dessert: sugar-sweet ginger-hot cakes and candy.

A Japanese family *(above left)* enjoys its Sunday dinner. Beside the rice bowls, others hold soybean sauce and other favorite seasoning dips.

Singapore cooking, called *nonya,* is a blend of Indian, Indonesian, Malysian, and Chinese influences, producing a rich variety of dishes which make choice difficult. So sidewalk restaurants parade push-carts loaded with fragrant steaming foods before the customer, who composes his menu from these samples. His dinner is prepared from the dishes he has chosen.

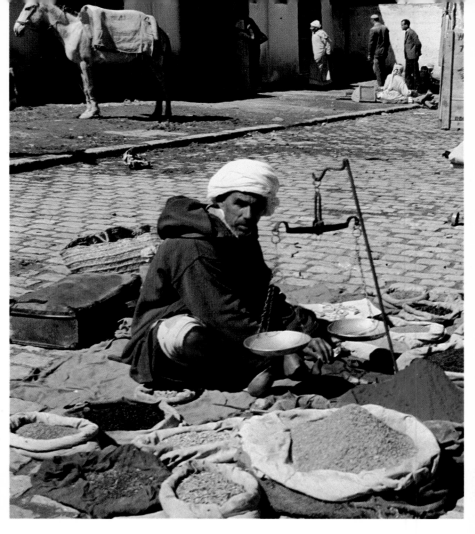

The Byzantine culinary zone starts in Iran, blankets the Middle East, throws out a northern branch to Romania and a southern one, mingled with Arab "tent cooking" through North Africa to Morocco *(map, opposite page)*.

Right: A spice seller in Rissani, capital of Tafilet, Morocco, runs a small-scale business, but with large-scale scales.

Opposite page, above:
The Bedouins, guardians of ancient culinary traditions, are famous for their hospitality. When they offer mint tea to their guests, they prepare it according to a time-honored ritual, which presents it three times, made each time in a different fashion. If they serve coffee instead, it is sweetened, not with sugar, but with cardamom.

Opposite page below: A typical Athenian taverna. The words on its corner (next to inn sign) read: "Bacchus Street."

A market in Mersin, on the southern coast of Turkey. Among its merchandise would be powdered sumac leaves, which would startle Americans, who think sumac poisonous: however, this is not the New World genus *Toxicodendron*, but the Old World *Rhus coriaria*. Either a condiment or a vegetable is *malukhiyah*, a viscous spinach-like plant used to thicken soups, like okra.

HEIRS OF BYZANTIUM

In the year of the Hegira 623 (A.D. 1226), Chamseddine Mohamed ben el Hassan el Baghdadi offered in his cookbook, *Kitab el-Tabih,* 159 recipes for "meats, poultry, fish, vegetables, dairy products, and sweets, seasoned with a variety of aromatic herbs, such as coriander leaves, parsley, mint, pennyroyal, fennel, rue, serpolet, dill, thyme, and bay leaf, and with exotic spices from China, the Islands of the Sound, the Indies, and East Africa: saffron, coriander, cumin, pepper, ginger, cinnamon, cloves, cardamom, mace, betel, musk, nutmeg, camphor, and hyacinth. He perfumed his dishes also with rosewater and orange-flower water, with the bitter juice of the sumac and of pomegranates, and with the tears of mastic gum. He also used lemon, vinegar, and honey. He mixed fruit and meat, the sweet and the sour, and sesame seeds, dates, grapes, and dried apricots, pistachios and all kinds of nuts." Add to this two other seasoners which became available only with the discovery of America, allspice and chili pepper, and this is a nearly complete list of the seasoners used today in what we might call, for want of a better name, Byzantine cooking, for it comes down to us from the heavily flavored food of Assyria and Babylonia through the Byzantine and Ottoman empires.

Despite their possession of an almost unlimited number of herbs, many of them sharp, and spices, many of them hot, the peoples of the Middle East have developed a seasoning essentially cool. Green herbs, aromatic and basically refreshing, but sometimes considered strong by Westerners because of their unfamiliarity, dominate the pungent spices, with an occasional exception like that of the Yemenites who brought back a hotly spiced cuisine from

164

southwestern Arabia when they returned to Israel after an exile which had lasted 2,500 years. Thus garlic, though common, is used with discretion, least so perhaps in Greece (where it probably arrived from the north, not the east) and Lebanon, the Middle Eastern country most altered by foreign influences; but even there it is eaten almost only fresh, when it is not as strong as after it has been dried. Iran considers it vulgar. As for the stinging chili peppers imported from America, they are most indispensable to the cooking of Bulgaria, on the fringe of this culinary area. Bulgarian cooking is spicier than that of its neighbor, Romania, whose cuisine is dominated by a local herb, *ciubritsa,* which resembles tarragon.

Though Middle East seasoning is not violent, it is complicated. A clue to the attitude toward flavoring is to be found in the fish recipes in Lebanese cookbooks, which describe in detail the herbs and spices which should go into each dish, but commonly begin "Take a five-pound fish," without bothering to specify what kind of fish should be used; obviously the seasoning is more important than what Westerners

the mouth-twisting quince, pomegranate juice and seeds, the grated rind of tamarind, which adds a sour taste, and citrus fruits, of which limes and lemons undergo a transformation peculiar to this region: they are dried until they become black, as hard as rock (and almost weightless), and are put into stews, their rinds pierced with tiny holes to release their concentrated bitter acidity into the dish. The chief cooking fat

SEASONERS OF NEAR AND MIDDLE EAST

Almonds, Bulghur, Chilies, Ciubritsa ("tarragon"), Coriander (leaves), Dill, Fennel, Fenugreek, Gourds, Lemons (dried), Mastic, Mint, Pine nuts, Pistachio, Pomegranates (juice, seeds), Quince, Sumac, Tamarind, Tree wormwood

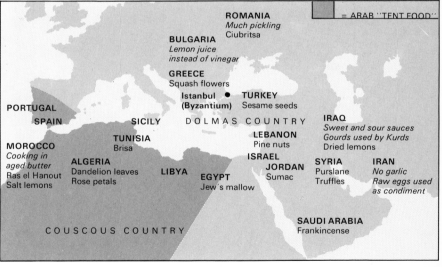

ROMANIA
Much pickling
Ciubritsa

= ARAB "TENT FOOD"

BULGARIA
Lemon juice instead of vinegar

GREECE
Squash flowers

PORTUGAL

Istanbul
(Byzantium)

TURKEY
Sesame seeds

SPAIN

SICILY

DOLMAS COUNTRY

IRAQ
Sweet and sour sauces Gourds used by Kurds Dried lemons

LEBANON
Pine nuts

MOROCCO
Cooking in aged butter
Ras el Hanout
Salt lemons

TUNISIA
Brisa

ISRAEL
JORDAN
Sumac

SYRIA
Purslane
Truffles

IRAN
No garlic Raw eggs used as condiment

ALGERIA
Dandelion leaves
Rose petals

LIBYA

EGYPT
Jew's mallow

SAUDI ARABIA
Frankincense

COUSCOUS COUNTRY

would consider the principal ingredient; the function of the fish is to carry the seasoners. Among familiar herbs, the favorites are dill, mint (especially pennyroyal), coriander leaves, fennel, and fenugreek. The most used nuts, often powdered or broken into small bits for seasoning purposes, are first of all the pine nut, followed by pistachios, almonds, and walnuts. Much use is made of

is olive oil, except where Bedouin influence is strong, when it becomes mutton fat.

To the more or less familiar condiments the Middle East adds a few of its own. Dried sumac leaves, particularly popular in Jordan, give a sour woodsy taste to the dishes in which they are used. *Shaybah* ("old man") is a dried curled grayish leaf, in English tree wormwood. A leaf used fresh is *kurrath,* which is chopped fine for seasoning, like

SEASONERS OF NORTH AFRICA

Coriander (leaves), Cumin, Dandelion leaves, Garlic, Jew's mallow, Jute, Lemons, Salt, Onions, Ras el Hanout, Saffron.

chives, and indeed belongs to the same family. Jew's mallow, a sort of jute, apparently acquired its name in Syria, for it was Jews who cultivated it there; jute proper is eaten in Egypt. The licorice-like flavor of mastic, which oozes from the lentisk tree and is sold in the form of small, irregularly shaped pebbles, is appreciated throughout the region. *Habbah sawda* is called in English black caraway, but is probably nigella. *Mahlab* is a condiment made from black cherry kernels, which gives a fruity flavor to bread. Grains of wheat are converted into a seasoner by being boiled, dried, and cracked into small bits; they are eaten almost everywhere in the Middle East under one form or another of the name "bulghur." You may class as a seasoner, if you wish, a food dear to Yemenites—baked desert locusts.

A few local specialties: Iran, the Kurdish condiment of gourd cooked in syrup sprinkled with chopped walnuts and cinnamon. Greece, its well-known egg and lemon sauce, *avgolemono;* its equally well-known carp roe, *taramosalata,* which becomes a dip when beaten into lemon juice and olive oil, with grated onion or garlic optional; its less well-known heavy garlic sauce, *skordalia,* in which the garlic is abetted by olive oil, lemon juice, sometimes walnuts or almonds, and, improbably, mashed potatoes; and its *vlita,* mustard-flavored greens with olive oil, thyme, and much garlic. Syria, purslane, not a strange plant, but this seems to be the only place where it is used in the Middle East.

Egyptians like their food spicy, in revolt perhaps against the uninspiring nature of the beans which in various guises constitute a large part of their diet. We are now in Africa, not only geographically, but also gastronomically, for it is here that we first meet with the most widespread dish of North Africa, couscous. It is comparatively rare in Egypt, and sometimes sweet, but the usual version is seasoned with brown gravy containing onions, fresh coriander leaves, and gum mastic. This is restrained flavoring for couscous, a dish which welcomes vivid seasoning. In the rest of North Africa it gets it.

Couscous is a dish of unlimited versatility —a versatility achieved almost solely by its seasoning. Basically it is steamed semolina, cooked in a pair of pots. The grain is in the upper pot, whose bottom is pierced with

small holes to permit the passage of vapor from the bouillon boiling in the bottom one. Tunisia, Algeria, and Morocco, have each their own type of couscous; within them are sub-types for their Arab, Berber, and Jewish ethnes, and within these, sub-sub-types which correspond to different localities or tribes. The most important factor which differentiates one from another is the seasoning, applied at four stages. The semolina acquires its first flavoring from the steam rising from the bottom pot, whose contents vary with the wealth of the cook. If he is poor, it will be a bouillon of vegetables, enlivened, according to his means, with parsley, coriander, raisins, saffron, marrow, and much black and red pepper. If

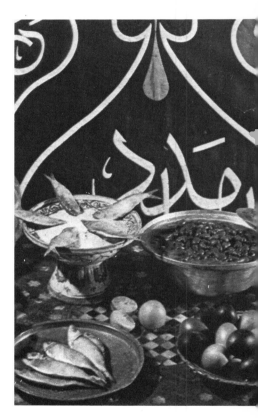

he is well-to-do there will be meat in the pot, most likely chicken or mutton. The second seasoning occurs when, after the cooking, some of the bouillon is poured over the grain, which dowers it with a pronounced flavor when, as in Tunisia, it is given heightened spicing with *brisa,* a condiment made of crushed dried hot red peppers, cumin, and salt. The third seasoning is then often added by pouring also over the semolina a thin hot sauce which gives further fire to the whole. The fourth seasoning consists of little sauces of varicolored highly spiced pastes offered as side dishes; some of them are so hot that nobody dares put them directly on the couscous. Instead a large tablespoon is filled with the bouillon and a minute amount of one or the other of these condiments is dissolved in it. Its sting thus adulterated, it may be added safely to the dish.

Couscous is purely Arab, the most characteristic dish of the nomad cuisine whose very name translates as "tent food." The variety of foods which can be conveniently carried on the march is limited. To relieve the monotony of the diet, much use is made of herbs and spices, whose small compass and minimum perishability, once they have been dried, makes them eminently portable. The result is often hot, but can on occasion be extremely subtle, with delicate blends of many herbs often perceived initially as unpleasant by Western palates, but this is a function of their unfamiliarity. They gain on longer acquaintance.

The marriage of rustic nomad Arab food with the sophisticated Byzantine cuisine reached its zenith in Morocco, where Islam established itself at the period when Arab culture had attained its highest level—in philosophy, in mathematics, in medicine, and in gastronomy. Morocco is the home of *ras el hanout,* which means "head of the shop," the best thing it has to sell. It is a blend of some thirty herbs and spices which has the reputation of being aphrodisiac, as it ought to be if it is true that one of them is cantharides. Legend has it that its formula is a secret of the spice merchants of Fez, but many of its constituents are generally known, among them ginger, cinnamon, black pepper, red pepper—and rosebuds!

Morocco is also the capital of the various dishes made from the fine many-layered pastry which was the invention of the Saracens—*brik,* a raw egg enveloped in a turnover, a trap for unwary eaters, and *bastilla,* in which pigeon is the most important of the several ingredients tucked into the pastry leaves. These dishes are elaborately flavored. Moroccan *bastilla* is apt to contain parsley, coriander, ginger, turmeric, cumin, and onions, with perhaps a little saffron as well; before serving, it is sprinkled with chopped almonds, cinnamon, and sugar. A third Moroccan contribution is *msir,* the

celebrated salt lemon. Preserved in brine, it is the North African counterpart of the dried lemon (or lime) of the Middle East, but it is more subtle. Half a lemon in a stew will flavor it more elegantly than salt.

North Africa favors both garlic and onion in its cooking, and makes lavish use of black and red pepper. Many of its dishes are elaborately, not to say extravagantly, seasoned. Snails, for instance, appear in a sauce which contains green anise seeds, caraway, licorice, thyme, green tea, sage, mint, bitter orange rind, sweet marjoram, hot red pepper, and gum arabic. Desserts are surprising and ingenious too. The Algerian cake called *ybba* is made of flour, olive oil, honey rose petals, and dandelion leaves. Dates are stuffed with a paste of pistachio nuts flavored with rose water.

The most used spices of North Africa include cumin and coriander seeds, the most used herbs coriander leaves and, of course, mint, which, as a flavorer of tea, gives rise to the ceremonious successive presentation of three different types of mint tea. It is a pleasant custom, but it is declining, because of the high cost of both mint and tea.

The name of the dish of bouillon, semolina, meat, and vegetables eaten everywhere in North Africa, *couscous,* is supposed to mimic the noise of steam hissing between the top and bottom sections of the sort of double-boiler in which it is cooked. There are spoons on the table at this couscous feast in Nuqub, but they are for serving. The correct way to eat couscous is to pick up a raisin or a chick pea in the right hand, use it as a kernel around which to roll a little ball of semolina, and pop it into the mouth with the fingers.

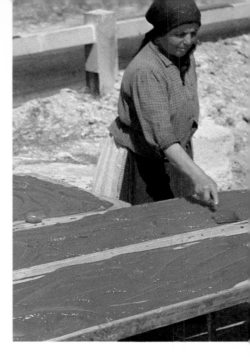

European seasoning has been tamed and modernized since the days when the Gauls doted on a sauce of honey, mint, and resin; but it is still based on ancient traditions. Side by side with modern factories, one finds old practices still honored by observance, as when olive oil is pressed from the fruit in Portugal or Spain by the same methods used 2,000 years ago.

Right: Time-tested ancient methods for preparing tomato extract are still used in Italy's Campania; but modern equipment produces the famous *concentrato, doppio concentrato,* and even *triplo concentrato* of Fidenza in Emilia-Romagna.

In one of the exotic outer zones of Europe, Sicily, a spice dealer *(facing page, bottom)* vends his wares from a gaily painted cart decorated, traditionally, with scenes from the legend of Charlemagne's Paladin, Roland.

Italian cooking is individualistic almost to the point of anarchy. Its diversity is such that no single seasoner can be cited as characteristic of Italy as a whole; yet Italy as a whole is characterized by great skill in the art of seasoning. This is a function of the kind of foods Italy eats, foods of which the principal characteristic seems to be that they are designed to serve as a background for flavoring. The universal pasta acquires its character from its stuffing or its sauce; the almost as universal *risotto* looks to condiments to lend it an interest which rice unadorned fails to inspire; and even the favorite meat of Italy is the most bland, the one which lends itself with least resistance

The menu for this wedding banquet in a Swiss restaurant is not given, but it should include Bündnerfleisch, paper-thin slices of dark-red beef, spiced, marinated in brine, and then cured for months in the pure mountain air of the Alps.

to the intrusion of other savors than its own—veal.

The finesse with which Italians apply tastiness to such foods is achieved with relatively conservative means. In her *Italian Food,* Elizabeth David describes the contents of "the

Italian store cupboard" as (among herbs) sweet basil, sweet marjoram, wild marjoram (another name for oregano), sage, thyme, mint (especially peppermint), rosemary, fennel (roots and seeds), celery, parsley, bay leaves, myrtle, borage, and juniper, and (among spices) nutmeg, cloves, cinnamon, vanilla, coriander seeds, saffron, black pepper (preferably freshly ground at the table; red pepper is not mentioned), and salt (preferably sea salt, of which there is no lack in Italy). Among other seasoners she lists garlic ("It is a mistake to suppose that all Italian food is heavily garlic-flavored"), but neither onions nor shallots; anchovies; dried mushrooms; pine nuts; white truffles (Umbria has excellent black ones); tomato paste; Parmesan cheese, of course; and also of course, olive oil.

The individualism which deprives Italy of any single characteristic flavoring bestows instead typical types of seasoning on its different regions, and even on single cities. Strangely enough, the two cities which were the greatest traders in Oriental spices after the Crusades, Venice and Genoa, make the most moderate use of them today. The city of Venice is content with its *salsa veneta,* of flour, butter, egg yolks, lemon juice, wine vinegar, minced onions, and cooked strained spinach, but some localities in its hinterland allow themselves somewhat more latitude: they use *pevara,* a pepper sauce to which cinnamon and cloves are added in Treviso. Vicenza bastes roast turkey with pomegranate juice, and Padua is wildly eccentric: the three condiments which are its trademarks are squash flowers, marrow, and cockscombs. As for Genoa, and its province of Liguria, "the most salient feature of Ligurian cooking is a presence—of aromatic herbs. Its second most important characteristic is an absence—of spices." The perfume of Genoa is basil. It is grown on every windowsill and is the soul of *pesto,* Genoa's famous sauce, in which it is combined with two kinds of cheese, garlic, and usually pine nuts—one of the three Genoa prefers, along with walnuts and hazelnuts. (A recipe for *pesto* appears on page 140.) Genoese ravioli has borage in its stuffing; the city uses bay leaves, oregano, sweet marjoram, fennel, mint, sage, rosemary, parsley, and wood mushrooms grown in Liguria, and it imports capers.

For the rest, it may be said that Italian taste favors herbs over spices, except in sausages; but the country follows what seems to be a general rule in the northern hemisphere: its seasoning is hottest in the south and becomes progressively cooler as one moves northward. On this principle, Sicily ought to use the most violent seasoners of Italy, but Sicily is a special case: its history has been largely non-Italian. It owes to the sweet tooth of the Saracens, who once ruled it, a penchant for the sort of spices which accord with sweetness—cinnamon, nutmeg, anise, and pistachio—and it is nontypical in its use of such condiments as sesame seeds, squash seeds, and the edible pods of the carob. Sicilian flavoring is assertive rather than hot; it is just across from it on the mainland that the most explosive foods are found. Almost all the dishes of the Basilicata are hot with pepper, and ginger is so ubiquitous in Calabria that its presence is taken for granted even when it is not named: a "strong" dish there is understood as one dominated by ginger.

In Apulia we are almost as far south, but there is more subtlety, as in the reputed preserved figs of Bari, stuffed with bay leaf, fennel seeds, and almonds. However, Apulia can go off the deep end on occasion; usually it prefers onions to garlic, but in its *spaghetti alla zappatora* it uses much chopped garlic along with the tiniest hottest red chilies it can find. We may doubt that this form of pasta enjoys much social standing: its name means "ditch diggers' spaghetti." The food of the Abruzzi is still hot. Wild thyme, which develops particular pungency in the higher altitudes of this region, is preferred to cultivated thyme, and locally grown poppy seeds and saffron are used extensively. Red pepper goes into soups, and the typical Abruzzi sausage, called crazy liver or alternatively *diavoletto,* devilish, owes the second name to its fiery spicing. Naples is the capital of garlic and flavors its pizza with oregano instead of the milder marjoram. Off the coast lies Sardinia, whose dominant flavorer is myrtle, backed up by borage, saffron, and mastic gum from the lentisk tree.

NOTABLE SEASONERS OF
EUROPEAN COUNTRIES

Spain-Portugal
Almonds, Chilies, Chocolate,
Coriander (leaves),
Cumin (native),
Olive oil (strong),
Turmeric, Vanilla

Italy
Borage (Genoa),
Cockscombs (Padua),
Ginger (south),
Marrow (Padua),
Mastic (Sardinia),
Myrtle (Sardinia),
Parmesan cheese,
Pomegranate juice,
Squash (flowers, seeds),
Truffles (white, black),
Vinegar of Modena

The north begins with Rome, which dislikes garlic; its own characteristic seasoner is wild mint. In Italy, Rome alone eats the potherb named *misticanza,* though it is not unknown in England, where it is called rockets. The capital also likes pine nuts and rosemary (which flavors its Easter specialty of milk-fed lamb), but this herb is more characteristic of Florence, where it flavors roast pork. One honored Florentine dish,

France
Bouquet garni, Caraway (Alsace),
Juniper (Alsace),
Truffles (black),
Verjuice (Touraine)

Germany
Anchovies, Hops, Juniper,
Peppercorns, Poppy seeds

Hungary
Lard, Liptauer cheese,
Paprika, Sour cream

Ever since the first chilies were brought to Europe by Spanish discoverers, Spain has made lavish use of them. At Campo Murciano, on the Mediterranean coast south of Valencia, whole acres are covered by chilies drying in the sun.

Perhaps no country in Europe is more sensitive to seasoners than Italy. Each region possesses its own special favorites.

PIEDMONT
White truffles **Padua**
Milan   Marrow   **Venice**
Saffron   • Salsa Veneta
• **Modena**• **Bologna**
Genoa Herb vinegar Ragú
Pesto   **Florence** NORTHERN
Basil   Fennel   COOKING
Borage   Rosemary
Pine nuts
Perugia •
Black truffles   Saffron
Rome •   Wild thyme
Dislikes garlic Poppy seeds
Wild mint   SOUTHERN
Rockets   COOKING
SARDINIA   • **Naples** Onions
Myrtle   Garlic   Fennel
Borage   Oregano   Bay leaves
Mastic   Almonds
Saffron
        SICILY
        Nutmeg   Ginger
        Anise   Citrus fruits
        Pistachio
        Sesame
        Carob
        Citrus fruits

pollo alla diavola, takes its name from the hot ginger sauce with which it is served, but this is uncharacteristic of Florence and of Tuscany, where the cuisine is sober.

One is tempted to describe the seasoning of the rest of northern Italy as dominated by the two M's—Modena and Milan. Though Modena has competition in its own region of Emilia-Romagna from the area which produces the commonest condiment of Italy, the Parmesan cheese which, grated, goes onto pasta and into minestrone, and from Bologna, whose *ragù* (chopped meat, tomato, parsley, marjoram, nutmeg) is a remarkable sauce for *tagliatelle,* it can still claim to cover the widest gamut in its flavoring. The griddle cake called *crescentina* is given the subtlest of seasonings by being fried between two chestnut leaves, the pig's foot sausage called *zampone* is given one of the strongest with its spicing of nutmeg, cinnamon, cloves, salt, and pepper. It is Modena also which makes the finest vinegar of Italy, *aceto balsamico,* herb-flavored to begin with, and then aged in a process during which it passes successively through a series of twelve barrels, each of which communicates to it some of the taste of the wood of which it is made—oak, chestnut, mulberry, juniper, etc.

A trademark of Milan is a dish, or more exactly a combination of two dishes, whose fame has spread around the world—*osso buco* accompanied by *risotto alla milanese.* The veal shank which is *osso buco* is distinguished by its gremolada sauce, flavored with parsley, rosemary, sage, garlic, crushed

anchovy, and grated lemon peel, to which some cooks add carrot, celery, and sweet marjoram. The Milanese rice is rich with saffron.

The diversity of Italian seasoning is endless, but let us stop with Piedmont, which uses more garlic than other parts of Italy. Its characteristic condiment is *bagna calda,* a hot dip for cold vegetables. It is composed of butter and olive oil mixed, much garlic, and thinly sliced white truffles, found almost nowhere else.

A country of which large parts were governed for eight centuries by the Moors might be expected to indulge in high heady spicing; Spain is on the contrary almost ascetic in its seasoning.

The list of Spanish herbs and spices is not long. Cloves and cumin (the latter native to Spain) are used sparingly. Among the herbs besides parsley, one finds occasionally a probable heritage from the Moors, mint (in the mint-flavored rice of Estremadura), tarragon (in Seville salads), bay leaves (in the tiny oyster-like *ostiones* of Cadiz), and in the Pyrenees, wild thyme and rosemary. Aragon, which uses more garlic than its neighbor, Castille, whose food is classic and sober, eats what seems like a dubious combination—calves' tongue with chocolate. Of the foods they found in America, Spaniards have adopted, besides chocolate, the tomato, whose ubiquity in sauces has perhaps also helped to discourage the development of other condiments, and chilies, which provide the heat for that spiciest of Spanish products, the fiery red *chorizo* sausage. Garlic is found everywhere in Spain, even in Castille, which usually prefers onions, in the comparatively mild form of one version or another of *sopa de ajo,* garlic soup.

The most used eastern spices are cinnamon, which is combined with chocolate, and saffron, which is combined with rice in the ubiquitous *paella.* Even the Spanish onion is sweet and bland.

The best-known gastronomic trademark of the Basques is *piperade,* the sauce which derives its very name from "pepper," but it is made with mild sweet peppers. Catalonia is more receptive to heat. It uses a great deal of garlic, and with many foods places on the table two bowls of sauce, of which one contains *ali-oli* ("garlic-oil"), and the other the sharp reddish-brown *romesco,* redolent of hot chili pepper. Nevertheless a Catalan saying maintains that *"la cocina catalana no admite trampas en lo cocina,"* which means that the region frowns on disguising the natural flavor of foods beneath an overlay of heavy seasoning.

The Portuguese, who, after all, were among the first to ferry Oriental spices to the West, are more receptive to exotic florid seasoners than Spaniards. The great days of Vasco da Gama have dowered southern Portugal, the Algarve, with curries redolent of turmeric, a spice little used elsewhere in Europe; the Algarve also grows large quantities of almonds, much used to flavor Portuguese dishes. From the other half of the world, Portugal acquired vanilla, much more favored here than in Spain, though it was the Spanish who met it first in Mexico. The New World is also represented on Portuguese tables by a porcelain jug containing a dark-red sauce made of olive oil and hot chilies, *piri-piri*.

Portugal's favorite herb is coriander, much grown in the province of Alentejo, used chiefly in the form of its fresh green leaves. Mint, bay leaf, cumin, and black pepper are also common; lemon juice is often applied to meat.

The cooking of southern Europe has oozed into southern France across frontiers which in any case have not always been in the same place. The *pesto* of Genoa is the *pistou* of Nice, both animated by fresh basil, but the French sauce is not as sharp as its Italian cousin. At the other extremity *piperade* is as characteristic of the French Basque country as of the Spanish Basque country, and the

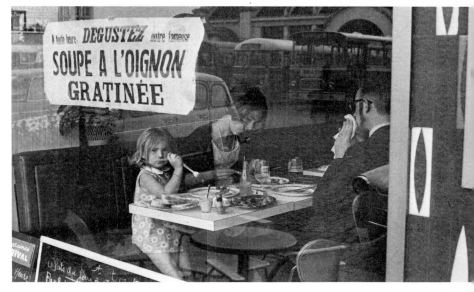

Catalan *ali-oli* is the southern French *aillioli*—the garlic mayonnaise which is called "the butter of Provence." Contrary to an impression which is general in America, garlic is not a trademark of French cooking in general, it is a regional phenomenon which characterizes the cooking of that part of France which once spoke the *langue d'oc*. There are not many exceptions to this rule—snails with Burgundian snail butter, for instance, or the slivers of garlic thrust into slits cut into a leg of lamb. Also typical of southern French cooking is skillful use of the wild herbs which are never so flavorful as when they grow in the higher altitudes of Provence or in the brush of Corsica.

Like the rest of Europe, France plunged into an orgy of heavy spicing after the Crusades; an almost universal condiment was cameline sauce, made of ginger, cinnamon, cloves, nutmeg, and vinegar. A revulsion against this tendency began with the advent of the *paquet*—chives, thyme, chervil, parsley, and only one hot spice (a single clove) wrapped up together in a strip of fat, placed as a whole in a dish to provide all the flavoring it was felt to need. Its modern descendant is the *bouquet garni,* the little bunch of herbs (parsley, thyme, and bay leaf is a common combination) which flavors many dishes with characteristic moderation.

Most of the survivors from the days of high seasoning are local. Saffron has almost disappeared except in the *bouillabaisse* of Marseilles (a southern phenomenon again). The acid verjuice pressed from green grapes, so

When is the onion a vegetable, when is it a condiment? It is a little of both if, as shown above, it appears in French onion soup, with a flavorful crust of melted cheese floating on top. It assumes the aspect of a festive dish in Paris, for there it is exotic: it was originally Alsatian.

An optimistic painting on the side of a Portuguese fishing boat shows two fishermen carrying between them a fish of a size becoming in-

creasingly rare. The Portuguese are particularly devoted to cod, which they claim they can prepare in 365 different ways (are they keeping one in reserve for leap year?). The secret of this versatility lies in varied seasonings.

Left: The Italian-speaking part of Switzerland likes Italian cooking, so Ascona, on Lake Maggiore, holds a festival in honor of risotto—a dish whose chief raison d'être is to intensify the fragrant sweetness or pungent sharpness of herbs and spices.

The famous Alsatian sauerkraut *(above)* is seasoned with spicy juniper berries. Germany adds peppercorns, caraway, allspice, and bay.

Taking no chances on freshness or adulteration, a wary woman shopper *(below)* bends down to sniff the spices offered by a Moslem merchant in the marketplace of Sarajevo, Yugoslavia.

Everywhere in the world, Wiener Schnitzel (boned breaded veal scallop) is looked upon as a dish typically Austrian: it was adapted from Italy's *costaletta alla milanese* during the Austrian occupation of Lombardy.

widely used in medieval and Renaissance times, is making its last stand in the Touraine, which also defies much of the rest of northern France by combining fruit and meat (prunes with roast pork); French purists inveigh against such dishes as duck with orange or trout with almonds. Burgundy still uses the ancient *saupiquet* sauce, meaning that it is strongly seasoned, for this word *sau* (from the modern *sel,* salt) refers to a meaning of salt commoner in earlier times as standing for spices in general. The capital of Burgundy is also, of course, the capital of mustards, many of them herb-flavored. Local peculiarities stemming from a later period include the caraway (in bread and on cheese) and the juniper berries (in sauerkraut) which have seeped into Alsace from the east, and the extensive use of onions which is the trademark of a city with a high gastronomic reputation—Lyons.

As a rule, however, French cooking and French seasoning remain remarkably uniform throughout the whole region which extends northward from the Gironde. Hot spices are rare, herbs are familiar and reassuring—marjoram, savory, tarragon, parsley, thyme, chervil, chives, and occasionally sage (one must look to the south for oregano, basil, and fennel). Salads are soberly seasoned with the classic French dressing of olive oil, vinegar (or lemon juice), salt, and pepper, often enlivened with chopped aromatic herbs. Sausages, the last refuge of spiciness in some countries, are as a rule mildly flavored in France, but fairly high seasoning remains in stuffings for poultry or meat (in breast of veal, for instance). On the whole, French flavoring, unobtrusive and thoughtfully employed, might be described as the seasoning of sanity.

"The Germanic peoples…had no real contribution to make to the art of cookery," wrote Richard Barber in *Cooking and Recipes from Rome to the Renaissance,* which makes short shrift of ham, bacon, and sausage. "German cooking is distinguished by its colossal character," Georges and Germaine Blond remarked in their *Histoire pittoresque de notre alimentation,* by which they seem to have meant that it is excessive in quantity and in kind. This might well be a result of Germany's climate, which, despite its two openings to the sea, is basically continental; continental climates call for hearty rather than for subtle foods. Germany's favorite foods are unlikely to encourage sensi-

tivity to fine nuances in seasoning: rye bread, particularly in northern Germany (consider the nature of pumpernickel); herring, fresh, smoked, dried and pickled (the runner-up in the fish category is probably smoked eel); cabbage and potatoes (the Germans were the first Europeans to accept the potato whole-heartedly in the late sixteenth century when almost everybody else was afraid to eat it); and beer in soups and stews. Consistently, German seasoners tend to be those with a sledgehammer effect.

The commonest is perhaps horseradish, eaten preferably fresh and grated. Caraway is frequently used; for one thing, it marries well with rye bread. A favorite condiment is the salty fillet of anchovy; the favorite herb is perhaps the sourish dill. Others which turn up often include marjoram (in dumplings), bay leaves, and savory, while hops are sometimes also eaten as an herb.

The favorite spices include mustard, capers, whole black peppercorns, poppy seeds (especially in Silesia), and juniper berries.

A country like Germany, once a mosaic of many small states each with its own peculiarities, must necessarily show many local differences in seasoning preferences. The trademark of Munich is *Radi,* salted white radish served sliced paper-thin; another Munich specialty, *Leberkäs,* which despite its name contains neither liver nor cheese, is a meat loaf of finely ground beef, pork, and bacon flavored with onion, marjoram, and nutmeg, as well as pepper and salt. Northern Bavaria makes a marjoram-flavored pork sausage, *Schweinswürstl.* In the Rhineland, pheasant is cooked with a stuffing which includes mushrooms, onions, chervil, parsley, tarragon, and grated lemon rind. In Baden salads are enlivened with dandelion greens, sorrel, watercress, and chervil. Frankfurt seems particularly receptive to herbs: one of its specialties is chervil soup, but its most characteristic contribution to condiments is its green herb sauce. Pomerania's black sauce is made from goose blood, vinegar, flour or groats, salt, nutmeg, cloves—and sugar.

One might be tempted to consider Austrian seasonings as relatively simple, if one happened to make contact with its cooking first through one of its two most characteristic dishes, *Backhendl,* fried chicken, often served with no other condiment than a slice of lemon, or, in a more orgiastic mood, with fried parsley. This is an opinion which would have to change on acquaintance with the other characteristic dish, *Tafelspitz,* boiled beef: it comes with grated horseradish mixed with vinegar, or applesauce, or whipped cream (!), plus one cold sauce (of chives, gherkins, or anchovies) and one hot sauce (of dill, tomato, mushrooms, onions, or cucumber). A seasoning not much found elsewhere is pumpkinseed oil, used in salads. This is a specialty of Styria, which has a number of ideas of its own, including capon stuffed with its own liver, stale bread, rosemary, parsley, marjoram, and pepper—a dish attributed, it is true, to the influence of Yugoslavia. Austria shares with Germany a predilection for onions, especially liked in the Tyrol, Italian as well as Austrian (but Austria uses a little more garlic than Germany does), wild mushrooms, marjoram, dill, savory, black peppercorns, caraway, and horseradish. Austrian roast pork with caraway seeds, garlic, and mustard, or alternatively with horseradish, seems to be of Bohemian origin, also exemplified by the version of the spicy Czech sausage served, with mustard, in Vienna, though there its heat is toned down.

Polish practice may have contributed to a use of marjoram in Austria even more extensive than in Germany. Yugoslavia has exercised considerable influence on Aus-

trian seasoning too, though it is often difficult to pin down, since Yugoslavian flavoring is in itself difficult to describe, because of its five principal ethnes, to say nothing of the effect of the long Venetian presence on the Dalmatian coast. It may be noted, at least, that Yugoslav food is basically peasant; strongly spiced meats are placed on the table backed up with relishes of chopped onion and small green peppers.

The country which contributed the most flavor to the cooking of the Austro-Hungarian Empire was probably Hungary; one thinks at once of paprika: modern Hungarian cooking is indeed based on paprika, lard, and onions. There is also a lavish use of sour cream as a condiment, and it may be that Liptauer cheese, though its name is German and its range covers much of Central Europe, is a Hungarian invention. This is not, traditionally, as many persons assume, a single separate cheese served ready to be

popped into the mouth. It might instead be described as a dish composed entirely of condiments, accompanied by just enough cream cheese to serve as the glue to hold them together. An order for Liptauer cheese brings to the table a host of small saucers, containing, respectively, the cheese, butter, crushed anchovy, caraway seeds, mustard, paprika, capers, onions, and anything else which appeals to local fantasy. The diner then makes his own combination. Liptauer cheese is the *nec plus ultra* of seasoning.

What would Hungarian cooking be without paprika, which has become the national spice, though it is of American origin? The country's best is supposed to be grown in the neighborhood of Szeged, whose women are shown here threading the individual peppers into long strings. They will then be hung up against sun-caressed walls to dry, and sold eventually in the celebrated market of Kossuth Square.

SLAVIC AND SCANDINAVIAN SEASONING

FAVORITE SEASONERS OF NORTHERN EUROPE

Slavic

Angelica, Dill, Horseradish, Kliukvy ("cranberry"), Nettles, Onion (raw), Parsley, Persimmon, Pomegranate, Quince, Sunflower seeds, Vinegar

Scandinavian

Allspice, Bay leaf, Berries, Capers, Chives, Cinnamon, Cloves, Cumin, Dill, Ginger, Horseradish, Marjoram, Mushrooms, Mustard, Nutmeg, Nuts, Onion, Parsley, Pepper (black, white), Thyme, Vinegar (strong)

If you pass, in Central Europe, from the territory of Teutonic cooking into that of Slavic cooking, you may not immediately perceive a marked difference, even in flavoring, which is the most sensitively variable factor in food and the one most intimately responsive to the nuances of ethnic character. You will still be in the presence of two foods hardly consistent with subtlety in seasoning—rye bread, tolerant of few added tastes except poppy seed and caraway, and cabbage, the basis of one of the two national soups (one might almost say meals) of Russia, *shchi*; the other is borsch, based on beets, not very hospitable to delicate flavorings either.

taste, a small cranberry. As in Germany, mushroom fanciers comb the woods for wild fungi, which are often pickled or dried. Other foods which are gathered wild include various greens, onions, garlic, and nettles, to which the south adds mallow and sorrel. Only a few herbs are used, those which can be grown locally, like dill, parsley, and for sweet pastries, that native of the far north, angelica. The Ukraine is partial to sunflower seeds.

One has the impression that in the vast domain controlled directly or indirectly by the Soviet Union, flavor is concentrated on the fringes and becomes progressively fainter as you move into the interior, until on the steppes of Central Asia taste has only minimum interest for peoples who eat much as their nomadic ancestors did, with a diet dominated by yoghurt and *koumiss* (fermented mares' milk). However, a good deal of onion is consumed in the center; after all, this is thought to be the area where the onion originated.

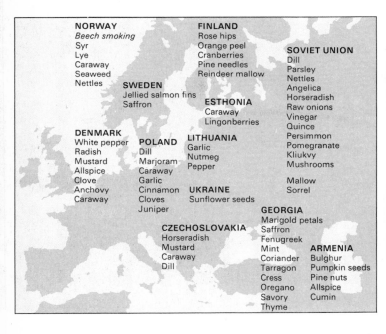

NORWAY
Beech smoking
Syr
Lye
Caraway
Seaweed
Nettles

SWEDEN
Jellied salmon fins
Saffron

DENMARK
White pepper
Radish
Mustard
Allspice
Clove
Anchovy
Caraway

POLAND
Dill
Marjoram
Caraway
Garlic
Cinnamon
Cloves
Juniper

CZECHOSLOVAKIA
Horseradish
Mustard
Caraway
Dill

FINLAND
Rose hips
Orange peel
Cranberries
Pine needles
Reindeer mallow

ESTHONIA
Caraway
Lingonberries

LITHUANIA
Garlic
Nutmeg
Pepper

UKRAINE
Sunflower seeds

SOVIET UNION
Dill
Parsley
Nettles
Angelica
Horseradish
Raw onions
Vinegar
Quince
Persimmon
Pomegranate
Kliukvy
Mushrooms

Mallow
Sorrel

GEORGIA
Marigold petals
Saffron
Fenugreek
Mint
Coriander
Tarragon
Cress
Oregano
Savory
Thyme

ARMENIA
Bulghur
Pumpkin seeds
Pine nuts
Allspice
Cumin

Above right: Soviet Armenians near the city of Yerevan celebrate a wedding beside a laden table. Armenian food is highly spiced and garlicky.

As in Germany, onions, often eaten raw, are commoner than garlic. As in Germany, grated horseradish is a favorite condiment. As in Germany, many vegetables and fruits are pickled in vinegar, and as in Germany, when fruit is eaten fresh it often accompanies meat. The fruits are not always the same: Russia makes considerable use of quinces, persimmons, pomegranates, and *kliukvy*, which resembles, in looks and in

One of the most unexpected flavors crossed the southern border from Moslem territory—rose petals in jam. Soviet Armenia has imported eating habits acquired farther south. Armenian kebabs are hotly spiced, their beef sausages redolent of strong pepper, allspice, cinnamon, and cumin, their dry salted beef flavored with cumin. Armenians also use pumpkin seeds, pine nuts, and the cracked wheat (*bulghur*) of the Middle

East, and differ from Russians by eating a good deal of garlic. So do Georgians, who are also adventurous in their seasoning. They use a paste made from crushed walnuts as a basis for the region's two distinctive sauces, *satsivi* and *hazha*.

The dominant flavor of Polish cooking is dill, the country's most important herb. A favorite Polish condiment is a small sharp-tasting pickled purple plum flavored with cinnamon and cloves; the famous kielbasa sausage contains, at its mildest, caraway and garlic and is sometimes smoked over juniper wood.

The Baltic States in general are more receptive to garlic than Russia proper. Lithuania uses it in sausage, along with chopped parsley, black pepper, and nutmeg. Estonia's habit of serving lingonberries with stuffed cabbage is attributed to Swedish influence. Scandinavians have a predilection, probably inherited from their Viking ancestors, for flavors which are apt to strike non-Scandinavians as overpowering: *lutefisk,* cod cured in lye; *surströmming,* fermented sour Baltic herring, which when canned develops so much gas that the can bulges visibly and has to be opened with caution, like a champagne bottle; *syr,* milk which, after being kept for several months, develops a taste like exceptionally bitter vinegar and is indeed used as a vinegar substitute; *rakørret,* fermented trout which becomes so buttery that it is spread on bread and, according to

an unsympathetic observer, "smells like raw petroleum and tastes like strong cheese."

These extreme examples of the sturdiness of Scandinavian taste buds are honored especially in Norway and Sweden. Danish flavoring is blander, Finnish is more woodsy. Allspice seems to be the favorite exotic flavorer of the Scandinavians; cinnamon, nutmeg, and cloves are apt to be saved for desserts (Scandinavians go in heavily for sweets, except the Finns). Denmark, however, despite the fact that its cooking is not spicy, uses the strong clove as well as allspice, white pepper, and anchovy to season its calves' liver paste. It is less extreme when it cooks cabbage with caraway seeds (which Norway saves for sauerkraut).

Dill is the favorite Scandinavian herb. *Gravlax,* raw salmon, is cured with it, aided by white pepper and salt (and sometimes sugar as well!), and is customarily served with a sweet-and-sour mustard-dill sauce. The Finns, who make a rite of eating crawfish, cook them with fresh dill, including the flowers. Dill is one of the seasoners at the disposition of herring fanciers, whose skill at seasoning is given full play in their innumerable fashions of preparing this fish with countless combinations of dill, red or white vinegar (Scandinavian white vinegar is gaspingly acid), carrots, red and yellow onions in rings or slices, parsley, chives, bay leaves, capers, allspice, ginger, mustard (powdered, or in the form of crushed seeds), horseradish, black and white pepper (chili pepper does not seem to appeal to Scandinavians), and once more, sugar.

Scandinavian seasoning is mildest when it comes from the woods—nuts, several sorts of wild mushrooms (particularly prized in Finland), and fruit, especially berries. Although other fruits are used as condiments, for instance when the Swedish stuff goose with apples and prunes, berries are dominant. Long exposure to the sun during the northern summer makes them exceptionally flavorful and performs the same service for some herbs—thyme, for instance, is more zestful in Scandinavia. The berries most commonly used as flavorers in Scandinavia include the lingonberry, something like the American cranberry, but only one quarter as big; the honeyberry (like a tiny raspberry), the fruit of the Arctic bramble; the rowan berry (fruit of the mountain ash); and the orange-yellow cloudberry.

"Blessing of the Bread" at Easter outside an Orthodox Christian church in Moscow *(left)*. Some of the dark rye loaves must contain poppy or sesame seeds.

Sweden's famous smörgåsbord is presented here on a table 7.60 meters (25 feet) long, bearing more than 60 dishes—herring in every guise, eggs, fish, vegetables, cold cuts, and hot dishes like meatballs in gravy.

175

THE WORLD
OF THE ANGLO-SAXONS

America's major contribution to the culinary art, the hamburger, has now taken to the high seas—or at least, the Father of Waters—and its servitors have exchanged chef's garb for sailors' uniforms *(right)*. One of the great assets of the Big Mac is the spicy sauce served with it, whose ingredients are a house secret.

London: Rule's restaurant, since 1798 faithful to tradition, symbolized by the tightly rolled umbrella, the bowler hat, and, no doubt, roast mutton with mint sauce.

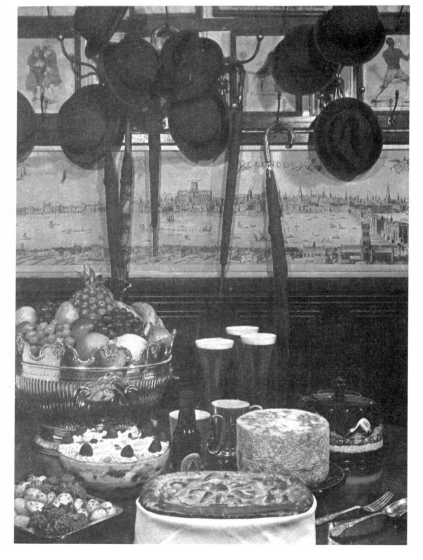

Americans and Britons are both descended, in the unsympathetic words of William Edward Mead *(The English Medieval Feast)*, from "men and women who were coarse-feeders, whose palates were dulled by sharp sauces, by spiced wines, and by peppers, mustard and ginger and cubebs and cardamom and cinnamon with which the most innocent meats and fruits were concocted." There is indeed a curious anomaly about the cooking of English-speaking countries, where food often described by foreigners as drab and tasteless coexists with violent seasoners, while in between there is almost nothing. Anglo-Saxon seasoning lacks a middle class.

The favorite foods of the British Isles are not such as encourage subtle seasoning, or indeed any seasoning at all more imaginative than salt and pepper. The prevailing cereal, wheat, does not inspire it, as does the rice of the Orient, while the oats of Scotland and the potatoes of Ireland are even worse. What the English cook best are roasts and chops, which allow little scope for seasoning. Usually they are gratified only with Worcestershire sauce or one of its fellows, which contain, but to a certain extent restrain, such pungent ingredients as anchovy essence, sharp vinegar, soybean sauce, garlic, and strong spices, or are accompanied by mustard or horseradish. If the meat happens to be lamb or mutton, it is flanked by mint sauce (sometimes caper sauce is substituted). The peppery mint is one of England's favorite herbs, added for instance to garden peas, which tend to be cowed by it. Shropshire and Yorkshire even put mint into sweet buns.

The average Briton is devoted to the two overwhelming seasoners at the sweet and bitter extremes of the taste scale—sugar and salt, which tend to blot out others. Observe him in a restaurant: he salts his food automatically without tasting it to find out whether it needs salting. His sugar consumption is 111 pounds (50 kilos) per person per year, compared to 99 pounds (45 kilos) for the United States, though Americans make excessive use of sugar also. Only three countries eat more; two of them belong to the British sphere of gastronomic influence, Australia and Ireland; Eire is the world's number-one consumer of sugar.

In addition to mint, herbs popular in the British Isles include savory, with beans; fennel or parsley, with fish; chives, in salads; and sage, to stuff roast leg of veal or, with onions, any kind of poultry. Fresh sage juice accounts for the green streak in Sage Derby cheese. One can only approve of the cooks who, in parts of England characterized by moors or heaths, use their juniper berries, cloudberries, and whortleberries to flavor game; but it is sad to see the delicate whitebait seasoned not only with lemon juice, but stunned with a sprinkling of cayenne pepper.

A few other herbs benefit from the promotion given them by localities where they are traditionally grown. Peppermint comes from Hertfordshire, chamomile from Lincolnshire, lavender from Norfolk, and licorice from Pontefract, Yorkshire, where it has been a specialty since 1562.

The British interest in spices, which had cooled after the Middle Ages (though there were some survivals, like the strongly flavored marigold flowers still found in stews in the Channel Islands), revived with the conquest of India; for a while sauces and stews were choked with coriander, turmeric, hot pepper, cumin, and cardamom. Then interest waned again, leaving as vestigial reminders curries, chutneys, and a few isolated dishes like the kedgeree eaten at breakfast. But these remain exotic borrowings which have never been integrated into British cooking and exert no influence on its basic nature. Spices subsist most commonly in pastry: Eccles and Banbury cakes (dried fruit and spices); the Bath bun (candied peel, caraway seeds, sometimes saffron); or barm brack, a raised bread served especially at Halloween (bits of fruit, nutmeg, cinnamon, cloves, and allspice). But the herb and spice content of meat pies, mincemeat, plum pudding, and the like has diminished. (However, the sweet biscuit-like parkin, of oatmeal and wheat flour, with a dosage of ginger and cinnamon which causes it to keep for weeks, improving as it ages, has not yet given up the ghost.)

Some hotly seasoned dishes remain from a more courageous past, with flavorings which strike us today as rather excessive: hot mustard in pickles; chilies in vinegar; potted shrimps with nutmeg, mace, and cayenne pepper; kipper paste with anchovy, cloves, mace, and cayenne pepper; dry spiced beef cured with salt, saltpeter, brown sugar, allspice, peppercorns, cloves, and juniper berries; or deviled beef bones with spicy sauce *and* Worcestershire sauce, mustard *and* curry powder, black pepper *and* cayenne pepper.

As for the future of the English cuisine, a contemporary French writer is hardly optimistic: "English cooking is becoming Americanized. It is falling from Charybdis

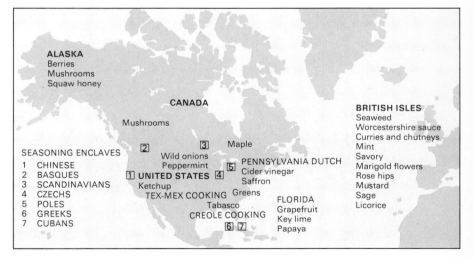

SEASONING ENCLAVES
1 CHINESE
2 BASQUES
3 SCANDINAVIANS
4 CZECHS
5 POLES
6 GREEKS
7 CUBANS

ALASKA
Berries
Mushrooms
Squaw honey

CANADA
Mushrooms

Maple
Wild onions
Peppermint
[1] UNITED STATES
Ketchup
TEX-MEX COOKING
Tabasco
CREOLE COOKING

PENNSYLVANIA DUTCH
Cider vinegar
Saffron
Greens

FLORIDA
Grapefruit
Key lime
Papaya

BRITISH ISLES
Seaweed
Worcestershire sauce
Curries and chutneys
Mint
Savory
Marigold flowers
Rose hips
Mustard
Sage
Licorice

into Scylla. It is not its renaissance that I can sing, but rather its requiem."

If this is true, Anglo-Saxon cooking is meeting itself coming back; for American cooking, including its seasoning, is based on English cooking. When the first English-speaking colonists arrived in North America, they picked up virtually nothing new from the Indians, except that Colonial

ANGLO-SAXON SEASONERS

British Isles
Capers, Chives, Cinnamon, Cloves, Fennel, Juniper, Licorice, Marigold flowers, Mint (esp. Peppermint), Mustard, Parsley, Rose hips, Sage, Salt (to excess), Savory, Sugar (to excess), Worcestershire sauce (and its fellows), Vinegar

United States—Canada
Chilies (southwest), Chocolate, Coconut, Greens (southeast), Ketchup, Maple syrup, Okra (south), Onions, Sage, Sugar (to excess), Tabasco, Vanilla

Health food stores represent a reaction against the adulteration of natural foodstuffs. Meanwhile, American "junk food," once eaten from the hand, often standing up, has become a national institution and been promoted in status *(below)*.

The nineteenth-century influx of immigrants dowered the United States with many enclaves of foreign cooking, often more sensitive to seasoning than are native Americans. In the photograph *(below right)* taken in a Wisconsin cornfield about 1895, a Scandinavian family displays its produce proudly.

housewives used maple sugar as often as salt for seasoning. (Today it has disappeared as a day-to-day spice, for maple sugar and maple syrup have become expensive luxuries.) They borrowed few flavorers from the Indians, but Negro slaves gave the South its "mess o' greens." Only a few favorite herbs were imported from England. Records of seventeenth-century gardens in Salem, Plymouth, and Charleston rarely list any except rosemary, coriander, and pennyroyal. Nevertheless these early Americans were fond of imported ginger: during the Revolution soldiers were issued regular rations of ginger, sugar, molasses, and rum—three of them condiments, or even all four, depending on what was done with the rum. After the war American cooking became spicier as American ships became faster. Their speed made Salem for half a century the world's leading port for spices, with a monopoly on Sumatra pepper, and a substantial interest in cinnamon, cassia, and cloves. The consequent stimulation of the taste buds no doubt contributed to increased demand for greater variety in herb gardens. One of their growers was Thomas Jefferson, who liked tansy pudding at breakfast, made from an herb which is now less often used. Mulligatawny soup, with its seasoning of turmeric, coriander, black pepper, and the western hemisphere's own cayenne pepper, was for a while a favorite American dish. Curries were relatively common, heavy doses of cloves went into sausage meat, and the

American housewife made in her own kitchen a large variety of sauces—with mint, with capers, with "nasturtians," with celery, with white onions or brown, with mushrooms or with anchovy.

The immigrant Pennsylvania Dutch brought with them a taste for lusty seasoning: their apple butter was spicier than that of New England, they used cider vinegar in their cooking for tartness, cloves went into scrapple, coriander and sage were popular, ham was smoked over hickory or sassafras wood, and by the accident that one of their families, the Schwenckfelders, had grown saffron in Germany, that plant was imported by them and planted on their land. The Pennsylvania Dutch taste for spiciness is still exemplified by their many relishes, of which "seven sweets and seven sours" are traditionally provided at important dinners.

The Shakers, of whom Charles Dickens wrote that they "are good farmers, and all their produce is eagerly purchased and highly esteemed," built up a business in herbs so important that they were at one time able to supply 350 different kinds of leaves, flowers, roots, barks, and seeds for culinary or medical purposes, while in their own cooking they made good use of chives, mint, chervil, rosemary, summer savory, borage, basil, sorrel, tarragon, and nutmeg. Their apple pies were flavored with rose water, their blue-flower omelets with chive blossoms. Before the Civil War, the United

States had reached the highest point of seasoning in its history.

But the military demand for unspoilable foods in forms easily handled gave a mighty fillip to the development of canning and meat processing. In the vulgarization and commercialization of flavor which followed, Americans lost their former appreciation of seasoning. Spices and herbs in the form of packaged powders failed to inspire the imagination or educate the taste buds. The American housewife accepted cassia and left cinnamon to Europeans, who recognized the difference in quality and were willing to pay for it. She used powdered or liquid vanilla substitutes while genuine vanilla beans, native to the New World, were shipped to the Old. Seasoning was reduced to its commonest elements—chives, onions (a recent recourse to garlic seems to have been more of a fad than a tribute), parsley and watercress used more for ornament than for taste, and sage in poultry stuffings. Native flavors—peppermint, wintergreen, beechnut, spruce—were abandoned to chewing gum. Subtle or assertive flavors had to be looked for in gastronomic enclaves of foreign inspiration—among the Chinese of the Pacific coast, the Spanish-Americans of Tex-Mex cooking, the Creoles of Louisiana, the Scandinavians and Poles near the Great Lakes. The French-Americans of New England contributed little, for the French who first settled Canada came mostly from Normandy, which

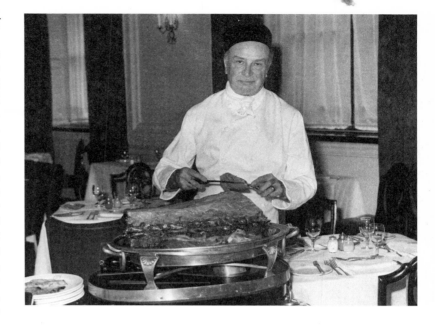

uses little seasoning even in France. British Canadians, like Americans, followed in the footsteps of the mother country. (So did Australians, willy-nilly, for they found no useful flavorers on their continent, except the macadamia nut and eucalyptus juice, used by the aborigines before the white man came, but not now.)

In 1975, in preparation for a projected joint operation by American and Russian astronauts and cosmonauts, they tasted each other's space foods. The Americans found the Russian food too spicy, the Russians found the American food too sweet.

London's most famous restaurant is probably Simpson's on the Strand. Simpson's most famous specialty is probably its roast beef. With it, horseradish or a spot of mustard.

Modern machine harvesting has not taken over everywhere in the United States. *Below:* Mexican migrant laborers use primitive methods to harvest onions in New Mexico.

Chili peppers everywhere are strung together and hung in the sun to dry. Such a string is being held up for the admiration of New Mexicans at Chimayo. Though individual peppers are light, this string weighed five pounds.

NATIVE SEASONERS OF LATIN AMERICA

Allspice, Cashew nut, Chilies, Chocolate, Peanuts, Squash (seeds, flowers), Vanilla

IMPORTED SEASONERS OF LATIN AMERICA

Almonds, Anise seeds, Bay leaf, Cinnamon, Cloves, Coriander (leaves, seeds), Garlic, Ginger, Lime juice, Malegueta pepper, Onions, Oregano, Palm oil, Pepper, Pine nuts, Pomegranate seeds, Sesame seeds

LATIN AMERICA

MEXICO
Chocolate
Annato

Allspice

VENEZUELA
COLOMBIA
Vanilla
ECUADOR Cashew nut
Quinoa
PERU **BRAZIL**
Peanut Manioc meal
Squash seeds Palm oil
Tomato **BOLIVIA** Chilies

PARAGUAY

CHILE
Hot chili **URUGUAY**
sauces

ARGENTINA

= CHILI COUNTRY

THE HOTTEST FOOD IN THE WORLD

The Latin American chili is so hot that some varieties literally blister the lips of those not used to them. The trade grades its countless kinds on a heat scale running from 1 to 120: the popular jalapeño, which numbs the mouths of northerners, is rated only at 15. The heating constituent in chilies, capsaicin, is so pungent that its taste can be detected in a solution of one part capsaicin to 100,000 parts of solvent. Another constituent, capsanthine, provides not heat but color: added to chicken feed it gives egg yolks a darker color.

reaches the temperate climates of Argentina and Chile, it seems that no dish is without it. This is, of course, the chili, which provides the red pepper now used throughout the world. It is the most important contribution of the New World to seasoning.

The second in importance is probably vanilla. One might put cacao, which gives us chocolate, ahead of it, if it were not for the fact that vanilla is always and only a seasoner, while chocolate must most often be considered primarily as a food or a drink; one of its chief uses as a flavorer comes precisely from its own area, in the chocolate *molé* sauces of Mexico, employed especially on poultry. Chocolate on chicken may sound barbarous, but in chocolate molé sauce you do not taste the chocolate as such unless you make a deliberate effort to single out its flavor from the riot of competing savors in which it is submerged—several kinds of chilies, black pepper too, almonds, sesame seeds, anise seeds, coriander seeds, cinnamon, cloves, garlic, onion, and tomato.

Another American seasoner which has become a citizen of the world is allspice. Universal too is the peanut, American also, sometimes a food, sometimes a flavorer, and sometimes the source of a cooking oil. Less widespread is the cashew nut, which depends like an overgrown comma from the base of the cashew apple, but had better not be pulled out and eaten fresh, for its acrid juice is dangerously irritating, and has to be processed out of it.

A Latin American plant which has not spread from its native land is quinoa, whose leaves are eaten like spinach, but its seeds are used as a spice; both leaves and seeds contain essential nutritive elements lacking in the potato, which grows side by side with it in the high altitudes of the Andes and is the basic food of the Andean Indians; for them quinoa is consequently an indispensable complementary element. Another native condiment with only faint flavor is *farufa*, manioc meal, of which large shakers appear on Brazilian restaurant tables, like Par-

One of the first new foods Columbus and his men noticed when they landed in the West Indies was the spice they called *agi* (it is *ají* today in Peru). It would have been hard not to notice it, for it was (a) fiery and (b) ubiquitous. It still is. From the Caribbean islands through Mexico, Central America, and South America until one

> Every kind of merchandise was kept separate and had its fixed place marked for it....
> There were sellers of kidney-beans and sage and other vegetables and herbs... also honey,
> honey-paste, and other sweets like nougat.... Much cochineal, is for sale too under
> the arcades of that market, and there are many sellers of herbs....
>
> Bernal Diaz, chronicler of the Cortez expedition, describing the Aztec market of Tenochtitlan
> in *The Conquest of New Spain*

mesan cheese shakers in Italy. Its function is less to add taste to the moist dishes over which it is sprinkled than to soak up juices and sauces so that no drop will be lost.

Latin American squashes are believed originally to have had virtually no flesh, but to have been filled with large edible seeds; throughout Latin America squash seeds are still roasted and eaten like peanuts; or crushed into a greenish meal which flavors sauces; or pressed for a likewise green oil which can be used for seasoning or cooking; the flowers are eaten as well.

Not native to America are coconuts, which probably took root first on the Peruvian coast after drifting across the Pacific, and now offer their meat for desserts and their milk or oil for flavoring and cooking. Coriander is one of the most used foreign herbs, chiefly in the form of its leaves, though the seeds are employed also; so are pomegranate seeds, while pine nuts are native and popular. As though chili pepper were not enough, tiny hot malegueta peppers have been introduced from Africa, and of course black pepper from Asia. Other commonly used seasoners are lime juice (on avocados), onions, garlic, cinnamon, ginger, bay leaves, and oregano.

Though the variety of spices used in Latin America is wide, the chili remains the king. On restaurant tables everywhere, very small, very hot ones are found whole, or larger ones chopped, in olive or dendé oil. Mexico provides one more example of the interdependence between basic cereals and seasoning. Of its twenty-nine states only one, Sonora, consistently prefers mild chilies to hot ones and even offers many dishes containing no chilies at all. Sonora is also the only Mexican state which, instead of maize, makes wheat its basic grain.

At an Andean stop near Oruro, Bolivia, passengers pile out of dinerless train to refresh themselves before resuming the journey.

Above left: A market scene in Peru—the country which gave the world one of its most important vegetables, also one of its most important condiments, the tomato.

Offerings of food are laid out at a Negro rite in Bahia de Todos os Santos, Brazil. Slaves brought many African foods to Brazil, which now grows 200 to 300 African plants—for instance, the palm which provides dendé, used in Brazilian cooking.

AFRICA

Africa south of the Sahara, one is almost tempted to say, has no seasoners; or, contradictorily, that it has them all. Before whites penetrated the Dark Continent, Africans, we are told, seem to have paid little attention to taste; their basic food was often curds and whey wherever the tsetse fly had not eliminated milch animals. Then the colonial period began, with the colonizers importing their own seasoners: Arabs from the north; spice ships from the Orient leaving on the east coast samples of their wares; Europeans and Asiatics in the south; and on the western coast, slavers from the New World deposited its new foods. The basic African grain became maize (mealie); there had been only millet before, and not much of that. The peanut took Africa by storm. But the most important arrival was the red chili pepper, which quickly became, and remains, the dominant spice of the continent. Africa itself originated very few of the flavorers it eats today. Among spices, the most important, after red pepper, are turmeric (from tropical Asia) and cloves (from the Moluccas), black pepper (from India) and vanilla (from America). The most popular herb is mint (probably from southern Europe) and after it thyme (from southern Europe also).

Except in the North African coastal strip, only one African territory achieved (in pre-colonial times) government above the tribal level: Ethiopia. It is also the only one whose seasoning presents a characteristic consistent native flavoring, perhaps not unconnected with the fact that it is also the only one which has retained millet as the basic grain. Ethiopia possesses an all-purpose seasoner, which goes onto or into almost all cooked dishes: *berberé* sauce, a fiery-red paste whose most essential component seems to be identified by the fact that even outside the sauce it is also called *berberé*. But as it is *Capsicum abyssinicum* and Capsicum identifies it as a descendant of the American chili, it cannot have been the original pepper of this age-old condiment. This was probably African or Guinea pepper, also called Ethiopian pepper and scientifically *Xylopia aethiopica,* although it seems to have originated farther south; or it could

Map labels

Myrtle leaves

WEST AFRICA
Cooking in Shea butter
Cassava leaves
Sweet potato leaves
Spicy cedar
Baobab   Cress
Kola nut

Musk mallow
Galangale
Cardamom

ETHIOPIA
Cooking in spiced butter
Berberé sauce

EAST AFRICA
Cooking in hippopotamus lard
Giraffe marrow
Horseradish tree
Baobab

ZANZIBAR
Near world monopoly of cloves

TROPICAL AFRICA
Garlic tree
Wild pepper
White mustard

MOZAMBIQUE
Cashew nut
Chilies
Curries

MADA-GASCAR
Zedoary root
Musk mallow
Vanilla

SOUTHERN AFRICA
Tamarind
Curries
Quince

SEASONERS USED THROUGHOUT AFRICA

Cloves, Dill, Mace, Mint, Nutmeg, Peanut, Pepper, Rosemary, Sage, Thyme, Turmeric, Vanilla
A curious fact: *all* the seasoners eaten throughout Africa are foreign to that continent. The few native spices and herbs are used locally, each in its own region. But it is possible that Africa possesses seasoners as yet unknown to Westerners.

have been Ashanti or Benin pepper, also called Guinea cubebs, which is *Piper guineense,* and thus a true pepper. Either or both of these may, indeed, still be ingredients of *berberé* sauce, for Westerners have not yet identified all the native herbs and spices which may enter it, a task rendered difficult by the probability that the recipe varies almost with every family. Among its chief ingredients, which, though originally foreign, have become naturalized in Africa, are, besides red pepper, black pepper (in the form of whole peppercorns), salt, cumin, coriander seeds, crushed fenugreek seeds and dried fenugreek leaves, basil, cardamom pods and seeds, allspice, nutmeg, cinnamon (in sticks), cloves, ginger, onions, and garlic. Every Ethiopian kitchen contains a cooking fat known as *niter kebbeh,* butter into which has been worked such seasoners as turmeric, cinnamon, nutmeg, ginger, garlic, basil, cardamom, and bishop's weed (an herb which probably reached Ethiopia from Asia Minor).

East Africa, the territory east of the Great Rift Valley (Kenya, Uganda, and Tanzania), likes milder food, despite the circumstance that Zanzibar, now part of Tanzania, enjoys what is very nearly a world monopoly of cloves. Arabs from the north probably brought into this region such subtle dishes as chicken cooked in pomegranate juice, which then becomes part of the gravy, along with crushed fried walnuts.

The most popular seasoners are fenugreek and coriander, plus several shared with tropical regions: malegueta pepper, cinnamon, ginger, dill, and hoary or American basil, also called the tea bush, since it is much used there for making tea. Of secondary popularity are sage and rosemary, while East Africa shares with West Africa the calabash nutmeg, called in French the false nutmeg; there is a false nutmeg in English also, eaten throughout equatorial Africa, probably native to Angola. The balloon vine of East Africa, whose pods are eaten as a vegetable, becomes a spice when its seeds are used, so it is known by the alternative name of heart seed. A thoroughly native delicacy is the marrow from giraffe bones, cooked, when it can be had, in what is said to be one of Nature's finest lards—hippopotamus fat.

The spice miscalled wild or Cameroon cardamom is actually a variety of malegueta pepper. Indian mustard is probably indeed

Indian as its name indicates, though it has been cultivated in central Africa for a long time. The horseradish tree, whose powdered root serves as a substitute for this seasoner, might well be native, for there is an African species, but in fact the one commonly eaten is probably the Indian variety. A seasoner native to West Africa is the plant called in English the spicy cedar and in French laurel, which gives an idea of its flavor; both seeds and flowers are widely used. A flavorer listed as "musk," between quotation marks, in the World Food Organization's roster of African aliments seems to be a spicy variety of the kola nut. It is a delayed action seasoner: a piece of it chewed before eating other foods makes them taste better. Palm nuts and palm oils are much used, the latter for deep frying, enriched by chili or nutmeg; when it is a case of cooking fish, crushed herbs, pepper, onions, and garlic are frequently combined with the palm oil.

Since West Africa is where the slavers arrived from America, this part of the continent has been particularly receptive to New World foods, but it uses them sometimes in fashions unknown in their land of origin—for instance both cassava leaves and sweet potato leaves serve as seasoners in cooking. The peanut is indispensable for sauces, and we must suspect Mexican influence behind a dish of plantains (vegetable bananas) embellished with hot chocolate sauce.

Elsewhere in tropical Africa, the former Congo is addicted to white mustard, while Mozambique grows, and uses, great quantities of two American seasoners, cashew nuts (to flavor chicken), which are recognized as foreign, and chilies, which are not. It is difficult to single out any dominant flavorings or national characteristics in South African cooking; its settlers have been too diverse—the Dutch at the end of the seventeenth century; the first non-African slaves from the East, the "Cape Malays," though there were as many Indonesians as Malays among them, who introduced the tamarind; the French Huguenots; in the nineteenth century, Indians, imported to work the sugarcane plantations, who brought along curries, mangoes, and papayas; there was even some German influence on the food. Meanwhile the cooks who put this mosaic of influence together were of course the indigenous Negroes.

A Kenyan woman prepares maize. First brought from America to feed Negroes waiting to be shipped into slavery, maize has become the mealie-mealie of Africa, its universal cereal.

Opposite page: African marketplaces are stirring and exciting, gathering places for every purpose from gossip to business. The one above is in Djenné, Mali. The imposing building in the background is the mosque.

In Mali, these women are shredding onion leaves. They will then be patted into small balls and eaten either for their own sake or to lend zest to other foods. Africa uses all the plants of the onion family—garlic, chives, leeks, shallots, and the rest.

GLOSSARY OF BOTANICAL TERMS

Achene : Hard, dry 1-seeded fruit.

Adnate : One organ united to another.

Alternate : Where leaves are arranged one after another.

Annual : A plant completing its life cycle within 12 months.

Axil : The upper angle formed by leaf and stem.

Axillary : Flowers borne at the axils of leaf and stem.

Bark : The outer rind of a tree's trunk or branch.

Berry : A fruit whose seeds are embedded in its own juice.

Biennial : A plant flowering or fruiting in the year following that in which the seed is sown.

Bifoliate : Double leaved ; with 2 leaflets.

Bracteoles : Small bracts attached to the base of the pedicels.

Bracts : Small (modified) leaves differing from the others and present on the flower stalks.

Calyx : The green whorl of leaf-like organs situated below the corolla of a flower.

Capitate : Growing in heads, as in Compositae.

Capsule : A dry, many-seeded fruit vessel.

Carpel : Free or united divisions of the ovary.

Caulin : Leaves belonging to or produced from the stem.

Climber : A plant with long straggling shoots requiring support.

Cone : A scale-like fruit containing seeds.

Cordate : A heart-shaped leaf with 2 rounded lobes at the base.

Corolla : A whorl of floral leaves known as petals.

Corymb : Raceme of flowers or pedicels which decrease in length as they approach the top of the stem.

Cruciferae : An order whose flowers of 4 petals are arranged in the form of a cross.

Cyme : A terminal inflorescence beneath which are side branches bearing a terminal flower.

Deciduous : A tree, shrub or plant losing its leaves each year.

Decumbent : Stems of a plant which lie flat on the ground.

Decussate : With 4 leaves arranged cross-like.

Dentate : Leaves with triangular teeth at the margins.

Dioecious : Plants with differently sexed flowers on different plants with stamens on one ; pistils on another.

Disk : Surface or central florets of a flower as in Compositae (Disc florets).

Division : Propagation by dividing a plant into pieces containing roots.

Entire : Leaves neither divided nor toothed at the margins.

Evergreen : A tree, shrub or plant retaining its leaves all the year.

Eye : The dormant bud of a plant.

Filament : The lower stem-like part of a stamen.

Fistular : The hollow stems of plants as in many umbellifers.

Florets : The small rayed petals of flowers as in Compositae.

Follicle : An inflated 1-celled carpel.

Genus : A group of related species.

Glabrous : A plant which is smooth, glossy — without surface hairs.

Glandular : A cellular secreting organ.

Glaucous : Leaves which are blue-green as in Rue.

Half-hardy : Plants needing protection in winter or spring.

Hirsute : Leaves covered in long silky hairs.

Imbricate : Arranged over each other, like the scales of a leaf bud.

Involucre : Whorled bracts at the base of a flower or flower head.

Keel : The pair of petals of Pea-like flowers.

Labiate : Lipped : the corolla or calyx divided into 2 unequal parts as in lavender, thyme.

Lanceolate : Lance-shaped leaves, tapering at each end.

Lateral : A shoot growing out sideways from the main stem.

Linear : Leaves which are long and narrow.

Nectary : Honey-secreting organs at the base of petals.

Node : A point or stem where a leaf is produced.

Obovate : Egg-shaped. Leaves with the broad end outwards.

Opposite : Leaves growing opposite to each other.

Palmate : Segments of a leaf spread out from a central point.

Panicle : Flowers borne in an elongated spray.

Pappus : The hairy appendage of a seed.

Peduncle : Stalk connecting leaves on flowers to stem.

Pellucid : Transparent. Dots or glands on leaves containing essential oil.

Peltate : A leaf with its point of attachment on the face.

Perennial : A plant which grows and blooms each year indefinitely.

Perfoliate : When a leaf encircles the stem.

Perianth : When calyx and corolla are indistinguishable.

Petiole : The stalk of a leaf where it joins the main stem.

Pinnate : Leaflets arranged in pairs.

Pollen : Dust or grains on the anther containing the male cells to fertilise the ovules.

Pratense : Growing in meadows.

Pubescent : Leaves or stems closely covered in hairs or down.

Raceme : Stalked flowers borne in a spike or cluster.

Radical : A tuft of leaves arising from the root.

Rhizome : A stem with a thickened base, growing horizontally, usually beneath the soil.

Rosette : Leaves radiating from a central underground stem, often overlapping to form a circle.

Sagittate : Leaves shaped like an arrow.

Segment : A petal of a flower, or parts of a leaf divided almost to the midrib.

Self-fertile : Flowers which fruit and set seed when fertilised by their own pollen.

Serrate : Leaves which are saw-edged or toothed.

Sessile : Leaves which are without stalks.

Simple : Leaves not divided or serrate.

Sinuate : Leaves with blunt lobes.

Solitary : Flowers borne singly, one to a stalk.

Spike : A raceme, except that the flowers are stalkless.

Spur : The extension of the lower part of a corolla.

Stamen : The male organ of a flower composed of filament and anther.

Stellate : Star-like, radiating from a central point as in Star anise.

Stigma : The cellular part at the top of a carpel or style to which pollen adheres.

Stipule : Leaf-like appendages at the base of the petioles.

Stolon : Runners growing out from a plant and rooting at the leaf nodes.

Style : Termination of a carpel bearing the stigma.

Taproot : The main root, descending far into the soil.

Tomentose : Leaves covered with entangled silky hairs.

Trefoil : A leaf composed of 3 leaflets.

Umbel : Stalked flowers arising from one point and radiating to the same level.

Whorl : Flowers of leaves arranged in a circle of 3 or more around a stem.

Wing : The lateral petals of a pea-like flower.

PICTURE CREDITS

Akademische Druck- und Verlagsanstalt, Graz (from Wiener Dioscurides Codex Vindobonensis Med. gr. 1) der Akademischen Druck- u. Verlagsanstalt, Graz 1965–1970): 21 bottom

Alfieri, Bernard, Horticultural Picture Library, Leatherhead: 49 (24), 55 (44), 59 (59), 72, 75 left below, 81 bottom right

Artus, *Hand Atlas*, Vol I+II+III: 13 far left, 14 right, 43 (5), 46 (15), 47 (17), 50 (26 and 27), 51 (30), 52 (34), 54 (40), 56 (48 and 49), 58 (57), 59 (58 and 60), 61 (66), 62 (70b), 67 (85), 68 (90), 75 center left

Atlas-Photo, Paris: 172 top (PH: Lauros)

Aurness, Craig, Los Angeles: 180 top

A–Z, Botanical Collection, Dorking: 41, 42 (2), 46 (16), 47 (19), 48 (20), 53 (37 bottom), 58 (55), 62 (69 and 70a), 65 (81), 67 (87), 68 (88), 69 (94a), 75 center right above, 80 top right, 80/81 bottom, 81 top right, 83 top, 84, 86 top right, 88 top right, 93 center right, 101 center, 122 center left, 154 above right, center right, 155 above right, 160

A–Z Collection, Dorking (PH: Brian Furner): 11 second from left, 12, 13 second from right and far right, 42 (3), 49 (22), 51 (32), 60 (61 and 64), 74 right above, 75 above right, 81 top left, 92 below left, top center left, top center right, below left, 93 top, 95 top and center left, 96 bottom, 97 left, 98, 99 above right, 102 center left, 122 top center, 162 center

Belser, Basilius, *Hortus Eystettensis sive diligens et accurata omnium plantarum, florum, stirpium.* Faksimile-Neudruck der Ausgabe von 1713, Munich-Allach 1964: 88 center

Bibliothèque Nationale, Paris: 16

Biedermann, Hans, *Medicina Magica*, Graz 1972: 11 top

Bock, Hieronymus, *Kreütterbuch*, Strassburg 1577: 27

Brake, Brian/Rapho, Paris: 17 top

British Library, London: (Beda's *Vita Sancti Cuthberti*, Add. Ms. 39943 f. 2r) 13 bottom, (Royal 11. E. xi, f. 2) 22 bottom

Bucher Verlag, Lucerne: 183 top

Buishand, Tjerk, Alkmaar: 65 (79)

Bullaty & Lomeo, New York: 76/77

Bulloz Photographie, Paris: 18

Bührer, Lisbeth, Lucerne: 14 left, 102 top

Catrina, Werner, Zurich: 126 top

Chesi, Gert, Schwaz: 182 top, 183 below

Ciganovic, Josip, Rome: 170 top

Coleman Collection, Uxbridge: 43 (5b), 70 (97), 71 (98), 75 right below, 80 bottom, 162 top and bottom

Coray, Franz, Lucerne: 42 (1), 43 (4), 44 (7 and 9), 45 (12), 46 (14), 47 (18), 48 (21b), 49 (25), 52 (35), 53 (36 and 38), 54 (43), 68 (89), 71 (99), 82 left, 90, 91 top, 94 center left, 100 top, 102 bottom left, 122 bottom, 123 bottom, 131 right and bottom, 135 right

Corradi, Pio, Zurich: 24

Culinas PR AG, Lucerne: 122/123, 128/129, 131 top

Dagworthy, Judith, Press and Public Relation Office, London: 179 top (PH: John Stone)

Da Spaloti, Cherubino, *Fior de Virtu*, Venice 1490: 19

Döbler, Hansferdinand, *Kochkünste und Tafelfreuden*, Munich 1972: 134

Duna Ungarn Anzeiger, Fahrwangen: 173

Elisofon, Eliot, New York: 176

Freeman, John, London: 137 above

Fuchs, Leonard, *New Kreuterbuch*, Basel 1543: 26, 118/119

Gehring & Neiweiser, Bielefeld (from *Kostbarkeiten ferner Länder*, eine Gewürz- und Teepflanzenkunde von Alba-Gewürze, Bielefeld): 75 top right

Genders, Roy, Worthing: 74 right below, 94 bottom left (PH: John Gledhill), 97 top (PH: John Gledhill), 101 top (PH: John Gledhill), 154 above center

Giacomelli, Carlo, Malters: 159 right, 163 below right

Gööck, Roland, *Das Buch der Gewürze*, München 1977: 4/5, 10 right, 86 top left and bottom left

Graf, S.U., Schwaig: 165 top, 167

Harding, Robert, Picture Library, London: 155 below right

Hauser, Prof. Dr. A., Wädenswil: 87, 104

Held, André, Ecublens: 9

Hirmer Fotoarchiv, München: 15

Holle Bildarchiv, Baden-Baden: 88 left

Hortus Sanitatis, Strassburg c. 1497: 10 left

Hyams, Edward, *A History of Gardens and Gardening*, London 1971: 79 top

Imber, Walter, Laufen: 154 bottom

Keystone – Press: 178 top

Köhler, ·*Medizinal-Pflanzenatlas*, Vol I+II+III, Gera-Untermhaus 1887: 13 second from left, 44 (8), 45 (11), 57 (51 and 52), 58 (54 and 56), 63 (72), 64 (76), 66 (82 and 84), 69 (92), 157 bottom

Library of Congress, Washington: 179 bottom (PH: Marcia Keegan)

Lohse, Bernd: 162/163

Lonicerus, Adamus, *Kreuterbuch*, Frankfurt 1679: 2

Losch, F., *Les Plantes Médicinales*, Biel: 55 (46), 56 (50), 61 (67), 63 (73), 70 (95)

Magnum, Paris: 156 bottom (PH: Burt Glinn), 161 (PH: Ian Berry), 171 top (PH: Henri Cartier Bresson), 175 top (PH: Eliot Erwitt)

Mairani, Guglielmo, Milan: 164 top

Mansell Collection, London: 17 below, 22 top, 23

Mau, Leonore, Hamburg: 181 bottom

Mengis & Sticher, Lucerne: 168 below

Metropolitan Museum of Art, New York (The Harrys Brisbane Dick Fund 1926): 89

Mohr, Jean, Geneva: 172 center left

Muggli, Doris, Hertenstein: 181 above left

Naltchayan, Harry, Annandale: 174 right

National Portrait Gallery, London: 79 center left

Österreichische Fremdenverkehrswerbung, Zurich: 172 bottom

Operakällaren, Restaurant, Stockholm: 175 right

Oronoz, Madrid: 20, 21 above

Otto, Monika A., Lucerne: 153, 181 above right

Picturepoint, London: 11 far right, 44 (6), 75 center right below

Publisher's Archives: 11 far left, 56 (47), 71 (100), 105 (PH: James Perret), 127 (PH: James Perret), 162 second from top and second from bottom

Rapho, Paris: 156 top (PH: Roland Michaud)

Rauh, Prof. Dr. W., Institut für Systematische Botanik und Pflanzengeographie der Universität Heidelberg: 66 (83)

Ringier Bilderdienst, Zurich: 177 top, 178 bottom

Roettges, Willy: 169 bottom

Rüedi, Ruth, Lucerne: 94 top right, 124, 125, 129 right, 130, 130/131, 133, 152, 158/159, 164 left

Salou, Phédon, Paris: 165 left

Schinz, Marina, Courtesy T & L Books, New York: 80/81 center

Schultess, Emil, Forch/Zurich: 163 top right

SEF, Torino: 168 top

Smith, Edwin, Saffron Walden: 6

Smith, Harry, Photographic Collection, Chelmsford: 11 second from right, 45 (10), 46 (13), 53 (37 above), 55 (45), 73 left, 75 left above, 78 below, 82 right, 83 center, 91 right, 92 top right, 93 center left, 95 center right, 99 left, 122 top left

State Historical Society of Wisconsin: 178/179

Stiftsarchiv, St. Gallen (from *Idea Sacra Congrationis Helveto Benedictinae anno jubilei saecularis* 1702): 78 top

Taddei, Fototecnica, Lugano: 171 bottom left

Tate & Lyle Limited, London: 155 below left

Tetrel, Pierre, Paris: 166

The John Carter Brown Library, Brown University, Rhode Island: 25

The Shakespeare Birthplace Trust, Stratford-upon-Avon: 79 center top

Thuillier, R., Chatellerault: 171 below right

Tobler, Pierre, Lucerne: 120

Topham, John, Picture Library, Edenbridge: 7, 54 (41), 64 (75), 69 (94b), 80 top left, 81 bottom left, 96 top, 99 below right, 100 center, 103, 154 above left

Treviso-Coll., G. Comisso: 135 above

Turner, William, *A New Herball*, Collen 1568: 1

Victoria & Albert Museum, London: 155 top

Von Matt, Leonard, Buochs: 14 top

Von Schuberts, Prof. Dr. G. H., *Naturgeschichte des Pflanzenreichs: Lehrbuch der Pflanzengeschichte*, Esslingen 1887: 48 (21a), 49 (23), 50 (28 and 29), 51 (31), 52 (33), 53 (39), 54 (42), 57 (53), 60 (62 and 63), 61 (65), 62 (68), 63 (71 and 74), 64 (77), 65 (78 and 80), 67 (86), 68 (91), 69 (93), 70 (96)

Wetzel, Adolf A., Uitikon: 73 right, 121, 126 bottom, 136

Wienerwald, Munich: 172 right

Wymann, Werner, Bern: 137 below, 157 above

INDEX

Numbers in italics refer to illustrations.
A symbol "(r.)" indicates recipes.

A

Africa, 74
  North, 165, 166–167
  seasoners used in, 152,
    154, 182–183
  see also individual
    countries
Alaric the Goth, 17
Allium, 22
Allium ascalonicum, see
  Shallot
Allium cepa, see Onion
Allium fistulosum,
  see Scallion
Allium porrum, see Leek
Allium sativum, see Garlic
Allium schoenoprasum, see
  Chive
Allium scorodoprasum,
  see Rocambole
Allium ursinum (Bear's
  garlic), 43
Almond *(Prunus amygdalus),*
  65
  culinary uses, 28–29
  cultivation of, 65,
    106–107
  description, 65
Almond soup (r.), 139
Aloysia citriodora, see
  Lemon verbena
Alpinia officinarum, see
  Galingale
American cress, *see*
  Winter cress
Amomum melegueta, see
  Melegueta pepper
Anchovy fillets, 15
André Daguin's pepper
  cookies (r.), 150
Anethum graveolens, see Dill
Angelica *(Angelica arch-*
  angelica), 16, *44, 74, 99*
  culinary uses, 28–29
  cultivation of, 44, 74, 88,
    106–107
  description, 44
Angelica archangelica,
  see Angelica
Anglo-Saxon countries,
  seasoners used in, 155,
    176–179
Anise *(Pimpinella anisum),*
  10, *63, 73*
  culinary uses, 23, 28–29
  cultivation of, 63, 95,
    106–107
  description, 63

Aniseed tree, 17
Anthriscus cerefolium,
  see Chervil
Apicius, 15, 16, 23
Apium graveolens, see Celery
Apple mint, 89
Appraylere, 18
Arabia, 74
Arachis hypogaea, see Peanut
Arkesilas bowl, *15*
Armoracia rusticana, see
  Horseradish
Artemisia abrotanum
  (Southernwood), 47
Artemisia dracunculus,
  see Tarragon
Artemisia redowskii
  (Russian tarragon), 46
Artemisia vulgaris, see
  Mugwort
Artichoke flan (r.), 144
Artichoke hearts in red wine
  (r.), 149
Asafetida *(Ferula assafoe-*
  tida), 15, *54*
  culinary uses, 28–29
  cultivation of, 54,
    106–107
  description, 54
Asia
  cultivation of herbs in, 74
  seasoners used in, 152,
    154–155, 156–163
  see also individual
    countries
Attila the Hun, *17*
Australia, seasoners used in,
  179
Austria, seasoners used in,
  173

B

Babylon, 16
Bacon, Francis, 79, *79,* 93
Badian, *see* Star anise
Baggeson's gold, 78
Balm *(Melissa officinalis),*
  12, 20, 21, *58, 73, 101*
  culinary uses, 28–29
  cultivation of, 58, 74, 88,
    106–107
  description, 58
  harvesting of, 98, 99
Bamboo *(Bambusa vulgaris),*
  47
  culinary uses, 28–29
  cultivation of, 47,
    106–107
  description, 47
Bambusa roseum, 47
Bambusa vulgaris, see
  Bamboo

Barbarea vulgaris, see
  Winter cress
Barber, Richard, 172
Bartram, John, 59
Basil, *see* Sweet basil
Basil sauce for roast lamb or
  chicken (r.), 139
Basil thyme, 82
Bastes, 132
Bates, Caroline, 156
Bay leaf *(Laurus nobilis),*
  57, 92
  in American cookery, 23
  culinary uses, 28–29, 122
  cultivation of, 57,
    106–107
  description, 57
  in garden, 86, 92
Bear's garlic, 43
Bede, the Venerable, 17
Bedouins, 164, *165*
Beef, seasoners and, 154
Beet sugar, 24
Berberé pepper, 14
Berberé sauce, 152,
  182–183
Bergamot *(Monarda didyma),*
  59, 73, 74, *88*
  culinary uses, 28–29
  cultivation of, 59,
    106–107
  description, 59
  harvesting of, 88
  ornamental uses, 88
Bergamot mint, 89
Black elder, *see* Elder
Black mustard *(Brassica*
  nigra), 12, 21, *48, 92,*
    101
  culinary uses, 34–35
  cultivation of, 48, 92,
    110–111
  description, 48
Black pepper *(Piper nigrum),*
  64
  culinary uses, 28–29
  cultivation of, 64, 96,
    106–107
  description, 64
  in history, 17, 20
Blond, Georges and
  Germaine, 172
Borage *(Borago officinalis),*
  48, 81, 101
  culinary uses, 28–29, 88,
    99
  cultivation of, 48, 82, 95,
    106–107
  description, 48
Borago officinalis, see
  Borage
Bouillabaisse, 18
Bouillon de santé, 20
Bouquet garni, 23, 92, 123
  recipes for, 122, 123
Brassica nigra, see Black
  mustard

Brazil, 74, 75
Breads, recipes, 150–151
Britain, *see* England
British East India Company,
  21, *23*
Buckwheat, 17
Burma, seasoners used in,
  158
Burnet *(Pimpinella*
  saxifraga), 63
  culinary uses, 28–29
  cultivation of, 63,
    106–107
  description, 63
Burton, Robert, 56
Bush basil, 60
Butters, recipes, 131, 132,
  140

C

Cacao *(Theobroma cacao),*
  69, 75
  culinary uses, 28–29, 180
  cultivation of, 69,
    106–107
  description, 69
Calamint, 87
Calendula officinalis, see
  Marigold
Canada, *see* North America
Caper *(Capparis spinosa),* 21,
  23, *49*
  culinary uses, 28–29, 130
  cultivation of, 49, 96,
    106–107
  description, 49
Capparis inermis, 49
Capparis spinosa, see Caper
Capsicum annuum, see
  Paprika
Capsicum frutescens, see
  Chili
Capsicum minimum, 49
Caraway *(Carum carvi),* 12,
  13, 20, *50*
  culinary uses, 30–31
  cultivation of, 50, 88, 95,
    100, 101, 106–107
  description, 50
Cardamom *(Elettaria*
  cardamomum), 53, 102
  culinary uses, 30–31
  cultivation of, 53, 75,
    106–107
  description, 53
  harvesting of, 102
  in history, 17, 21
Carrot salad (r.), 141
Carthamus tinctorius, see
  Safflower
Carum carvi, see Caraway

Cassia, 20
Catchup, *see* Ketchup
Catmint, 90
Cayenne, *see* Chili
Celery *(Apium graveolens),*
  46
  culinary uses, 30–31
  cultivation of, 46, 88,
    106–107
  description, 46
Ceylon, 75
Chamomile, cultivation of,
  80, 83
  as ornamental, 82
Charlemagne, 17, *18*
Cheese, 29–39, 131
  recipes with, 144–145
Chenopodium bonus-henricus,
  see Good-King-Henry
Chervil *(Anthriscus*
  cerefolium), 12, 17, *45,*
    92
  culinary uses, 23, 30–31
  cultivation of, 45, 74, 88,
    106–107
  description of, 45
Chicken, 29–39
  recipes with, 147–148
Chicken livers on croutons
  (r.), 147
Chicken with forty cloves of
  garlic (r.), 147
Chicken with Moroccan spice
  mixture (r.), 147
Chicory, 74, 88
  indoor cultivation of, 92
  harvesting of roots, 102
Chili *(Capsicum frutescens),*
  22, *49,* 75, *180*
  culinary uses, 30–31, 165
    170, 180, 181, 182
  cultivation, 49, 108–109
  description, 49
Chili con carne (r.), 145
China, seasoners used in,
  160–162
Chinese five powders, 14,
  160, 162
Chinese ginger, 71
Chinese steamed fish (r.), 144
Chive *(Allium*
  schoenoprasum),
  14, 17, *44, 101*
  culinary uses, 30–31, 129
  cultivation of, 44, 74, 96,
    108–109
  description, 44
  in garden, 79, 86, 87
  grown indoors, 92, 94
  harvesting of, 98
Chive butter for grilled fish
  (r.), 140
Chocolate, *see* Cacao
Chorizo sausage, 15
Chutney, 14, 21, 157
Cinnamomum zeylanicum,
  see Cinnamon

Cinnamon *(Cinnamomum zeylanicum)*, 12, 18, 22, *50–51*
  culinary uses, 30–31
  cultivation of, 12, 50–51, 75, 108–109
  description, 50–51
  in history, 15, 16, 17, 20
Citrus aurantifolia (Lime), 51
Citrus aurantium (Bitter orange), 51
Citrus limonia (Lemon), 51
Citron *(Citrus medica), 51*
  culinary uses, 30–31
  cultivation of, 51, 108–109
  description, 51
Citrus medica, see Citron
Classic white butter sauce (r.), 140
Clove *(Eugenia caryophyllata), 12, 21, 53,* 101, 102, *162*
  culinary uses, 30–31, 150, 162
  cultivation of, 53, 75, 108–109
  description, 53
  in history, 17, 20
Clove orange ice (r.), 150
Cocoa, *see* Cacao
Cochlearia officinalis, see Scurvy grass
Cod, 171
Coffee, 74
Cola, 75
Compost, 91, 94
Condiments:
  definition of, 14
  history of, 15–16
  see also Seasoners
Constantinople, *20*
Cooked tomatoes and sweet green pepper salad (r.), 141
Cooking, 28–39, 120–135, 138–149
Coriander *(Coriandrum sativum), 12, 17, 51,* 100
  culinary uses, 30–31, 157
  cultivation of, 51, 87, 95–96, 108–109
  description, 51
  oil of, 101
Coriandrum sativum, see Coriander
Corsica, 85, 87
Corsican mint, 82
Corylus avellana, see Hazel nut
Costmary, 17
Cotton lavender, *72,* 86, 87
Couscous, 166–167, *167*
Cowslip, 74, 88
Cranberry sauce, 14
Crème anglaise (r.), 135

Cress *(Lepidium sativum),* 12, 17, *57,* 97
  culinary uses, 30–31
  cultivation of, 57, 97, 108–109
  description, 57
Crocus sativus, see Saffron
Crusades, 17–18, 20, 21
Cuba, 75
Cubeb *(Piper cubeba), 64*
  culinary uses, 30–31
  cultivation of, 64, 108–109
  description, 64
Cucumber salad (r.), 141
Cumin *(Cuminum cyminum),* 17, *52,* 101
  culinary uses, 32–33
  cultivation of, 52, 108–109
  description, 52
Cuminum cyminum, see Cumin
Curcuma longa, see Turmeric
Curcuma zedoaria, see Zedoary
Currant, 20, 21
Curry, 11, 14, 102, 156–157
Cypress roots, 17

D

Daguin, André, 150
Dandelion *(Taraxacum officinale), 69, 99,* 101, *101*
  culinary uses, 32–33
  cultivation of, 69, 88, 108–109
  description, 69
Dates, 20
David, Elizabeth, 13, 23, 57, 168
de La Quintinie, Jean, 20
de Serres, Olivier, 20
Desserts, 29–39, 135
  recipes, 135, 150–151
Diaz, Bernal, 181
Dickens, Charles, 178
Dill *(Anethum graveolens),* 17, *45*
  culinary uses, 32–33, 175
  cultivation of, 45, 95, 108–109
  description, 45
  seeds of, 100, 101
Drying herbs, 98–103
  by hanging, 98
  by rack, 99–100, *100*
Dumas, Alexandre, 23

E

Eau-de-Cologne mint, 89
Egg and cheese dishes, 29–39, 131
  recipes, 144–145
Eggs in brioche with mustard tarragon sauce (r.), 145
Egypt, seasoners used in, 166
Elder *(Sambucus nigra),* 67
  culinary uses, 32–33
  cultivation of, 67, 108–109
  description, 67
Elderberry wine, 23
Elecampane, 102
Elettaria cardamomum, see Cardamom
England:
  cultivation of herbs in, 73, 74, 75
  use of seasoners in, 17, 18–20, 176–177
  see also Tudor era
Eruca vescaria subsp. sativa, see Rocket
Eugenia caryophyllata, see Clove
Europe, seasoners used in, 154, 168–175
  see also individual countries
European four spices, 14
Evelyn, John, 21, 23, 54, 66, 83

F

Fennel *(Foeniculum vulgare), 11,* 12, *54, 73*
  culinary uses, 11, 32–33
  cultivation of, 54, 74, 88, 108–109
  description, 54
  harvesting of, 101`
  in history, 17
Fenugreek *(Trigonella foenum-graecum), 70*
  culinary uses, 32–33
  cultivation of, 70, 108–109
  description, 70
Fertilizer, natural, 83, 85, 87
Ferula assafetida, see Asafetida
Field poppy, *see* Poppy
Figs, 21, 78
Filbert, *see* Hazel nut
Filbert crisps (r.), 150
Fine herbs, 123, 130 (r.), 131
Fines herbes, 123, 130 (r.), 131

Fish, 8, 28–38, 131
  recipes, 143–144
  seasoners and, 154, 155
Five-Spice Powder (China), 14, 160, 162
Florence, use of spices in, 18
Foeniculum vulgare, see Fennel
Fool Midammis (broad bean salad) (r.), 166
France, seasoners used in, 17, 23, 169, 171–172
Fried chicken with sesame seeds (r.), 148
Fried halibut or pollock with parsley sauce (r.), 143

G

Galingale *(Alpinia officinarum), 44*
  culinary uses, 32–33
  cultivation of, 44, 97, 108–109
  description, 44
  in history, 17, 18, 25
Gallimaufry, 21
Gardening, 72–103, *76–77,* 105–117
  herb gardens in history, 73, 78–79
  layout and planning, 78–90, 95
  planting, 83–90
  in pots and tubs, 75, 80, 91–94, 96
  weather and, 74–75, 78, 79, 85–86, 87, 88, 90
  see also Propagation; Soil
Garden thyme, *see* Thyme
Garlic *(Allium sativum),* 10, 14, *43*
  culinary uses, 32–33, 125, 126, 165, 171, 175
  cultivation of, 43, 108–109
  description, 43
  in history, 18, 20, 21
  propagation of, 97
Genoa, and spice trade, 18
Gent, John, 47
Geranium, scented-leaf, *see* Scented-leaf geranium
Gerard, John, 78
Germander, 92
Germany, seasoners used in, 169, 172–173, 174
Geum rivale, 54
Geum urbanum, see Herb bennet
Ginger, *13,* 17, 18–19, 20, 21, 25, *71, 154*

culinary uses, 23, 32–33
cultivation of, 71, 74, 108–109
description, 71
propagation of, 97
source of, 12, 101
Gingered chicken stew with chick peas (r.), 148
Glycine max, see Soybean
Glycine soja, see Soybean
Glycyrrhiza glabra, see Licorice
Good-King-Henry *(Chenopodium bonus-henricus), 50*
  culinary uses, 32–33
  cultivation of, 50, 74, 88, 108–109
  description, 50
Grated potato cake stuffed with leeks (r.), 148
Greek mixed salad (r.), 142
Gremolata (r.), 140
Ground ivy, 94

H

Halva, 68
Hanging baskets, 93–94
Hatfield House, Harfordshire, 79
Hawaii, seasoners used in, 159
Hazel nut *(Corylus avellana), 52*
  culinary uses, 32–33
  cultivation of, 52, 110–111
  description, 52
Helianthus annuus, see Sunflower
Hemlock, 10
Hemphill, Rosemary, 12
Herb and spice chart, 28–39
Herb bennet *(Geum urbanum), 54*
  culinary uses, 32–33
  cultivation of, 54, 110–111
  description, 54
Herb bouquet, *see* Bouquet garni
Herb brandy (r.), 135
Herb-of-grace, *see* Rue
Herbs:
  advice on use of, 122, 125, 126
  defined, 10–12, 123
  in drinks, 11, 75, 98
  drying of, 22, 98–103, 122, 126
  fresh, 123, 125

geographical distribution of, 74–75, 152, 154–155
medicinal, 10–11, 16, 18, 22, 73, 78, 87
nonculinary uses, 73, 79, 81, 85
storing of, 98, 101
transplanting of, 82, 95
see also Gardening; Plant Lexicon; Seasoning; Seasoners
Herrick, Robert, 86
Hickory nut, 22
Hippocrates, 16, 23
Holland, 18
Honey, 24–25
Honey cinnamon cake with walnuts (r.), 151
Honeysuckle, 78
Hop *(Humulus lupulus), 55*
culinary uses, 32–33
cultivation of, 55, 110–111
description, 55
Horseradish *(Armoracia rusticana),* 14, *14, 46,* 89, *92*
culinary uses, 32–33
cultivation of, 46, 110–111
description, 46
propagation of, 97
Humulus lupulus, see Hop
Humus, 83, 87, 88
Hungary, seasoners used in, 169, 173
Hyssop *(Hyssopus officinalis), 56*
culinary uses, 32–33
cultivation of, 56, 110–111
description, 56
Hyssopus officinalis, see Hyssop

I

Illicium griffithii, 56
Illicium verum, see Star anise
Incense, herbal, 100
India, 21, 23
seasoners used in, 154, 156–158
as spice-growing region, 75
Indians of America, 22
Indochina, seasoners used in, 158, 159
Indonesia, seasoners used in, 158, 159

J

Jamaica, 74, 95
Japan, seasoners used in, 160, 162–163
Jasmine, 86
Jefferson, Thomas, 178
Juglans regia, see Walnut
Juniper *(Juniperus communis), 56*
culinary uses, 34–35
cultivation of, 56, 110–111
description, 56
Juniperus communis, see Juniper

K

Keats, John, 75
Kedgeree, 21
Ketchup, 14, 23
Khava bush, 64
Khichri, 21
Kirsch, 15
Knot gardens, 79, *79*
Korea, seasoners used in, 163

L

Lady's smock, 88
Lamb's lettuce, 88
Lamb's tails, *72*
Lamb steaks with olive sauce (r.), 146
Lamb stew with marjoram (r.), 145
Laos, seasoners used in, 158–159
Lapinia officinale, (Chinese ginger), 71
Laserwort, 15
Latin America, seasoners used in, 154–155

Laurus nobilis, see Bay leaf
Lavandula nana compacta, 57
Lavandula spica, see Lavender
Lavender *(Lavandula spica),* 17, *57, 81*
culinary uses, 34–35
cultivation of, 57, 74, 100, 110–111
description, 57
in garden, 79, 86
Lawson's cypress, 78
Leek *(Allium porrum),* 14, *43*
culinary uses, 34–35
cultivation of, 43, 110–111
description, 43
"Le Livre de Rustican", 78
Lemon herb butter (r.), 131
Lemons, 21
Lemon thyme, 69
Leomon verbena *(Lippia citriodora), 58*
culinary uses, 34–35
cultivation of, 58, 110–111
description, 58
Lentils, in khichri, 21
Lepidium sativum, see Cress
Leslie, Eliza, 22–23
Lettuce, 21
Levisticum officinale, see Lovage
Licorice *(Glycyrrhiza glabra),* 17, *55,* 74, *162*
culinary uses, 34–35
cultivation of, 55, 89, 102, 110–111
description, 55
propagation of, 97
Limestone, 85, 91
Lippia citriodora, see Lemon verbena
Liptauer cheese, 173
Liver brochettes with bay leaves (r.), 146
Lovage *(Levisticum officinale),* 17, *58,* 74, 101
culinary uses, 34–35
cultivation of, 58, 110–111
description, 58

M

Mace *(Myristica fragrans),* 20, 23, *59*
description, 59
see also Nutmeg
McKendry, Maxime, 17
Madagascar, 75
Madame Chu's star anise

beef (r.), 146
Maître d'hôtel butter (r.), 132
Maize, 183
Malaysia, seasoners used in, 158, 159
Maple sugar, 24
Maple syrup, 22
Marigold *(Calendula officinalis), 49*
culinary uses, 34–35
cultivation of, 49, 82, 99, 100, 110–111
description, 49
Marinades, 133–134
recipes, 134
Marjoram, *see* Sweet marjoram
Masala, dry, 157
May, Robert, 20–21
Mayonnaise (r.), 14, 130
Meadowsweet, *72*
Mead, William Edward, 176
Meats, 29–39, 131–132
recipes, 123, 145–147
see also Marinades
Mediterranean fish soup (r.), 138
Meleguetta pepper *(Amomum melegueta), 44*
culinary uses, 34–35
cultivation of, 44, 110–111
description, 44
Melilot *(Melilotus officinalis), 58*
culinary uses, 34–35
cultivation of, 58, 110–111
description, 58
Melilotus officinalis, see Melilot
Melissa officinalis, see Balm
Mentha aquatica (Water mint), 59
Mentha citrata, 89
Mentha piperita, see Peppermint
Mentha spicata, see Spearmint
Menthol, 87
Mexican fish soup (r.), 138
Mexico, cultivation of spices in, 75
Middle Ages, use of herbs and spices in, 18–20
see also Crusades; Monasteries
Middle eastern lamb tartlets (r.), 146
Mildew, 99
Mint, *see* Peppermint; Spearmint
Molasses, 24
Molé sauces, 180
Moluccas, seasoners used in, 18, 159

Monarda didyma, see Bergamot
Monardes, Dr., 59
Monasteries, cultivation of herbs in, 73, 78, 98
Montezuma, garden of, 22
More, Sir Thomas, on rosemary, 86, 87
Moroccan bread (r.), 151
Morocco, seasoners used in, 152, 165, 167
Moslems, 20, 21
Moss, for hanging baskets, 94
Mountain thyme, 69
Mugwort *(Artemisia vulgaris), 47*
culinary uses, 34–35
cultivation of, 47, 86, 110–111
description, 47
Mulligatawny soup, 23
Mushrooms, 130
Mustard, *see* Black mustard; White mustard
Mustard sauce (r.), 131
Mutton, 23
Myristica fragrans, see Nutmeg; Mace
Myrrhis odorata, see Sweet cicely
Myrtle *(Myrtus communis), 60, 101*
culinary uses, 34–35
cultivation of, 60, 112–113
description, 60
Myrtus communis, see Myrtle

N

Nasturtium *(Tropaeolum majus),* 12, 23, *70*
culinary uses, 34–35
cultivation of, 70, 92, *95,* 112–113
description, 70
in hanging basket, 93, 94
Nasturtium officinale, see Watercress
Near East, 74, 95
seasoners used in, 164–166
Neolithic Man, 8
Nero, *14,* 16
North Africa, 74
seasoners used in, 165, 166–167
North America, cultivation of herbs in, 73 74, 75
use of seasoners in, 22–23, 25–26, 155, 177–179
Nuoc mam, 14, 158

Nutmeg *(Myristica fragrans),* 16, 18, 20, *59, 154*
culinary uses, 34–35
cultivation of, 59, 112–113
description, 59
see also Mace

O

Ocimum basilicum, see Sweet basil
Ocimum minimum (Bush basil), 60
Okra, 75, 96
Olea europaea, see Olive
Olive *(Olea europaea),* 21, *61*
culinary uses, 34–35
cultivation of, 61, 112–113
description, 61
Olive and caper relish (r.), 140
Onion *(Allium cepa),* 10, 14, *42*
culinary uses, 34–35, 126, 171, 183
cultivation of, 42, 88, 112–113
description, 42
in history, 18, 20, 22, 23
propagation of, 97
Orange and grated carrot salad (r.), 142
Orange-scented thyme, 69
Oregano *(Origanum vulgare), 11,* 20, 23, 25, *61*
culinary uses, 34–35
cultivation of, 61, 112–113
description, 61
see also Sweet marjoram
Oriental meatball soup (r.), 138
Origanum majorana, see Sweet marjoram
Origanum onites (Pot marjoram), 61
Origanum vulgare, see Oregano
Osso buco, 140, 170
Ostia, 17
Oswego tea, *see* Bergamot

P

Paella, 15 (r.), 149
Palmyra, *17*
Papaver rhoeas, see Poppy

Paprika *(Capsicum annuum), 49, 154, 173*
culinary uses, 34–35
cultivation of, 49, 96, 112–113
description, 49
Parsley *(Petroselinum crispum),* 10, 12, 23, 45, *62, 92, 93*
culinary uses, 36–37, 122, 125, 129
cultivation of, 62, 88, 89, 92, 95
description, 62
drying of, 100
harvesting of, 98
historical reference, 20
propagation of, 95, *96*
Platt, Sir Hugh, 92
Peanut *(Arachis hypogaea), 46*
culinary uses, 36–37
cultivation of, 46, 112–113
description, 46
Pelargonium capitatum, see Scented-leaf geranium
Pelargonium clorinda, 62
Pelargonium tomentosum, 62
Pennsylvania Dutch, 178
Pepper, *see* Black pepper ; Chili ; Paprika
Pepper, hot, *see* Chili
Pepper cookies (r.), 150
Peppermint *(Mentha piperita),* 21, 23, *59,* 85, *92*
culinary uses, 36–37, 176, 177
cultivation of, 59, 89, 102–103, 112–113
description, 59
harvesting of, 99
varieties of, 89
Pesto, 169
recipe, 140
Petroselinum crispum, see Parsley
Philippines, seasoners used in, 158, 159
Phytolacca americana, see Poke
Piper methystcum (Khava busch), 64
Pimenta officinalis, see Allspice
Pimpinella anisum, see Anise
Pimpinella saxifraga, see Burnet
Pine (nut), 18, *64*
culinary uses, 36–37
cultivation of, 64, 112–113
description, 64
Pineapple sage, 67
Pinus edulis, see Pine (nut)
Pinus sylvestris (Scots pine), 64

Piper cubeba, see Cubeb
Piper nigrum, see Black pepper
Pistachio *(Pistacia vera),* 18, *65*
culinary uses, 36–37
cultivation of, 65, 112–113
description, 65
Pistacia vera, see Pistachio
Pittosporum tenuifolium mayi, 78–79
Plant Lexicon (descriptions of plants and their cultivation), 40–71
see also Gardening ; Herbs ; Spices
Platt, Sir Hugh, 92
Pliny the Elder, 15, 60
Poke *(Phytolacca americana), 63*
culinary uses, 36–37
cultivation of, 63, 112–113
description, 63
Poland, seasoners used in, 173, 174
Poppy *(Papaver rhoeas),* 62
culinary uses, 36–37
cultivation of, 62, .112–113
description, 62
Portugal, seasoners used in, 18, 22, 169, 171
Portulaca oleracea, see Purslane
Pot herbs, 123
Pot marjoram, 61
Potpourris, 79, 85, 86, 87
Pots, growing herbs in, 91–94
see also Window boxes
Potted salmon (r.), 144
Poterium sanguisorba, see Salad burnet
Poultry and game, 29–39
recipes, 147–148
Propagation :
from seed, 95–96
from stem cuttings, 96, 97
by root division, 96–97
from root cuttings, 97
from bulbs or sets, 97
Prunes, 17
Prunus amygdalus, see Almond
Pureed green celery with coriander seed (r.), 148
Purslane *(Portulaca oleracea),* 65
culinary uses, 36–37
cultivation of, 65, 112–113
description, 65
Purslane salad (r.), 142

Q

Queensland, 74, 97
Quinoa, 180

R

Rabbit, 22
Raisins, 17, 20, 21
Ras el hanout (Morocco), 14, 167
Recipes, 123–135, 138–149
Renaissance, use of herbs in, 18, 20–23
see also Tudor era
Rib steaks in the style of Rome (r.), 146
Rice, seasoners and, 154, 155, 157, 159, 168
Roast lamb, Arab style (r.), 147
Rocambole *(Allium scorodo-prasum),* 14, *44*
culinary uses, 36–37
cultivation of, 44, 112–113
description, 44
Rocket *(Eruca vesicaria subsp. sativa),* 53
culinary uses, 36–37
cultivation of, 53, 112–113
description, 53
Rome, and the spice trade, 16–17, 21
Rosa gallica officinalis, 87, *88*
Rose, Giles, 65
Rosemary *(Rosmarinus officinalis),* 10, *66, 73, 154*
culinary uses, 36–37
cultivation of, 66, 74, 75, 114–115
description, 66, 81, 86, 87
harvesting of, 98
medicinal value, 86
oil of, 85
propagation of, 96
Roses, 78
for potpourris, 86
Rose water, 18, 152
Rosmarinus officinalis, see Rosemary
Rue *(Ruta graveolens), 66, 73,* 78
culinary uses, 36–37
cultivation of, 66, 114–115
description, 66
Rule's Restaurant (London), *176*
Rumex acetosa, see Sorrel

Rumex scutatus, see French sorrel
Russian fish soup (r.), 139
Russian tarragon *(Artemisia redowskii),* 46
Ruta graveolens, see Rue

S

Safflower *(Carthamus tinctorius),* 50
culinary uses, 36–37
cultivation of, 50, 114–115
description, 50
Saffron *(Crocus sativus), 13,* 21, *52*
culinary uses, 36–37
cultivation of, 52, 74, 114–115
description, 52
in history, 15, 16, 18
source of, 12
Sage *(Salvia officinalis),* 10, 21, 67, *73, 81, 83*
culinary uses, 36–37, 87
cultivation of, 67, 74, 78, 96, 100, 114–115
description, 67
drying of, 98
varieties of, 83, 87
St. Gall, monastery of, 78, *78*
Salad burnet *(Poterium sanguisorba),* 65
culinary uses, 36–37
cultivation of, 65, 114–115
description, 65
Salade niçoise, 15
Salad herbs, 123
Salads, 28–38, 135
recipes, 141–142
see also Vinegars
Salem, Massachusetts, 22
Salt, 8
with other seasoners, 126
Salvia officinalis, see Sage
Salvia purpurea, 67
Salvia rutilans (Pineapple sage), 67
Sambucus nigra, see Elder
Sand, 82, 84
Santha Rama Rau, 156
Sassafras beer, 23
Satureja hortensis, see Summer savory
Sauce béarnaise (r.), 140 130
recipes, 131, 139–141
Sausage, 60
Sautéed apples with lemon or orange marmalade (r.), 150

Savory, *see* Summer savory;
  Winter savory
Scallion *(Allium fistulosum),*
  42
  culinary uses, 36–37
  cultivation of, 42,
  114–115
  description, 42
Scandinavian cooking,
  seasoners and, 174, 175
Scented-leaf geranium
  (Pelargonium capitatum),
  62
  culinary uses, 38–39
  cultivation of, 62, 85, 93,
  94, 114–115
  description, 62
''Schrebergarten,'' *24*
Scots pine, 64
Scrambled eggs with chervil
  (r.), 145
Scurvy grass *(Cochlearia officinalis), 51*
  culinary uses, 38–39
  cultivation of, 51,
  114–115
  description, 51
Sea scallops in papillote with
  watercress and tomatoes
  (r.), 144
Seafood, ham, and okra
  gumbo (r.), 143
Seafood sausage Le Plaisir
  (r.), 143
Seasoned breadcrumbs (r.),
  132
Seasoned salt (r.), 126
Seasoners, effect of industrialization, 25–26
  history of, 8, 15–26
  in international cuisines,
  152–183
  see also Condiments;
  Herbs; Spices
Seasoning, 120–135
Sedum reflexum, see
  Stonecrop
Seeds:
  as spices, 12, 75
  harvesting of, 100–102
  from herbs, 74
  propagation from, 95
  sowing of, 83, 95
Senna, *101*
Sesame *(Sesamum indicum),*
  68
  culinary uses, 38–39
  cultivation of, 68,
  114–115
  description, 68
Sesamum indicum, see
  Sesame
Shakers (U.S.), 25–26, 178
Shakespeare, William, 7, 53,
  71, 83, 86
Shallot *(Allium ascalonicum), 14, 42,* 88

culinary uses, 38–39
cultivation of, 42,
  114–115
description, 42
propagation of, 97
Shallot vinegar (r.), 133
Sicily, seasoners used in, 169
Silk Road, 16
Silphium, *15*
Simpson's on the Strand, *179*
Sinapis alba, see White
  mustard
Singapore, seasoners used in,
  163
Slavic cooking, seasoners
  and, 174–175
Smorgasbord, *175*
Soil:
  treatment of, 85–86, 87,
  88, 89, 90
  types of, 83–86, 87
  see also Compost; Humus;
  Sand
Song of Solomon, 52
Sorrel *(Rumex acetosa), 66,*
  101
  culinary uses, 38–39
  cultivation of, 66,
  114–115
  description, 66
Soups, 28–38, 129
  recipes, 138–139
South America, 75
Southeast Asia, seasoners
  used in, 158–159
Southernwood *(Artemisia
  abrotanum),* 47, 86, 98
Soviet Union, seasoners used
  in, 174–175
Soybean *(Glycine max), 54,*
  160
  culinary uses, 38–39, 160
  cultivation of, 54,
  114–115
  description, 54
Soybean sauce:
  in China, 160
  in Japan, 162, 163
Spaghetti with olive sauce
  (r.), 141
Spain:
  cultivation of herbs and
  spices, 74
  seasoners used in, 22,
  169, 170–171
Spearmint *(Mentha spicata),*
  20, 59, 89, *92*
  cultivation of, 114–115
Spenser, Edmund, 86
Spice brandy (r.), 135
Spice chart, 28–39
Spice Islands, 18, 159
Spice mixture for coffee (r.),
  141
Spices:
  advice on cooking with,
  122, 126–127

climate and, 74–75
cultivation of, 74–75
definition of, 12–13
geographical distribution,
  152, 154–155
history of, 15, 17–22
transport of, 73
Spruce beer, 23
Star anise *(Illicium verum),*
  56, 101, 162
  culinary uses, 38–39
  cultivation of, 56,
  114–115
  description, 56
Stonecrop *(Sedum reflexum),*
  68
  culinary uses, 38–39
  cultivation of, 68,
  114–115
  description, 68
Storage of seasoners, 100,
  107–117
  containers for, 102
Stratford-on-Avon, *79*
Stuffed tomatoes (r.), 149
Sugar, 23–26, 155, 176
Sugar cane, 18
  in history, 17, 21, 23–26
  importance in American
  cookery, 24–25
Summer savory *(Satureja
  hortensis), 67*
  culinary uses, 36–37
  cultivation of, 67, 79, 82,
  87, 91, 94, 95, 96,
  114–115
  description, 67
  harvesting of, 101
  see also Winter savory
Summer truffle, 70
Sunflower *(Helianthus
  annuus), 55,* 96
  culinary uses, 38–39
  cultivation of, 55,
  116–117
  description, 55
  in garden, 86, 88
Supermarkets, 25
Sweet and sour cherries with
  mace (r.), 150
Sweet and sour relish, 14
Sweet basil *(Ocimum basilicum), 60–61, 81, 95*
  in American cookery, 23
  culinary uses, 38–39
  cultivation of, 60–61, 95,
  116–117
  description, 60–61
  indoors, 92, 94
Sweet cicely *(Myrrhis
  odorata),* 60
  culinary uses, 38–39
  cultivation of, 60, 88,
  116–117
  description, 60
Sweet fern, *see* Sweet cicely
Sweet herbs, 123

Sweet marjoram *(Origanum
  majorana), 61, 73, 93*
  culinary uses, 38–39, 173
  cultivation of, 61, 75,
  100, 116–117
  description, 61
  as hedge, 79, 86
  in history, 20, 25
  indoors, 92, 94, 98
Sweet pepper, *see* Paprika
Sweets and baking, 29–39,
  135
  recipes, 135, 150–151
Szechwan cooking, 162

T

Tabasco sauce, 14
Tahina, 68
Tahiti, seasoners used in, 159
Talewort, *see* Borage
Tamarind *(Tamarindus
  indica), 68*
  culinary uses, 38–39
  cultivation of, 68,
  116–117
  description, 68
Tamarindus indica, see
  Tamarind
Tanacetum foliis crispis, 68
Tanacetum vulgare, see Tansy
Tannahill, Reay, 23
Tansy *(Tanacetum vulgare),*
  68, 74, *80,* 86, 88
  culinary uses, 38–39, 86
  cultivation of, 68,
  116–117
  description, 68
  harvesting of, 78
Taraxacum officinale, see
  Dandelion
Tarragon *(Artemisia dracunculus), 16, 46–47,* 88,
  116–117
  culinary uses, 38–39
  cultivation of, 46–47, 74
  description, 46–47
  harvesting of, 98, 99
Tartar sauce (r.), *130*
Tempura cooking (Japan),
  163
Thailand, seasoners used in,
  158
Theobroma cacao, see Cacao
Thyme *(Thymus vulgaris),* 10,
  20, *69,* 73, 82
  culinary uses, 38–39, 122
  cultivation of, 69, 74,
  100, 116–117
  description, 69
  drying of, 98
  as hedging, 79, 86, 87
  varieties of, 69, 82, 91

in windowbox, 92
Thymus citriodorus (Lemon
  thyme), 69
Thymus fragrantissimus
  (Orange-scented thyme),
  69
Thymus herba barona (Baron-
  of-beef thyme), 69
Thymus nitidus, 69
Thymus serpyllum (Mountain
  thyme), 69
Thymus vulgaris, see
  Thyme
Trifolium subterranean, 46
Trigonella foenum-graecum,
  see Funugreek
Tropaeolum majus, see
  Nasturtium
Truffle *(Tuber
  melanosporum), 70*
  culinary uses, 38–39
  description, 70
  raising of, 70, 116–117
Tuber aestivus (Summer
  truffle), 70
Tuber brumale (Winter
  truffle), 70
Tuber melanosporum, see
  Truffle
Tudor era, herb cultivation in,
  20–22, 86, 92
Tunisian mixed salad (r.),
  142
Turmeric *(Curcuma longa),*
  53, 75, 101, *157*
  culinary uses, 38–39, 157
  cultivation of, 53,
  116–117
  description, 53
Turner, William *(New
  Herbal),* 24, 65
Turnip, 10
Tusser, Thomas, 20, 23

U

United States,
  cultivation of herbs in,
  73, 74, 75
  seasoners used in, 22–23,
  25–26, 155, 177–179
Urbanization, 25–26

V

Vanilla *(Vanilla planifolia),*
  22, *71*
  culinary uses, 38–39, 135
  cultivation of, 71, 75,

116–117
description, 71
Vanilla planifolia, see
Vanilla
Veal, seasoners and, 154,
168
Vegetables, 8, 29–39
herbs as, 10, 14, 18, 88
recipes, 148–149
see also Potherbs
Venetian spice trade, 17–18
Verbena, *see* Lemon verbena
Vermouth, 11, 134
Versailles, 79
Vietnam, seasoners used in,
158
Vietnamese sour soup (r.),
139
Vinegars, 14, 21, 132–133
Violet *(Viola odorata)*, 21,
71, 74, 88
culinary uses, 38–39, 99
cultivation of, 71,
116–117
description, 71
Viola odorata, see Violet

Wintergreen, 73
Witches, 10, 11
Winter savory *(Satureja
montana)*, *67*
culinary uses, 36–37
cultivation of, 67, 86, 92,
94, 98, 114–115
description, 67
see also Summer savory
Winter truffle, 70
Worcestershire sauce, 14,
176
Wormwood, *72*, 87

Y

Yew, 10
Yougoslavia, seasoners used
in, 173

Z

Zedorary *(Curcuma zedoaria)*,
53, 75, 97
cultivation, 53, 116–117
description, 53
see also Turmeric
Zéphirine Drouhin (rose),
78, *78*
Zingiber officinalis, see
Ginger
Zucchini and caraway salad
(r.), 142

W

Walnut *(Juglans regia)*, *56*,
78
culinary uses, 38–39
cultivation of, 56,
116–117
description, 56
Watercress *(Nasturtium officinale)*, *60*, 74
culinary uses, 38–39
cultivation, 60, 116–117
description, 60
Water mint *(Mentha
aquatica)*, *81*, *103*
Weather conditions, 73–75
Welsh onion, *see* Scallion
West Indies, 75
Wheat, seasoners and,
154, 157
White mustard *(Sinapis
alba)*, 12, 21, 23, *48*, 92,
101, *155*
culinary uses, 34–35, 155
cultivation of, 48, 92,
110–111
description, 48
Wild mint, 17
Willan, Anne, 154
Window boxes, 91–92
Winter cress *(Barbarea
vulgaris)*, 47
culinary uses, 38–39
cultivation of, 47,
116–117
description, 47